Jeffrey Epstein

Secret
Black Books &
House Manual

CONTENTS

Epstein Black Book # 1

The largest and most significant of the two Epstein "black books," this address book contains 1,510 people listed in the late sex offender's ill-famed Rolodex, including dozens of billionaires, politicians and diplomats, and royalty.

This is a true reprint, published from the digital scans of the original document.

The black book was first revealed in court after Epstein's former Palm Beach, Florida, house manager Alfredo Rodriguez attempted to sell it to an attorney representing an Epstein accuser in 2009. It was subsequently was made public by Gawker in 2015.

This address book, dated 2004-05, was a significant moment for journalists and voyeurs, becoming a key source of information about Epstein and his network of associates, which included politicians, academics, celebrities, and royalty.

Abby
07944 574 202

Abousleiman, Joanna
0603 338 787
Email:
joannachevalier@hotmail.c

Adam, Nick
19 Rue De Lille
75007, Paris
00 331 538 97260(w)
00 331 40150061(h)
00 33 607 341 980 (p)

Agag Alejandro
00 44 771 730 6038
Email:
aagag@aslinvestments.com

Agnew, Marie Claire & John
51 Eaton Square
London SW1 0QY
0207-235 7589 (h)
0207 621 0011 (w)

Alai Azzedine
00 331 4272 1919

Albermarle, Rufus & Sally
511 6th Ave
p.o. box 394
New York, NY 10011
1 212 465 9867(w)
Email: rufusa@mac.com
1 917 969 2168 (p) Rufus
1 917 257 9735 (p) Sally
212 271 3481 (try this first)

Aldridge Saffron
47 Ladbroke Rd
London W11 3PD
0207-727 1006
001 212-879-7653
Email: saffya@aol.com
0207-221-3627

Alexander Pam
01 415 644 3055(w)
01 415 515 9708(p)
Email: palexander@alexanderrogil

Algranti Giacomo
Flat 4 83 Dilke St
83 Dilke St
Flat 4
London, W1
0207-493 6171
0385 261 390
0208-969 0027 (h)
0208-746 1181 (w)
0207-746 1157 (f)
0207-930 3703 (gw)
0386 438 218 (p)

Allan Paul
001 206 355 5777
Email: paul@vulcan.com

Allan, Nick & Sarah
B5 Banyan Villas
9 Stanley Village Road
Hong Kong,
00-852-813-0762

Althorp, Charlie
Althorp
0207-229 1573 (h)

0207-637 8655 (w)

Alun-Jones, Carella
34 Eaton Place
London SW1,
0207-235 7500 (h)
0372 58158 (c)

Alun-Jones, Jeremy & Deborah
Old Park
Fishbourne
West Sussex, PO18 8AP
0207 878 3381(w)
0124 357 2102(h)
Email: daj@old-park.co.uk
(Hm)21 St. James Square
London SW1Y 4JP
(Jeremy)
0777 412 1212 (Dp)
0207 930 4237 (wf)

Alvarez, Senor Vincente
00 34 1 276 8697 (h)
011 34 915 903490 (w)
00 34 1 563 8466 (I)

Amon, Mr Philippe
Domaine de Bougy
1170 Aubonne
Switzerland,
41 21 681 5555(w)
00 41 21 821 2222(h)
Email:
philippe.amon@sicpa.com
(Hm)25 Eaton Square (2nd
home)
Flat D
London SW1
41 21 821 2200 (hf)
00 41 792103175 (p)
00 41 21 627 5920 (w)
0041 21 821 2200 (hf)
41 21 627 5925 (wf)

0207-235-7769/9169 (2nd home phone & fax)

Amon, Roberta & Maurice
4 East 72 Street
New York NY 10021
001 212 535 9877 (h)
001 212 319 2020 (w)

Anastos, Lisa
200 E 72nd
New York
NY
10021
001 212 446 4761(w)
001 212 737 1722(h)
001 917 923 4513 (p)
001 212 446 4900 (wf)

Anderson, Lulu
0207-937 7730
0976 287 202

Appleby, Robert & Alex
16 Grafton Square
London SW4,
0207-498 3400 (h)
RA@Asia.debl.com
Email: alex@rockgecko.com
(Hm)House 7
3 Consort Rise
Pok Fu Lam
HK,
00 852 9104 2651 (Ap)
00 852 2817 4181 (h)
00 852 2817 4281 (hf)
00 852 2536 4567 (Rw)
00 852 2147 2813 (wf)
00 852 9104 2615 (Rp)

Arango, Maite
Espaller #10 (home)

9C
Madrid, Spain 28014
Email: marango@mail.vips.es
011 34 91 590 6710 (w)
011 34 91 420 3776 (h)
00 34 63 913 6063 (P)

Arellano, Victor

15 Cadogan Square
London, England SW1X OHT
0207-245 6064
0207-245 6065(f)
001 212 606 7795 (w)
001 212 772 3880 (h)

Arion Joaquin Fernandez de

Cordoba
Castillo de Malpicas
Malpicas de Tago
Provincia di Toledo,
(Hm)Bidasoa 6
28002
Madrid
Spain,
00 34 25 877113 (h)
00 34 1 411 7575 (h)
00 34 1 262 4531 (w)

Arion, Férnando
120 & 1/2 E 65th Street
NY, NY 10021
001 212 826 7426(w)
001 212 772 1029 (h)

Armstrong, Arthur & Cathy
001 212 737 7290 (h)

Aron, Herve & Marine
32 East 67th Street
New York, NY 10021
001 212 535 8623 (h)
001 212 988 5248 (m)

Ash, Lorinda
765 Park Ave
#8B
001 212 535 8835(h)
001 212 734 0100(w)

Ashley & Allegra Hicks
32 Walpole St.
London
SW3 4QS
07973 134277 (p)
0207 7303130 (h)

Ashley, Nick & Ari
57 Ledbury Rd
London
W11 2AA
0207-2211221(w)
0207-937 1068(h)
0207-937 1086 (h)
0207-736 6700 (w)
0207-221-1221 (w)
0159 12461

Assaf, Charlotte & Vittorio
21 East 66th St (h)
New York
NY, 10021
001 212 688 3820 (h)
001 212 593 9040
Email: bellacharlotte@aol.com
001 917 3314656 (p)
646 431 3052 (emergency contact)

Astaire, Mr Simon
60 Cathcart Road
London SW10
001 212 353 1285 (h)
0207-351 7973 (h)
001 212 235 5757

Astor Viscount William
0207-412 0703(w)

Atkin Helene
508 and a half conneticut St
SF 94107
001 650 851 2669
001 650 851 2689
001 650 9876 (w)
001 650 224 2198 (p)
650 851 2689 (h) Home

Atkin, Mike & Ami
825 Washington Street #5A
Hoboken NJ 07030 USA

001 201 659 3299 (h)
001 201 831 2152 (w)

Aznar Jose
S&S Capital
140 West 57th Street
7th Floor
New York, NY
001 646 831 1929
Email: jose@slscapital.com

Baddeley, Jean
Finca Las Colinas
Lista de Correos
29100 COIN
Malaga, Spain
Email: queenbee@mercuryin.es
34 952 11 28 14 (h)
00 34 52 783865
0295 768 285
0385 770 977 (p)

Bahrke Peter
0207-973 8250
00 46 707766655
Email: pb@arkwright.co.uk

Baker Danny
001 917 647 9649

Bakhtiar, Shariar
Church Palm Cottage
Coats Cirencester Gloss

0285 770067 (f)
0285 770146 (h)

Balazs, Andre
The Mercer
142 Greene Street #5A (h)
New York, NY 10012
212-226-1555 (h)
212-226-8224 (wf)
Email: hotelsab@aol.com
(Hm)33 Nostrand Parkway
Shelter Island, NY 11965
212 869 3050 Ans.Svc.
212 226 1555 Home
213 656 1010
646 286 4170 (p)
646 221 7221 (p)
631 749 0494 (h)
631 749 0512 (hf)
212 226 5656 x 201 (w)

Baldwin Alec
001 212 769 7975(h)
001 516 205 2532(c)

Balliol College, Oxford
Oxford, Enlgand OX1 3BJ
0865 277803

Bamford George/alice
Daylesford House
Moreton- in- Marsh
Gloucestershire
GL56 OYH
01608 659777
Email: alice@scbpartners.com

+44 7831 136 210 Alice (p)
00 1 917 873 9156 George p
+44 7836 747546 George UK cell

Bamford Sir Anthony and Lady C
018895 90312(sa)
01608 659777(lc)

Bands, Doug
Office of William J. Clinton
55 West 125th St
New York
NY 10027, 001 212 977 112
202 320 4109 p
212 348 8882
Email: wjc@imcingular.com
(Hm)200 West 60th
Apt. 22G
New York
NY, 10023
212 348 6751 David Slade
202 406 8002 Mike Lee (w)
301 627 8125 Mike Lee (h)
914 806 0462 Mike Lee (car)
877 741 2905 Mike Lee (b)
Mike Lee email
mlee@usss.treas.gov
07 787 524 101 Sara Latham
646 227 4930 Denise Diorio
spking scheduler
212 348 0452 Joe Cashion asst.
director sch
202 236 5546 Uma
914 806 0463 Mark Galespie
202 288 5192 Mike Lee(p)
212 828 8321 Jim Morrison
212 348 9245 fax
212 348 4963 Hanna Richert
212 348 1779 Laura (Clinton's

scheduler)
941 349 6467 doug bands h
917 887 8468 Jim Kennedy(press)
212 977 1120 (guy Doug friend h)
914 861 9380 no.42 do not use

Bannister, Clive
HSBC Investment Bank plc
8 Canada Square
London, E74 5HQ UK
011442079916182(w)
44 207 991 4320 (wf)
44 777 1840 228 portable
44 20 7221 1878 home
011442079914320 fax
011442079916182 Clive Direct at work

Banon, Javier
IFB International Finance Bank
55 East 59th Street
New York, NY 10022
001 212-308-0300 (p)
001 212-250 7545(w)
001 212 249 0259 (h)
001 212 687 2816
001 646 734 7618 (p)

Barham, Nicholas & Gretal
95 Eaton Terrace
Belgravia
London SW1W 8TY,
0207- 823 6760(h)
0207 389 5010 (w)
Email:
nbarham@arlingtongroup.co

(Hm)103-87/97 Yarranabbe Gardens
Darling Point
Sydney, Australia
NSW 2027
07836 569480 Portable
01734 713398 Country
001 917-826-5946 (p)
0207 730 3856 (hh)
612 9327 3565 (h-Australia)
612 9328 3856 (hf-Australia)
00 614 0209 7007 (other portable)
020 7389 5019 w-direct line
020 7389 5015 (Asst. Helen Andrews)
020 7389 5011 (wf)

Barnes, Peter
001 213 621 2332 (w)

Barnett, Craig
983 Park Avenue
001 212 272 4012
001 917-754-7456 (p)

Bastone, Hillary
0207-259 6070

Batstone Hillary
8 Holbein Place
London SW1 W8NL
0171-730-5335(w)
(Hm)24, 1st Street
London SW1 W8NL
0171-581-2554(h)

0836-594-908(p),

212 249 6801 (Asst Erin Eagan

Batstone, Tim Natasha
01492 580274(h)
01492 876593(w)
0492 860584 (h)
0492 76593 (w)

Benson, Steven
001 212 715 7352 (w)
001 212 832 0091 (h)

Baumer, Lorenzo
00 33 1 4286 9933
00 33 1 4286 9944(f)
Email: www.lorenzbaumer.com

Bentinck, Baron
Moyns Park
Birdbrook near Halstead
Essex, England CO94BP
01 440730396(o)
001 917 734 4663(p)
Email: Steven_Bentinck@msn.com
00 468 864 224 (p)
01440 730073 (h)

Beaumont, Lord & Lady
40 Elms Road
London SW4,
0207-498 8604

Beckwith, Tamara
001 323 864 4005

Berggruen, Nicolas
Alpha Investment Management
110 East 59th Street (w)
33rd Floor
New York, NY 10022
001 212 421-0110 (w
001 212 421-0169 (f
Email:
nicolasb@alphamgmt.com
(Hm)Pierre Hotel (h)
795 Fifth Avenue
Suite 3104
NYC 10021
001 212-838-8000 (h)
001 786 553 7277 (p)
001 212 702 0611 (w)
646 824 0111 (Emergency Contact)

Belzberg, Lisa
7 E. 67th Street
New York, NY 10021
001 212 647 7777(mw)
001 212 517 5009(h)
(Hm)Pencil
30 West 26th Street
2nd Floor
New York, NY 10010
001 914 234 3087 (h)
212 249 7742 (hf)
646 638 0565 (w)

Berkman, Bill
The Associated Group
650 Madison Avenue
25th Floor
New York, NY 10022
212 301 2800 (o)
212 301 2811 (f)
(Hm)158 Mercer St (home)
10012
001 917 520 8910
001 212 625 0066(h

Bernard, Tara
07 770 523 149(p)

Birchall, Martyn
44 E. 12th Street
New York, NY 10003
212 254 1548 (h)
212 253 0437 (o)
212 253-0438 Office Fax

Birley, Robin
35 Brompton Square
Flat 2
London SW3 2AE
0207- 591 1940 (h)
07730 396 656 (p)
Email: rbirley@birleys.co.uk
(Hm)Birleys Limited (w)
Suite K3 Cubrian Hse
217 Marsh Wall
London, E14 9FJ
0207- 513 8886 (w)
00 34 52 781621 (Mar)
020 7538 1347 (wf)

**Bismarck, Debbie &
Bola Von**
1 Gerald Road
London, SW1W 9EH
0207-808 4800 (h)
0207-808 4801(hf)
Email: bis-
marck@netcomuk.co.uk.
0207-730 6224
07 77 05 23 026 (p)

Bismark Vanessa Von
43 West 13th St.
Apt. PHF
New York
NY, 10011
001 917 497 4970
001 212 741 0141(w)
(Hm)112 West 27th (w)
Suite 401
New York
NY, 10001
001 212 645 6331 (h)
001 212 529 3400
001 212 517 5697
001 212 741 0630 (wf)

Bisson, Jean Marc
001 212 989 4228 (h)
001 917 699 4523 (p)
001 917 983 0642 Beeper

Bjorlin, Jean Paul
Juilliard School
60 Lincoln Center Plaza
Box 800
NY, NY 10023

917 822 9168

Black, Conrad & Barbara
Hollinger International
712 Fifth Avenue
New York, NY 10019
0207 938 1177(f)
1 416 441 2748 (h)
Email: cblack@poststamp.net (Co
(Hm)(London home)
14 Cottesmore Gardens
London, England W8 5PR
1 305 655 8175 (w)
1 416 216 0401 (w)
0208 341 3693
0207 538 6219 (w) London
1 416 441 0591 (f) Toronto
0207 460 8888) (London home)
1 212 586 5666 Hollinger
1 212 452 1301 (h)
1 917 754 3721 (p)
1 212 988 4853 Penny (Barbara's
Asst.)
1 416 363 2454 (wf) Toronto
442074608888 (h)
561 833 7139 PB
44 20 7937 2686 London (hf)
212 452 1306 NY (hf)
212 452 1306 NY (hf)

Blacker (Blogs & Jill), Mr & M
Oak Hanger
Reeds Lane
Liss Hants
01730 892114

Blaine David
917 523 4567(p)
917 771 7977 (colin hiss asst.)

Blair Tony
sec Katie Kay
0207-321 0905,

Bloomberg Mike
499 Park Avenue
15th Floor
New York, NY 10022
001 212 772 1081 (h)
Email:
mbloomberg@bloomberg.net
(Hm)17 Est 79th St
1 212 318 2000 ext 2005 (w)
001 914 273 2198
001 917 692 9244(p
001 212 772 1081(h

Boardman Samantha
001 212 737 4058
011 561 659 7899

Boardman Serena
001 212 628 7542(h)
001 471 1329(w)

Boden, Johnie & Sophie
1 Dawson Place
London W2 4TD
0207-221 6013 (w)

0208-964 2662(h)

Bodini, Daniel
American Properties
400 Park Avenue
New York, New York
001 212 826 9700 (w)
212 935 0773 (h)
(Hm)(Home)
800 Fifth Avenue
New York, NY 10021

Boisgelin, Edward de
69 Stanhope Mews East
London SW7.
0207-584 1456 (h)
0207-867 4056 (w)

Boisguilbert, Pierre de
00 33 1 45 63 03 62
00 33 1 47 71 08 54
00 33 1 4026 1529 fax

Bond Anabelle
0776 6012181
Email: ab@annabellebond.com

Bonomi, Andrea & Giola
Via della Spiga 26
Milano, 20121
02 454 71579
0041795426093(Gp)
Email: gcbonomi@aol.com

Bookis Nicholas
001 212 265 6930(h)

Booth Mark & Lauren
NetJets
60 Sloane Avenue
London SW3 3DD
020 7590 5110(w)
0207-373 9847(h)
Email: mbooth@netjets.com
(Hm)13 Collingham Gardens
London
SW5 OHS (h)
0207 7590 5117 (wf)
07711 110123 (p)
020 7373 1350 (hf)
07711 795782 (car)
020 7590 5112 (w-direct)
Maria Bevan (asst)

Boothe, Christina A.
0207 -774 9857 (w)
Email: christina.boothe@gs.com

Borgese Paulo
00 39 06 320 3804(h)
00 39 07 44 710294
00 39 6 6680 46 51 (p)
00 39 348 410 9589

Borrico, Michael
President
Certified Contracting Inc.
623 West 51st St. (h/w)
NY, NY 10019
001 212 397 1945(w)

001 212 397 4454(h)
Email: mgbcert@aol.com
001 646 641 6511 Cell

0207-589 8919

Bossom, Hon Bruce and Penelope
34 Princedale Road
London W11 4NJ.
0386 89303 (h)
0386 89528 (fax)
0207-727 5127 (h)

Brachetti Peretti ferdinando
Via Pincina 13
Rome
00198
0039 335 377 377(p)
00 39 0684 93 775(w)
0039 0688 45000 (h)

Boucherie Sylvianne
90 Ave Du Maine
Paris
75014
00 33 1 4321 6090(h)
0033 1 4321 0786(f)
Email: sylvibou@club-internet.fr
33 607 559712 (p)

Brachetti, Hugo
00 39 0688 41867 (h)
00 39 335 377 377(p)
Email: u.brachettiperetti@apioil
00 39 0684 93404/3 (w)

Braine, Caroline
0207- 351 1499 (h)
0207-351 1499 (h)

Bourke, Rick
Fort Hills Lane
Greenwich, Conneticut, 06831
001 203 853 7515(h)
001 203 661 3753(h)
001 914 646 4000
001 203 629 0157

Braine, Ms Katie & Serge
20 Cheney Row
London SW3 5JB.
0956 505 321(h)
0372 58158 (c)
0207-351 6216 (h)
0207- 350 1614 (w)
0207- 352 0030 (p
00 39 5 85700795 (Carera)
0956 505321
00 33 90 05 7956

Bowles, Hamish
Vouge
001 212 286 6077
001 212 675 8608(h)
001 212 286 6037 (w)
00 33 1 4544 1489 (h)
0033 1441178 31/37 (w)

Bram, Ben
212 902 8620

Brand Tony
Plein Sud
212 431 6500
212 431 6724 (f)
Email: tony@pleinsudny.com

Brandolini d'Adda
President-Exor
Georgina & Tiberto
19 Avenue Montaigne
Paris 75008
060 751 7935georgina
01 44 4343 35
01 4 952 0916 fax

Brandolini Nuno & Muriel
167 E 80th (h)
NY NY 10021
001 212 288 6930 (h)
212 288 6946 (hf)
Email: murielbran@aol.com
(Hm)(2nd home)
108 Newtown Road
Hampton Bays
917 655 6193 (p)
631 723 2961 (Hampton)
212 249 4920 (w)
212 288 6946 (wf)

Brandt, Peter
001 561 798 0460 (h)

001 561 795 4128 (f)

Branson, Richard
80 Oxford Gardens
London SW10,
08675 3163 (h)
0207-229 1282 (h)
0207-286 1213 (w)

Briatore, Flavio
Fingest Manoz
Fingest
Hanley on Thame
44 1608 678 000 (w)
44 1608 678 804 (f)
Email: flavio.briatore@uk.renaul
(Hm)Renault F1 Ltd. (w)
Enstone
Chipping Norton
Oxfordshire, OX7 4EE U.K.
+44 7785 307 306 (p)
+44 1491 639 610 (h)
+44 7831 675 888 Rosella
(Flavio's asst.)
+44 1491 638 012 (hf)
+44 1608 672 410 Direct
00871 3232 71 610 Boat/Plane
+44 7785 307 306 Emer

Broadhurst, Julia
Speedo
4 Apple Lane
Newlands 7700
Capetown, SA
00 27 21 881 3235(h)
00 27 21 534 1431(w)
Email: julia@cygnet.co.za

Broglie, Louis Albert de
14 rue de Franqueville
Paris 75116 France
84 rue de Ranel
Paris, 75016

Bronfman, Jr. , Edgar
Lexa Partners, LLC
390 Park Avenue
New York, NY 10022
212 433 1212 (w)
212 422 1213 (wf)

Brooks, Christoper & Amanda
191 Chrystie Street
Apartment 5R
New York, NY
10002
212 614 2870 (h)
001 212 583 3234(aw)
Email: BrooksACC@aol.com
0011 917 496 9772 (ap)
347 865 1847 (cp)

Brooks, Miranda
34 King Street
New York 10014
001 212 255 0395
001 917 378 3718
Email:
mirandabrooks@mindspring.
(Hm)001 212 243 2062(w)
212 982 2860 Emergency Contact
- Brother

Brown, Chris & Alison
1 East 62nd. Street
New York, N.Y. 10021
001 212 772-6435
0207- 259 6441
Email: cfbrown62@aol.com
001 213 644 9150 (h)
001 212 582 3400 (w)
001 212 560 5559(aw)

Bruce, James & Lucinda
1st Peter's Square
London W6 9AB,
0208-741 2276 (h)
0207-382 8617 (w)

Brunel, Jean-Luc
Karin Models
99, Boulevard Haussmann (h)
75008, Paris, France
9 Avenue Hoche (w)
Paris, France 75008
1 212 226 4100(w)
1 212 226 4060 (f)
Email: jeanluc@karinmodels.com
(Hm)(h) 721 Fifth Avenue, 49J
(w) 6 W. 14th Street 3rd floor
bel. 5th/6th
New York, NY
011 331 4265 1835 (h)
001 331 4563 0823 (w)
1 212 750 3649 (h)
011 336 0956 2000 (p)
+3314640 0503 Pamela (h)
011 331 4563 5818 (w f)
1 516 537 3014 (Pamela h)
1305 672 8300 Karins
+3314563 8949 (Pamela w)

pboulet@easynet.fr Pamela
646 286 7000 (p)
011 336 1472 7262 Michael
646 638 3722 x222 Eve (Jean
Luc's P/A)
646 638 3738 Eve's fax #
011 5511 8135 8000 (p) Brazil

Bryer Tania
Flat 2 Walton Hse
London SW3
0207- 584 4410

Buck Joan Juliet
001 505 983 8683

Buffet, Jimmy & Jane
540 South Ocean Drive
Palm Beach, Florida 33480
001 407 655 3668

Bull, Bartle
Jones, Hirsch, Conners & Bull
439 E. 51st Street
New York, NY 10022
212 593 1694 (h)
212 527 1360 (w)
Email: bbull@jhcb.com
845 373 8586 (h)

Bullough, Hamish and Emma
Ashbocking Hse67 Abingdon Vill
Ashbocking

Suffolk IP6 9LG
01473 890130(h)
01473 890131(hf)
207 986 0260 (w)
7831 191770 (p)
7774 728698 (car)

Burckle, Ron
9130 West Sunset Blvd. (w)
LA, CA 90069
310 995 6995p
310 789 7295w
310 271 0098 (h)

Burney, Mr Jules
58 Bradbourne St
London SW6 3TE
London SW6,
0207-736 2644(h)
0207-352 4001(w)
001 917 859 9090
0207-352 4001 (w)

Burtril, Martin
001 212 941 1105

Bushnell, Candice
001 212 886 3787
001 212 734 3877 (h)
001 212 757 8100
001 212 472 7400

Busson, Arki
125 East 64 Street
New York, NY 10021 USA
0207-290 6100
00 41 22 3636464
001 212 472 8757 (h)
001 212 751 4510 (w)
00 33 1 4727 2021 (w)

Butter, Charlie
12 Pelham Crescent
London SW7 2NP, UK
0207-589 7250(h)
0207-589 7245(f)
0207-495 4939 (w)
01796 472 006 (h) Scotland
07 909 918 718 mobile

Button Terri
Visa International
17 Smith Terrace
London SW3 4DL
0795 842 0063 (p)
0207 351 7638 (?)
Email: terri_button@hotmail.com
(Hm)9 Sympson Close (parents)
Abingdon
Oxfordshire
OX14 5RB
01865 437505 (sister)
01235 529226 Parents
0207 795 5897 (w)
0207 351 7638 (h)

Byng, Robert
Belgravia Court
33 Ebury Street
London SW1,

0207-730 4665 (h)
0207-836 2002 (w)

Cadenet de Alain
30 Queensgate Place Mews
London SW7
0207-373 3802(h)
0207- 584 5511(w)

Calacanis, Jason
601 W. 26th Street (h)
212 475 8000x101
917 597 6209
212 627 9907 (h)

Caledon , Nicky
Caledon Castle
Caledon
Nr Armagh Co Tyrone
Northern Ireland,
0861-568232
00 41 263 14777 (Verbier)
0861 568125 (f)
0207-828 2178 (f)
0861 568 232 Ireland
0207- 351 4544 (h)
3 Pelyt Place London SW3 5D

Calvo-Platero,
Mario/Ariadne
251 West 19th St.
New York, NY 10011
212 620 9081 (h)
212 463 8897 (hf)
Email: aplatero@aol.com
001 212 755 7766 (MW)

001 212 620 9081 (h)
001 212 755 7766 (AW)
001 631 283 1966 hampton
001 212 847 2759 car
001 212 463 8897 (hf)
001 917 355 5337 (mp)
001 917 854 2088(p
001 917 856 9980 (p)

Cambell Roddy
0207-221 4264(h)
0370 606081(p)
0207-292 5699 office

Cambell, Alistar
10 Downing St
0207- 930 4433
0207 930 4433 #10 Downing
Street

Camerana, Giancarlo
00 41 1 201 5930 (w)
00 41 1 910 3735 (h)

Cammy
917 859 5005

Campbell, Naomi
126-127 Pier House
31 Cheyne Walk
London
SW3 0XX,
0207-376 7308(h)

001 310 625 5500(p)
Email: 4284063@skytel.com
(Hm)c/o NC Connect
601 West 26th Street
Suite 1150
New York, NY 10001
07785 363 369 cell
310 276 6780/8 home
347 922 1456 (p)
212 320 3636 NC Connect (w)
001 347 922 1456 (p)
00 55 11 9998 6257 (p) Brazil
001 212 489 0039 (h)
212 320 3640 Asst. Arrel
212 320 3725 (wf) NC Connect

Campo del Brooke & Emilio
33 Hyde Park Gate
London SW7 5DN
0207-584 7886(h)

Candole, Andrew de
Flat 1
6 Lowndes St
London SW1
017 823 3737 (w)
0467 777666
0207-736 9669
0831 121988

Candy, Nicholas A C
Candy and Candy Ltd
50 Lower Belgrave St.
London, England SW1W 0NR
Email: nick@candyandcandy.com
(o) 44 (0) 20 7824 7526
(p) 44 (0) 7770 888 130

(f) 44 (0) 20 7824 7521

Caprice
0797 476 7885 (p)
0207-834 3840 (h)
001 310 344 8904 (p)

Carello Sara Massimo
0207-584 6919

Carey, William & Carina
57 Basuto Road
London SW6 4BZ,
0207-731 1826 (h)

Carlbom Camila
157 W 4th St
NY NY10014
001 212 2422 8445
001 917 539 1033

Carmine
00 39 0823906750
00 39 3933323678

Carrera, Barbara
001 213 476 6885 (h)
001 213 476 9867 (fax)

Caruth, Sophie
0705 0096823
14B Belle Vue Road
Wandsworth Common
SW17 7EG,
0208-672 8276

Carvalho, Michel & Charlene
35 Egerton Cresent
London SW3,
0207-730 1679 (h)

Casagrande, Guido
5 Via Borgonuoo
Milan Italy
00 39 2 86464802 (h)
00 39 2 878451 (w)
00 39 3053341 (c)
00 39 2 878734 (f ax)
00 39 335284407 (p)
001 516 537 5487

Case Simon
00 62 21392 9866
00 62 811 803090

Case, George & Pauline
34 Talbot Rd
London W2 5JG,
0207-229 1022

Castaneda Debbie
335 634 9863

01672 521 237

Cecil, Dr. Mark
7 Alexander Square
London
SW3 2AY, UK
207 225 0031 (h)
207 225 0081(hf)
Email: mark.cecil@glgpartners.co
07456 262626 (p)
784 488 8890 (Mustique)

Cator, Alby and Victoria
55 Melbury Road
Flat 1
London, W14 8AD
0207- 602-9377 (h)
01603 721050
Email: 0585 336319

Cecil Mark & Mini
PO Box 49428
Nairobi Kenya
00 501 506/7/8
00 501 754(f)

Cerina, Fabrizio
Credit des Alpes
Via Nassa 56
6901 Lugano
001 917 496 0606(p)
011447900 888683(p)
Email: fc@creditdesalpes.com
00 39 29 006 262 (h)Milan
00 39 02 659 5803 (wf)
00 39 026318 (w)
001 212 371 6353 (h)
00 41 91 923 7185 (w)Lugano
00 41 91 923 1436 (wf)
00 41 22 731 8001 (w)Geneva
00 41 22 731 8077 (wf)
+44 7900 8888 83 (p)
+39 335 4214 14 (p)
917 496 0606 (p)
+41 91 923 7185 (Giancarlo
Cammarata, PA)

Cecil Mark & Mini
The Lawn Hse
Hatfield Park
Hatfield
Herts,
01707 251395

Cecil Stephenson, Aurelia
Hugditch Cottage
Ramsbury
Wilts
SN8 2HL,
0207-351 2227(w)
0207-584-2001(h)
Email: cecil@aurelia_london.co.u
0468 992400

Cerutti Gian Carlo
Via Adam 66
15033, Casave Monferrato
00 39 142 459443 (w)
00 39 142 459439 (w)

1e

Chatwal, Vikram
Hampshire Hotels & Resorts
595 Eleventh Ave.
bet. 44th & 45th St.
New York, NY 10036
1 212 474 9880 (w)
1 212 320 2900
(Hm)1 Central Park West #32F
10023
1 917 442 7425 (p)

**Chenevix-Trench, John
& Lucy**
4 Albert Place
London, W8 5PD
0207-376-1193
0385 778862
00 33 53 90 3937 (c)
0207-425 7672 (w)
0207-376 1193 (f)

Cicogna Gianluca
1020 5th Avenue
14th floor
New York, NY 10028
001 646 521 8510(w)
0207-225 0350(h)
Email: gc@zanett.com
001 212 388 0224 (h)
001 917 554 8110 (p)

Cicogna, Geoconda
15 Queens Gate Gdns
London SW7
0207-589 1953/581 451 (h)

00 34 52 855247 (marb)
00 34 52 855010 (little house)

Cicogna, Gianfranco
70a Fulham Road
London SW3,
Email: gcicogna@ursustel.net
0207-584 5656 (h)
0207-581 3880 (h)
00 27 11 8041996 (f)
071 976 1224 (fax)
0860 363891
010 27 54 33 11191 (S. Africa-h)
00 27 833 23 0000 (p)

Cicogna, Marina
00 39 6 6788234 (Rome)
00 39 6 9026023 (Rome)
00 41 82 34584 (S t M)

**Cicognani, Pietro
&Alejandra**
125E 74th St
New York, NY 10021
001 212628 7661(h)
001 212 245 4860(w)
001 212 249 8812 (h)
001 212 308 4811 (w)
001 212 249 7514 (w)

Cierach, Linska
The Studio
1c Clareville Grove
London
SW7 3AU,

0207 373 3131
0468 275 050(p)

Cipriani Guiseppi
212 499 0599 (w)
917 353 3445 (p)

Cisneros, Gustavo and Patty
950 5th Avenue
New York, New York 10021
001 212 717-5880 (h)

Claverino, Amadeo
00 39 2 600 3666 (h)
00 39 2 583 05 00 7 (w)

Claverino, Isabel
00 3902 7231 8479
011 39 0272 3181(w)
(Hm)00 39 335 820 0541

Cleese John Alice Fay
sec gary
0207-229 6344(h)
0207-221 2472(w)

Clempson, Graham & Emma
30 Sloane Court West
London SW3,

0207-730 2851 (h)
0207-982 2085 (w)

Clive, Lucy
45 Elgin Crescent
London
W11 2JU
0207-221-7677 (h)
07957-544-262 (p)
Email: lclive@boden.co.uk
0208-453-1345 work
001-908-234-2554 New Jersey
0207-235-1186 Uncle
001 516 353 1926 (p)

Coben, Larry
Sunrise Capital Partners
101 W 12th Street Appt 35
NY NY 10011 USA
001 212 996 6266
212 582 3015 (w)
Email: lcoben@hlhz.com
(Hm)685 Third Ave, 15th floor
New York, NY 10017-4024
001 212 675 3385 (h)
001212 582 3015 (w)
212 497 4259 direct dial (w)

Cochrane, Ms Mandy
2 Poplar Grove
London W6 7RF
0494 672492 (w)
0207-603 6807 (h)

Cohen Dalit
76 Elm Park Mansions

Park Walk
London SW10
0207-995 8984(w)
0207-349 0310h)
07 880 736 286 cell
0207 573 0055 (wf)

Cohen Peter
400 South Point Drive
Apt. 2402
Miami Beach
FL 33139
001 305 531 5370(h)
001 305 772 3966(p)
Email: peter@thebox.com
305 588 9938

Coleman, Jo
001 212 260 7210 (w)
001 212 751 8654(h)
(Hm)166 E. 63rd St.
12A
New York
NY10021,

**Coleridge, Nicholas &
Georgia**
38 Princedale Road
London, W11 4NL
01144 207 221 4293(h
Email:
ncoleridge@condenast.co.u
020 7499 9080 Nick (w)
020 7499 0052 Nick (wf)
020 7221 4293 (h)

Colle Jeffrey
001 212 308 8555(w)
001 212 988 4410(h)
001 407 798 0808(h)
001 516 537 2203(h)
001 516 324 8500 (w)
001 516 443 8500(p)

Collins Phil & Oriann
41 22 994 40 14 (w)
Email: oriannecollins@littledr
41 22 994 40 11(h)
41 79 414 94 05(p)

Conrad, Henrietta
4a Pembridge Mews
London W11
0207-221 6370 (h)
07831 372264 (ph)
0207-792 3933 fax
0207-712 9300 (w)
72435101

**Constantine, Susanna
Sten Ber**
40 Brymer Rd
London, SW11 4EW
0207-376 3212(w)
0207 720 8882(h)
Email:
SContantine@breathmail.ne
(Hm)Susannah@ready2.com(
0797 181 5695(p)
00 33 9054 3592 (Fra)

Cooke, Clive

Home:
721 Fifth Avenue #63H
New York, NY 10022
001 212 421 5085 (h)
001 212 668 9668(w)
NY, NY 10038 W: 199 Water
Street
W: 001 212 668 9668
516 283 1839 Southhampton:
07 715 172 772

Cordle, Ms Rachel

54A Radcliffe Square
London SW15 6BL
0207-370 3943 (h)
0207-581 7034 (w)

Cordle, Rupert & Camilla

33 Albert Bridge rd
London
SW11 4PX
0207-738 8997
0836 323616 (Cp)
Email: rupert.cordle@ukonline.co
(Hm)34C Albert Bridge Road (w)
London SW11 4PY
207 498 5649(w)
07831 584 053 (Rp)
207 498 5689 (Asst. Alise)

Cordova Hohenlohe, Fernando de

Bidasoa #6
28002 Madrid
120 1/2 East 65th St.

New York, NY 10021
001 212 772 1029
00 34 11 75 75 Spain
001 212 826 7425 (w)
001 212 421 1430 (h)

Cotterell, Harry

Byford Court
Byford, Herefordshire
HR4 7LD
0981-22227 (h)

Courcel Martine De

00 33 6 07 55 96 99

Cowdray, Marina

The Viscountess Cowd
Cowdray House
Cowdray Park, Midhurst
West Sussex
GU29 OAY
01730 812461
01730 812122 (f)
Email:
house@cowdray.demon.co.uk

Cowie, Colin

11 E. 68th Street
New York, NY 10021
001 212 396 9007
001 212 396 9012(f)
Email: cawcowie@aol.com
001 917 601 1203 Stuart
917-667-7870 Colin Portable

Crabbe, Sophie
223 Cranmer Court
Whitehead Grove, London
SW3 3HD
01144207-581 8920(h)
07768 208 209 cell

Cudro, Alaistar
00 3315 389 4762 (h)
00 3314 252 7234 (w)

Curry, R. Boykin
Eagle Capital Management
499 Park Avenue
New York, NY 10022
212 293 4001 (w)
212 293 4045 (wf)
(Hm)106 Central Park South
Apt. 27A
New York, NY 10019
001 917 572 4659 (p)

Cutter, Amanda
and Brooks, Christopher
191 Chrystie Street
Apartment 5R
New York, NY
10002
212 614 2870 (h)
917 496 9772 (ap)
Email: BrooksACC@aol.com
347 865 1847 (cp)

d'abo, Henri & Tatiana
West Wratting Park

West Wratting
Cambridgeshire
0223 290341 (h)
0207—352 7755

d'abo, Mrs Jennifer
13 Wilton Cresent
London SW1X 8RN,
0207-245 6447 (h)
0223 290328 (c)

D'Alessie, Carman
001 212 245 9914

d'Arenberg, Prince Pierre
125 est 72nd
0033609186420(p)
212 752 8888 (NY)
(Hm)1, Route de la Batiaz
1008 Jouxtens-Mezery
Switzerland
0207-225 0404(w)
0207-351 5428 (f)
00 33 4864 8016 (h)
00 33 248 64 80 16 (f)
001 212 734 9400(sylvia)
01152 315 35 10157 Mexico (w

d'Uzes Jacques de crussol
00 33 66 221896 (w)
00 33 42 888688 (h)

Dabbagh, Amr A.
011 966 2669 7220(w)
011 966 2669 6184(f)
Email: amrdabbagh@aol.com
01144 778 533 3365 (p)

Dahl, Sophie
01 212 925 8484(h)
01 646 244 7739(p)

Darrin, Drake
1 West 81st Street
New York
NY
10024,
001 212 580 0555 (h)
001 212 644-6001 (w)
001 212 273 0643 (p)

Dartmouth William
16 Westbourne Terrace
London W2 3UW
0207-723 6728
0207-224 8446 (f)
Email: william@williamdartmouth.

Davies Jeff
001 213 280 6686(p)
Email: megajeff@mac.com
818 9954 7363 Robert Maron (ent magr)

Davies, David & Linda
85 Eaton Place
London SW1,
0207-730 1517 (h)
0207-730 2931 (f)

Davis Michael
001 310 503 2233(p)
001 212 9882386(h)
Email: midav@earthlink.com

Day, Nick and Heather
P&D Development Company
PO Box 34
2 Rumuruti Kenya
12 Fawcett Street Flat #3
00 2545899483 day
00 2549374811 nit
00 254744008 (fax
0207-352 2553 (h)

de Andrade, Marcelo
Rua Euclides Figueiredo 76
Jardin Botanico, RJ Brazil
22261-070
001 212 717 7109 (w)
Email: mcadoc@attglobal.net
(Hm)Av. Presidente Wilson 164
Cobertura, Centro RJ Brazil
20030-020,
001 917 699 8496 (p)
00 55 21 2532 5184 (w)
00 55 21 533 2350 (f)
00 55 21 2527 9256 (h)
00 55 21 9986 5233 (p)
001 917 699 8496 (p)
00 33 1 5359 9798 (w)
00 33 1 1544 4713 (p)

55 21 2524 5682 (wf)

de Baecque, Patrick
33 6 11 87 9260
Email: pdebaecque@lefigaro.fr

de Cabrol, Milly
150 East 72nd Street
New York, NY 10021
001 212 988 4912
001 516 725 7225
(Hm)001 917 533 5580   Jef p

De Cadenet, Alen
0207-5 84 5511
001 213 654 0384

de Clermont-Tonnerre, Hermine
Princess
19 Rue de Saules
Paris 75018
00 331 4050 90 11(h
00 33 6 07243091 p
0771 886 0683

De Georgiou, Anouska
28 Porten Road
London, W14 OLQ
07775 738784(p)
0207 602 7213 mom's friend

De Soto , Fernando
Ninez De Balboa 81
Madrid, Spain 28006
00 341-575-9595

Dedieu, Jean & Paulette
Port de Lanne Maison Tartas
40300 Peyrehorade
France,
00 33 58 891623 (h)
00 33 1 4233 03 19

Del Bono, Luca
Quintessentially
15-19 Great Titchfield Street
London, United Kingdom W1W 8AZ
0207 908 7270 (w)
0207 908 7495 (wf)
Email:
ldelbono@quintessentially
(Hm)80 Broad Street
5th Floor
New York, NY 10004
1 212 837 7740 (w)
1 917 320 6405 (wf)
0164 632 5689
0796 629 0008 (p)

Dell, Adam
001 917 414 2676 (p)
001 212 219 3931 (w)

Deluca Dina & Fouard Chartuuni
1001 Fifth Avenue
New York, NY 10028

011 917 592 6424(dp)
(Hm)28 E. 63rd St.
New York
NY 10021
001 212 605 6824 (p)
001 212 570 0751 (h)
001 212 838 1400 (w)
001 516 267 3643 (c)
001 212 687 3500 (fw)

Derby Earl /Cntess Cass & Ted

1 Netherton Grove
London, SW10 9TQ
0207-352 5959 (l)
0207-352 4468 (f)
Email: derby@knowsley.com
(Hm)Vinowsley
Prescot
Merseyside, L34 4AF UK
0151 489 6147 (h)Merseyside
0151 482 1988 (f)Merseyside
07000 0DERBY personal
07785 904 624 D- portable
0774 130 526 CD-portable
0207 409 5600 (w)
0207 409 5710 (w-direct)
0151 482 1988 (wf)

Derby, Ros & Jonathan

659 Radcliffe Avenue
Pacific Palisades, CA 90272
001 310 230-3041 (h
001 310 230-3051 (f
001 310 280 7855(w)

Di Vita, Charlotte

917 539 0769 (p)

Dickenson, Debbie

240 E. 75 St
NY, NY 10021
001 212 734 3455

Dickinson, Janice

001 310-441-0048 (w
001 310-441-0068 (f
001 212-245-6713 Chris Royer

Dietrich Marc Antoine and Cath

51 Ave Montigne
Paris 75008
00 331 4256 9672

Dietrich, Paul & Laura

President
Meridian Emerging Markets, Ltd
1141 Custis St. (h&w)
Alexandria
VA
22308.
001 703 660 9080 (h)
001 703 768 9780(w)
Email: ljdvo@worldnet.att.net(L)
703 768 9779 (h&wf)
001 703 927 7090 (Lp)
001 703 927 7090 (Lp)

Dimbelby Johnathan

0207-221 4545
0207-792 1068

Email: 0171-243 1643(f)

Diniz, Pedro
PPD Sports
Rua Amauri, 255-1. Andar
San Paulo, Brazil
01448 000-SP
01133 614 14 84 84
55 11 3077 5151
011 5511 9981 7005 Brazil
0115511 388 601666 (Paula)
55 11 3079 9938 (wf)

Dixon, Alexandra
17 Seaton Close
Lynden Gate.
Putney Heath
London, SW15 3TJ UK
+44 20 8785 2518 (h)
01144794 768 9936(p)
Email:
alexandra@dixon91073.free
(Hm)Kismet
Traviesa 7
Los Monteros
Marbella, Malaga Spain
808 887 7599 office in Hawaii
+34 952 82 5331 Spain h
+44 20 8788 3975 Parents

Djerassi, Dale
001 650 747 0608
001 415 699 0636(p)

Dolbey, Alex & Suzie
Short Hoo

Haskeion
Nr. Woodbridge
Suffolk, IP13 6JQ UK
01473 738 130 (h)
01473 735 180 (w)
Email: sdolbey@msn.com /
dolbey@
(Hm)Domaine de Badia
St. Aulin
09500 Mirepoix
France.
07778 305 335 (p)
0207-221 6158 (h)
0842 765800 (Norfo lk)
0207 307 8886 (Alex-direct w)
0207 307 8868 (Alex-main w)
0207 307 8880 (A -wf)
07960 71 88 69 (Answering svc)

Donne, Alegra
416 Fulham Road
London SW6.
0207-381 1568 (h)
0207-498 2355 (w)

Dori
1 917 476 7742

Dorrit
0207-235 5957

Doss, David & Christy Prunier
315 Riverside Drive
New York, NY 10024

Douglas, Diandra
123 East 69th Street
New York, NY 10021
001 212 246 6411
01 917 362 8442
Email: diandra_m@yahoo.com
(Hm)936 Hot Springs Road
Santa Barbara, CA 93108
917 251 4959 other cell
646 361 2967 Zack Bacon (p)
212 585 1127 (w)
212 585 1127 (h)
212 585 1149 (hf)
805 969 9090 (CA home phone)

Dr Eli Wiesel
001 212 371 7029

Drax, Jeremy
326 Fulham Road
SW6
0207-352 2090 (h)
0207-978 2318 (w)

Dreesmann, Bernard
5 Pier House
Cheyne Walk
London   SW3,
0207-351 0449 (h)
0207-274 6246 (w)
0372-272911 (c)

Driver, Minnie
001 323 656 8199(w)
Email: minxed@earthlink.net

Dubb, Anthony V.
6 East 79th st
NYC, NY
10021
212 734 6060
Email: tony@avdub.com

Dubbens, Peter
0207 376 8755 (h)

Dubin, Glen
Dubin & Swieca
1010 Fifth Ave - Apt 11D(h)
NY, NY 10028
9 West 57th Street, 27th floor
New York, New York 10019
212 287 4977 (w)
212 287 4936 (f)
Email: glenn@hcmny.com
(Hm)9 Turkey Hill Road
North Salem, NY 10560
212-288-4844 (h)
212 396 1843 (hf)
917 887 6349 Car
212-287-4977 direct
914-669-4651 North Salem
914-669-8157(f)

Dubin, Louis & Tiffany
The Athena Group
001 212 327 0883(h)
Email:

Louis.dubin@theathenagrou
(Hm)29 E.64th St.
Apt. 5A
NY 10021
 001 212 459 2602(lwf
 001 212 327 0883(h)
001 212 506 0662 (lw)
001 212 506 0673 (tw)

Dubin, Peter
0207 376 8755

Duchess of York
Sunninghill Park (h)
Ascot, Berkshire SL5 7TH
011447768 151215(p)
01344 845688
Email: dofy@dofy.co.uk
(Hm)2nd floor (w)
33 Ridinghouse Street
London, W1W7DZ UK
212 938 4800 NYO - John
O'Sullivan
01144020-79786110 Kate
Waddington
917 930 7805 (p)
+44 207 307 1750 (w)
20-7725 9956 (f)
0207-585 3515 Arebella (h)
242-357-5568 Bahamas
917-743-3377 John O' Sullivan
port
917 743 3377 p Johnnie
917 202 6260 Janine-assistant as
of 1-10-03
+44 1344 8731 87 (h)
+44 1344 8456 88 (hf)
+44 207 307 1753 direct
+44 207 307 1751 (wf)
212 419 7493 Jenean

212 419 7493 Jenean f

Ducrey-Giordano, Francesco
Str Antica Di San Vito 36
Torino Italy
00 39 11 6505432 (h)
00 39 11 8221015 (w)

Duesing, Paul
Leisure & Lifestyle Ventures
2600 Fairmount
Bernward House
Dallas, TX 75201
214 720 0212
214 704 1691 cell
214 720 0082 (wf)

Duke of York
Buckingham Palace
London
SW1 1AA
011 44 7768 630630
0207 024 5955(wd)
Email: aace@dial.pipex.com
(Hm)Sunninghill Park
Ascot, Berkshire SL5 7TH
0207-350 1920 Lance (h) x
01344-873 070 Sunning Hill
0207-930 1224 (wf)
01344-873 080 Sunninghill (f)
01485-540 502 Wood Farm,
Sand. x
0207-930 2134 (Palace ex direc)
0776-863 0630 (p)
0207-218 5246 Modern x
0207- 024 58888 Sophie x
0207-930 2007 (w) x

07930-382 959 Sophie (p) x
0207-589 8626 Sophie (h) x
01553-772 675 Balmoral x
0207 7024 4275 Equerry - Robert
Olney

18 rue Montaliver
75008 Paris
00 33 1 42652237 (h)
00 33 3 2379282 (c)

Dunbar Johnson
Miranda & Steph
27A Leamington Rd Villas
London W11 1HT
0207-229 1894(h)
0207-873 3606(w)

Dunne, Griffin
145 6th Avenue
New York, NY 10013
001 212 343 8830 (w)
001 212 614 0921 (h)
 001 212 603 4337(cynth)

Dunne, Philip &
Dominice
3 Sterne Street
London, W12
0208-743 4985 (h)

Duong, Anh
353 W. 12th, 10014
01 212 627 0955(h)
01 917 213 7515(p)

Durso Luigi
Ines de la Fressange

Duthie, John & Charlotte
34 Queens Gate Terrace
London SW7,
0207-589 7993 (h)

Dzhabrailou, Umar
00 7 095 233 7000(p)
00 7 095 745 5228(w)
Email: umar@umar.ru
00709 5920 5000 (p)

Ecclestone, Bernie
28 Chelsea Square
London, SW3 6LX UK
44 207 584 66 66 (w)
44 207 589 03 11 (f)
(Hm)6 Princes Gate
Knightsbridge
London, SW7 IQJ UK

Eckon, Paul
0378 77 8888 (p)
00 27 82 9901111

Edsel, Lucinda
53 The Chase
London SW3,
0207-622 8738 (h)

Edwards, Andrew & Tracy
9 Eaton Mews South
London SW1W 9HP,
0207-235 4121 (h)

Elian, Johnathan
7 Hill Road
Greenwich, CT 06830
001 203 422 7711(w)
001 203 496 6251(p)
Email: elianj@starwood.com
1 203 249 8645 cell

Elias, Brian
001 305 798 3831 (p)
001 305 789 9242(w)
Email: 001 305 538 0010 home

Eliasch, Johan & Amanda
31 Chester Square
London, SW1W 9HT UK
+44 207 730 6459 (h)
+44 207 629 4399 (f)
Email: aeratbag@aol.com
(Hm)71 South Audley STreet
W1K 15A,
+44 77 67 87 2059 Amanda (p)
917 330 6039
001 347 672 7268 (p)
00 43 66 4381 4724 Johan (p)

Elingworth, Charlie & Amanda
The Basement
80 Oxford Gardens
London W10,
0208-968 679
0208-743 5129 (h)
0747 870754 (car)
0208-994 3782 (w)

Elizabeth
0033 660 596 267

Ellenbogen Eric
22 Gramercy Park
NY NY 10003
001 212 659 1970(w)
001 212 353 1275(h)

Ellingworth, Mr & Mrs
The Old House
Laughton Lutterworth Leics
0208-994 3782 (w)
0208-734 5129 (h)
0747 870754 (c)

Elliot, Ben
Quintessentially
80 Broad Street
5th Floor
New York, NY 10004
001 212 837 7740 (w)
001 917 320 6405(wf)
Email: ben@quintessentially.com

(Hm)15-19 Great Titchfield Street
London, United Kingdom W1W
8AZ
0207 908 7270 (w)
0207 436 6980 (wf)
001 917 553 6784 (p)

Elliot, Gail & Joe Coffey
72 Reade Street #5
New York, NY 10007
001 212 571 6153 (h)
001 917 692 2299(p)
01 212 571 6178 fax

Ellison, Mandy & Ralph
218 Mediterranean Road
Palm Beach, FL 33480
561-881-5748
561 881 5749 (f)
561-881-9093 (h)
561 863 4791 Voice Mail
561 881-5748 (h)

Elwes, Anabel
41A Limerston Street
London, SW10
0207-629 5955

Epstein, Ed
430 East 86th St.
New York, NY 10028
001 212 249 4003

Erba Noona
(tall blonde armanal)
00 39 02 481 7343(h)
0039 02 550 0510(w)

**Espirito Santo, Manuel
and Ros**
00 35 113974740(w)
00 35 936 445877(p)
0207-730 7768(h)

Estlin, Jean-Marc
7 Rue des Saints-Peres
75006 Paris
00 331 5375 0333(w)
00 331 5375 0376(f)
00 55 11 852 2466 Home
00 331 4020 0763
001 212 769 9760(frnd h)
001 212 751 9600 (w)
00 55 11 9935 3391 Brazil p

**Estrada Juffali, Chris-
tina**
Juffall, Walid
50 Hyde Park Gate
London
SW7 5DH
0207-823 8822 (h)
07789 678776(p)
Email: christinaestrada@hotmail.
(Hm)P.O. Box 1049
Jeddah 21431
Saudi Arabia
00 9662 6600005 Home and
fax-Saudi Arabia
07789 678 776 (p)

Evans Chris
0207-663 3601
0441 077441

Evehart Angie
001 310 560 5150(h)
Email: eke722@aol.com

Faber David
0207-598 4300

Faber Sally & Brook Johnson
Charlton Down Estate
Charlton Down, Tetbury
Gloucestershire, GL8 8TZ
01666 880 011(h)
07770 988 908(p)
Email: sallyfaber@hotmail.com
01666 880022 (hf)
0798 611 4004 (car)

Faibairn, Charlotte
& Hamish Fraser
109 Elsley Road
London SW11
0207-223 1801 (h)

Fairfax, The Hon Rupert
The Coach House
Logner Hall
Uffington Shrewsbury
Sy4 4TG
441 922 714009
Email: rupertfairfax@thorowgood.
01922 711676 (w)
07801248146 (port)
01743 709353 (h)
0468 857769(p)

Fairweather Natasha
Moscow
00 795 2436722(h)
00 795 2439762(f)

Fairweather, Ms Catherine
162 lancaster rd
London W11
0958 726887
0207-4395000 (w)5560
0207-792 8247(h)
0207—792 8247

Fairweather, Ambassador & Lady
Patrick & Maria
flat 1
18 Wetherby Gdns
London SW5 OJP
0207-244 9602(h)

Fakhre, Armado & Jasmine
19 The Boltons

London SW10,
0207-823 3990(h)
0207-352 2707(w)

Fakhre, Danny & Chris-tine
97 Eaton Place
London SW1,
97 Eaton Place

Fall, Meredith
114 Rue du Bach
Paris, France
00 331 4222 0741

Fallah, Mrs
4 Bolney Gate
Ennismore Gardens
London SW7,
0207-584 7307 (h)
0207-584 8238 (w)
0207-371 5877

Fallah, Ms Christina & Jon Robe
41 Fitzjames Ave
London
W14 0RR,
0207-610 4449(h)
0207-371 5877(l)
Email: 0850 398979

Falletans, Olivier de
18a Alexandra Ave
London SW11,
0207-622 9550 (h)
0207-489 2017 (h)

Fanjul, Pepe
561 655 6303 (w)
561 655 1814 (w)
212 472 6696(N

Faulkner, Terence & Cornelia
0207-580 0381 (h)
0207-937 1992 (w)

Feeley, Fiona
19 Chester Row
London
SW1X 9JF
U.K.
0207-352 7033(w)
Email: (NY) HEPICAAU@aol.com
(Hm)Ashe House
Overton
Hampshire
01256 771 411
07778 000 170 (p)
0774 130 526

Fekkal, Frederic
Frederic Fekkal Beauty Center
15 East 57th Street
NY, NY 10022
(btwn 5th & Madison)

212-753-9500
917 748 8989(p)
Email: ffekkai@ffekkai.com, ffek
(Hm)525 E. 72nd St #10E, 10021
212 396 9517(h)
212 583 3275 (f)
212 583 3220 Salon Dir.
212 753-9500 Brandon (appt.s)
310-385-4555 LA Salon
310-385-1638 LA Dir. line
212 583 3225 Assistant-Paige
212 622 9894 Phillipe (h)
917 816 3376 Phillipe(p)
011133621887196 french cell
583 3688 Sebastian-makes appts.
646 226 8989 (p)
917 826 8817 (AJ p)

Feldman, Andrew
001 212 945 2274 (w)
001 212 799 1229 (h)

Felix, Helena
12 Middle Way
Hornstead Gdn Suburb
London, NW1165P
0208-455 0807 (h)
0207-734 6090 (w)
0207-439 4781 (f)

Fell, David & Anne
001 212 744 0341 (h)
001 212 376 1225 (o)

Ferragamo, Leonardo & Beatrice
Villa Le Rose
Via Brancolano 2
Tavarnuzze, Italy 50029
00 39 55 237 4731 (h
00 39 55 336 0334 (w
00 39 55 375 242 (f)

Ferranti, Hugo
38 Evelyn Gardens
London SW7,
078 534 5345
0207-627 4727 (w)
0836 369118
01276 696912 (w)

Ferry Brian
Studio One
Avonmore Place
London, W14 8RY
0171 602 3330
0171 603 0549
Email:
E-Mail.@denejesmond.demon

Fiennes, Martin
Broughton Castle
Banbury
Oxon
OX15 5EB
0207-372 1967
0836 717333
Email: dirs@hbleisure.co.uk
0208- 968 5957 (h)
0295 262624 (c)
0253 290451
0207—373 2634(h)

01253 2901297(h)
01492 860815(w)

Fiennes, Martin
44 Cathcart Road
London SW10,
0208- 968 5957 (h)
0295 262624 (c)
0253 290451
0207—373 2634(h)
01253 2901297(h)
01492 860815(w)

Fiennes, Ralph
001 917 250 6629(p)
001 212 334 7333(h)
Email: ralphfiennespost@ralphfie
(Hm)0208-995 7398 (Terri asst)
0208- 743 8785 (h/f)
07973 261659 (p)

Fiennes, Suzzana
9 Bank Street, 2nd floor
between West 4th Street and
Greenwich Avenue
001 212 807 1157(w)
001 212 741 8658(h)
07 790 231 537 (UK-p)
01295 262624

Fifer, Chuck
001 212 744 5707 (h)
001 212 832 1177 (w)

Figg, Christopher & Charlotte
Little Hampden Farm
Great Missanden
Bucks HP16 9PS
0494 488254 (h)

Finch Charles
0207-257 8720
0207-937 9870
Email: finch@artistsindependant.
07768 722 235 (p)
0207- 792 3163
001 212 343 0069
079 795 95706 (p)

Finklestein, Howard
310-392-4893

Firyal Princess
1 East 66th St
NY NY
00 212 879 3900
(Hm)34 Chapel St
London SW1
0207- 235 2143

Fisher, Dan
721 5th #739
NY
001 212 421 4067 (h)
001 212 421 4222 (w)
001 212 421 4067 (c)

Flick Mook

Park House
7-11 Onslow Sq
London SW7 3NJ
0171-225 3147(w)
0171-581 1186(h)

Foman, Bobby & Jeanette

212-628-1561 (h)
212-888-6100 (w)
0207-235 9972 Home

Forbes Zandy

001 212 353 9755
001 212 829 4051 (w)
001 917 846 7617 (p)

Forbes, Chris (Kip) Astrid

Vice Chairman
Forbes Magazine
95 Old Dutch Road (h)
Far Hills
NJ
07931-2695,
212 620 2240
212 243 1509
(Hm)60 Fifth Avenue
New York
NY
10012,
908 234 1058 (h)
719 379 3263
719 379 3608

Forbes, Steve & Sabine

Southdown
Burnt Mills Road
Bedminster, N.J. 07921

Ford, Katie

Ford Models
142 Greene St. #5 (h)
New York, NY 10012
212 219 6500(w)
212 226 1555(h)
Email:
katieford@fordmanagement.
(Hm)33 Nostrand Parkway
Shelter Island, NY 11965
331 4029 9868 Work - Paris
212 752 3709 Katie - Parents
212 219 6126**** Katie direct
rings work & home
631 749 0494 Shelter Island
212-219- 6190 Downtown Office
646 541 2800 (p)
212 343 3884 (wf)
212 226 8224 Andre's private
fax
212 226 8224 KATIE'S FAX
631 749 0512 (hf)
212 219 6119 (w)

Ford, Tom & Richard Buckley

Gucci
011 44 207 898 3000
Email: fxterrier@aol.com

Forman John

001 212 930 8545 (W)

001 212 664 1734 (H)
001 917 359 3280 (P)

Forman Johnathan
001 212 930 8545
00 1212 664 1734
(Hm)001 917 359 3280

Formby, Nicola
4353 Fulham Road
London, SW10 9TX
07831 127575 (P)
Email:
formby@tueblonde.demon.co
0207 352 3600 (N) 0207 352 0504
(A)

Forte, Rocco & Aliai
10 Lowndes Place
London SW1,
0207-235 6565 (h)

Fox Andrew
00 61 3 822 0735(h)
00 61 3 206075
00 613 206 030 00 613 869
8333(w)
00 613 869 8398 fax

Fox, William & Lucinda
110 Chesnut Grave
London SW12,
0208-675 5625 (h)

Fraiser, Violet
001 917 414 0922
Email: vze2sxvy@verizon.net
212 242 5607(h)

Francesco de la Garda, Mr
Cameli & 10 spa
Via Roma 81A
16121 Genoa Italy
0207-581 1044 (h)
00 39 10 55081 (w)
00 39 10 550830 (w)

Francey, Kathy
001 917 497 4510 (p)
001 212 734 0747 (h)

Fraysse, Isabel
14 rue des Filles
Calvaire Paris, 75003
00 33 1 4277 9106 (h)

Freud Mathew
0207-291 6400
0410 637383
0207-351 2626 (w)

Frost, Mr David & Lady Carina
22 Carlyle Square
London SW3 6EY
0207-351 3035 (h)
0207-241 0317 (h)

Frostrup, Mariella
07970 727 272
0207-792 2976
Email: mariella@brazenhusky.com

Fry, Cosmo & Amanda
29 Stnhope Gdns
London SW7
0207-373 6435(h0

Fulhurst Teresa
001 917 705 7230

Furstenberg, Heinrich & Milana
771 Donaueschingin
Hofserberg Germany
00 49 771 86508 (h)
00 49 771 86423 (w)

Furstenbug Alex , Alexandra V.
001 212 396 4393(h)

Furstenburg Buravelli, Nina
via Delle Mantellante 26
Rome, Italy
00 39 3384671195(p)
00 39 0658331144(h)
Email: 00 39 0564609077(coun
try)

Fyson, Edwina
13 Ives Street
London SW3
0207-584 5577 (h)
00 345 661 30 30 (w)

Gaetani, Gelasio
Via Gregoriana, 5
Roma, 00187
06 678 1781

Gaetani, Rufreido
001 212 371 4136

Gallman, Kuki
Box 45593
Gigiri Road
Nairobi
Kenya,
00 25 4 2520048 (h)

Ganero, Mario Jr.
55 11 9970 1020 (p)

001 646 251 2211

Ganoza, Esteban Juan
Avenida El Rosario 450
San Isidro, Lima 27 Peru
+511 442 8734 (h)
+51 1 264 4278 (hf)
Email: jganoza@terra.com.pe
(Hm)Pizarro 428 (h&w)
Trujillo, Peru
+511 735 2000 (p)
001 212 625 2331 (friend in NY)
001 212 941 9341 (when in NY)
+51 44 2454 02/01 (w)

Garcia, Ludmila
Los Jeronicos Apt 4-22
Calle de Moreto 9
28014 Madrid Spain
00 34 1420 0211 (h)
00 34 1420 2560 (h)
00 34 1396 5613 (w)
& Villa las Libres
Camino Real
Marbella Spain
00 34 52 774594 (h)

Gardner, Adam
001 212 691 9660

Garland Michael
0777 5787777(p)
0207-235 2729(h)

Garson Jeremy
0207-771 3264

Gaspar, Nacho
43 Camino del Sur
La Moraleja
Madrid Spain 28409
00 34 1 6500325 (h)
00 34 1 5645030 (w)

Gaul, Harriett
Percy Lodge
15 Christ Church Rd
London SW14 7AB
0208-878 0111(h)
0208-392 9171(f)
 0208-878 0111
 0207—499 9080(w)

Geary Tim
001 917 566 0551
Email:
tim@sohohouseny.com/tim@t

Gelardin, Jack
28 Mallard St
London SW3
0207- 376 8497(h)
0207- 409 2324(w)
 0101 212 734 7905 (h)

German-Ribon Catriona
0779 965 1673

Email: cribon@pfd.co.uk

Gertler, Eric
Privista
11 E. 26th Street
15th floor
New York, NY 10010
212 653 8224(w)
917 797 5459(p)
Email: egertler@privista.com
212 653 8221 (f)

Getty, Mark
0207-446 0560 (w)
0207-495 8865(w)
0207-821-8581 (h)

Getty, Pia and Chris
20 East 78th Street
New York, NY 10021
001 212 717 6590(h)
001 212 297 1727(w)
Email: piag@aol.com
001 917 921 6788

Gibbs, Emma
Garden Frat
61 Ifield Road
London, SW10 9AU UK
0207-351-3772(h)
+44 7710 815 355 (p)
Email:
emmagibbsuk@hotmail.com
0207-352 3040 work

Gibson, Caroline
43 Camberwell
London SE5
0207-703 5974 (h)
0207-937 6044 (w)

Gillfilan, Andrew
Box 65014
Beamarie
Sandtan 2010 South Africa
00 27 11 7832650 (p)
0207-730 3412 (w)

Gillford, Lord & Lady
12 Ashcombe Street
London SW6
0207-384 2129 (h)
0207-245 1245 (w)

Gillmour, Andrew & Emma
001 212 533 0656 (h)

Ginsberg Gary
001 212 852 7016(w)
001 917 679 7445(p)
Email: gginsberg@newscorp.com

Gittis, Howard
MacAndrews
35 East 62nd Street
New York, NY 10021

212-572-5090
212-572-8400
407-835-8760 Palm Beach

Giussani Luca
011 305 673 9811
011 305 467 7737(p)
Email: lgiussani@dorial.net

Glanville Mary
58a Radnor Walk
London SW3
0207-352 3436(h)

Glass, Charlie
07 727 7638(h)
07 979 857 810(p)

Glentworth, Edmund & Emily
0207-735 2832 (

Goess, Pilar
00 43 1 505 1775
00 43 1 713 3905
00 33 1 4722 4137
00 16 4 453 3098

Goldberg, Ellen
Sante Fe Institute
505 946 3643 (w)

Goldsmith, Isabel
1362 Angelo Dr.
Beverly Hills, CA 90210
11 Tregunter Road
London, England SW10 9LS
4471 373 7867
4471 373 1762
818 783 7048 Home
310 271 7150 LA - Home
52 5 540 7657 Mexico City
52 5 540 7658/9 Mexico City -
Office Fax
52 3 337 0161 (hf)
0836 285 485 London - Car
LA Fax 310 271 3273
Sec. 52 328 555 00
(0468) 90 8514 Mobile

Golinkin, Sandy
220 E 72nd Apt. 17C
NY NY 10021
001 212 772 6949
001 212 286 7666(w)
Email:
Sandy_Golinkin@condenas
917 270 4002 (p)

Gomez, Thomas
220 E. 65th Street
Penthouse B
001 212 826 2766

Gomme, William & Emma
27 Ladbroke Square
London W11
0207-221 0899 (h)

Gordon, Jacobo
CG Investments
Ppe de Vergara, 128.
Entreplanta
28002 Madrid
34 917 453 540 (o)
34 914 111 988 (f)

Gore, Juliet
49 Smith Street
London SW3
0207-352 1317 (h)
0207-581 4178 (w)

Gottlieb, Steve
001 212 713 0572 (h)
001 212 979 6410 (w)

Goulandris Dimitri
0207-221 2532(h)
0207-425 3640(w)
0468 615060

Grabau, Lorenzo
0207-370 6454 (h)
0207-867 2925 (w)
00 39 6 320 1435 (Rome)

Graff, Francois
Managing Director
Graff
721 Madison Ave.
NY
10021
001 212 355 9292(w)
0207 584 8571/4
(Hm)6 & 7 new bond Street
London
W1S 3SJ

Granby, David
51 Seymour Walk
London SW10
01476 870798(h)
0207-352 4074 (h)
0629 812014 (h)
01476 870246 (ph)
01629 812014

Grange, Jacques
9 rue de Beaujolais
75001 Paris France
00 33 1 47034455 (h)

Grant Jamie
001 212 861 6571(h)

Greece Princess Olga
001 212 628 1237

Greece, MC & Pavlos
hrh Prince Pavlos
001 212 452 1542(h)
001 860 868 1737
Email: pavlos@ivorycapital.com
(Hm)001 917 770 2922(pp)
001 212 692 6362(pw)
001 212 861 6492(ph)
212 861 6963 MC (w)

Green, Deborah
0207-235 8305
00 41 30 45 671
001 213 858 8625 (h)

Green, Jeremy
4 Avenue Fontainbleu(h)
Fresnaye, 8001
Capetown, South Africa
27 83 323 7007(p)
07947 131910
Email: jeremy@bugan.com
(Hm)121 Victoria Junction (w)
Prestwich Street
Green Point, 8005
Cape Town, South Africa
27 21 434 8189 (h)
00 27 21 461 3832(f)
27 21 425 6383 Jeanine

Green, Judy
555 Park Ave.
New York, NY 10021
001 212 486-1077

Gregg Geordie &Katherine
36 Kensington Park Grdns
0207-499 9080(w)
0207-221 5758(h)
0207- 351 1413
077 47 695 830 cell

Grenfell, Natasha
19 Cheyne Place
Royal Hospital Road
London SW3.
0207-351 1413 (h)

Griffen, Ted
001 646 486 6573

Griscom, Nina
asst. Kelly
640 Park Avenue
New York, NY 10021
001 212 744 0442
001 631 283 8505
Email: ninaggg@aol.com
001 212 879 8883 (h)
212-744-1805 Home fax

Gross, Pamela & Jimmy Finkelst
655 Park Avenue
New York, NY 10021
212 737 4292 (h)
631 283 1144 (h)
Email: pgflo@aol.com (pamela)
(Hm)505 First Neck Lane

Southampton, NY 11968
212 717 7743 (hf)
631 287 5597 (hf)
212 830 5025 (w)
917 613 5275 Pamela p
917 613 5697 James p
917 825 0299 car
212 689 1470 James w
212 288 8600 Pamela w
212 689 4018 (wf)

Grossman Lloyd
0207-736 7376

Gubelmann, Marjorie
40 East 62nd St
New York
NY
10021
212 758 0508
917 282 2112

Guccioni, Tony
001 212 941 8303(w)
001 212 226 6751 (h)

Gudefin, Christian
Deutshce Bank
01 212 250 6468(o)
01 212 722 3747(h)
Email: christian.g.gudefin@db.co
001 212 722 3747 (h)
0207-584 9668 (h)
0207-901 3333 (w)

Guedroitz, Solina & Nicolas
Sally & Rufus' bestfriends
24 Pimlico Road
London, England SW1W SLJ
011 44 207 730 3111
011 44 207 730 1441f

Guerini Maraldi, Alessandro
11 Elm Park Rd.
London SW3
0207-860 9057 (w)
0207 795 1060 (h)
0776 823 1728 (p)

Guerrand-Hermes, Valesca
mathias
1 West 67th
#614
New York
NY, 10023
1 212 579 7572
1 917 400 1144 (p)

Guest, Cornelia
001 917 861 0426(p)
001 516 997 2576

Guggenheim, Barbara & Bert Fie
Barbara Guggenheim
8328 Marmont Lane

Los Angeles, CA 90069 (h)
63 East 82nd Street
New York, NY 10028
212-772-3888
212-772-3380
323-650-4427 Home
323-650-3060 Home Fax
212-265-6686 NY - Barbara Home
310 275 2133 (w)
001 33 1 6495 0939
001 33 1 6495 0487
310 201 7454 Burt's work
212 265 6633 Burt NY home
310 801 9621 Barb (p)
310 456 8824 beach house

Guiness, Sabrina
001 561 964 8316
001 213 656 0470 (h)

Guinness, Mr Hugo
29 Brechin Place
London SW7,
0207-370 1947 (h)

Guissaini, Luca
001 305 673 9811(h)
011 305 467 7737

Gumberg, Ira
001 412 244 4007

Guttfreund Susan &John
212 517 3455
212 956 1283 john work
 508 228 1776
508 325 5480 Sec Diana

Hahn, Dr & Mrs
PO Box 383
Porto Rotondo Sardinia
& Rothehof 3180 Wolfsburg
Germ

Hall, Pippa
0804 25302

Halpern Jen
38 Ringmarthe Street SW6
(Hm)Halpern Associates
250A Kings Road
London SW3 5UE
0207 351 2888,
0207-736 9940 (h)
0207-589 3614 (w)
0777 419 7871 (p)

Hambro, Clementine
001 917 405 6490
0207-823 4115

Hamilton, George
21 Eaton Mews South   SW1

(Hm)139 South Beverly Drive
Suite 233
Beverly Hills
CA, 90212
0207-235 5338 (h)
001 310 276 5646
001 312 543 5513
001 310 278 6578 (peggy w)
001 303 925 1000 (Aspen)
001 310 702 8055 (p)
001 310 503 1930

Hammond, Dana
117 East 72nd Street
001 212 283 0403 (f)
001 212 288 5047
001 561 588 7632

Handler, Sharon
530 Park Avenue
Apt 5H
New York, NY 10021
001 212 888 7676 (w)
001 212 758 9129 (h)
212 230 1445 (hf)
917 230 1445 (p)
212509 1500 In July try John
Loeb's office
914 684 6165 weekends

Hanover Ernst & chantal
Hurlingham rd
London SW6
0207-7314422(h)

Hanson, Brook
65 Eaton Square
London SW1
0207-235 8179 (h)
0207-245 1245 (w)

Hanson, Lord & Lady
Kimber Cottage
Chieveley
Nr Newbury Berks
0635 248835 (h)
001 619 320 9980 (PSpr)
001 212 355 2088 (NY)

Hanson, The Hon Robert
The Garden House
Westonbirt
Tetbury Glos GL8 8QQ
01666 880 491(h)
01666 880 313 (hf)
(Hm)
48 Eaton Place
SW1 X8AL, England
0207- 235 3889 (48 Eaton home)
01666 880 334
760 320 9800 (h)
0207-647 0900 (w)
07836 543 474 (p)
0207-351-6660 (h)
0207-245 1245 (w)
0860 502722
0207- 351 4380 (Fax)
001 619 320 9800 Parents
001 908 406 1429(p)
001 212 355 2514(h)
0207 235 3892 hf

Hapsburg, Marie
31 Fernshaw Road
London SW10
0207-352 1987 (h)

Harvey Victoria
07 798 555999

Harvie-Watt, Isabelle
0207-602 6944 (ph)
00 39 2 801481 (w)

Haslam, Nick
0207-730 0808(w)
0207-584 0978(h)
Email: n.h.design@btinternet.com
0 410169700 cell

Hatkoff, Craig & Jane
Victor Capital Group
1 West 72nd St.
NY NY 10023
001 212 877 7042(h)
001 212 501 7024(h)
Email: CHatkoff@aol.com
001 212 273 1626 car
001 516 537 0673
212 579 4393 Direct Line
917 434 1600 cell

Hauteville, Marc de
00 33 1 4224 4385 (h)

Hay, Henry & Patricia
24 E 84st
NY NY 10028
001 212 452 1485(h)
001 646 387 3513(hp)
Email: 001 603 5194 (pp)

Hayworth Reggie
Bradwel grove
Burford
Oxon
01993 822734

Hazell-Iveagh, Clare
Elveden Farms Limited
Thetford
Norfolk
IP243TQ, UK
01 842 890 787(h)
01386 584200 (Mom)
0208- 960 3571 (aunt)
01386 584200(mump)
079331 382731 victoria
0114479326227596 (p)
0207- 881 9847 (UK w)
01842 890 223 (w)

Hearn Barry & Susan
Matchroom
10 Western Road
Romford, Essex
01708 782200
01708 723425(f)
01277-217-116 home

Hefner III, Bob
001 405 843 4773 (h)
001 405 948 9898 (f)
001 303 925 4927 (Aspen)
001 405 948 9800 (Oklah)

Heiden Lisa
30 East 81st #11B
NY NY 10028
001 305 865 3436(par
(Hm)6494 Allison Islan
Miami Beach 33141
001 305 538 1795(h
001 917 518 5210
917 319 5507 sister Leslie (p)
0776 6044218 (p)

Heineken, Mr Fredie
Domaine de Grange
Cap d'Antibes
France
00 33 93 614101 (h)

Helen and Tim Shifter
784 PArk Ave
NY NY 10021

Helvin, Marie
0207-834 5321 (h)

Herbert Jason
0207-292 9600
07974 084233

001 646 872 9583
001 646 613 6100

Hermes, Olga & Olaf
165 West 66th Street
New York, NY 10023
001 212 874 2527 (h)

Herrero, Juan & Helen
Fransisco Morenol
Madrid, 28001
00 34 1 276 6157 (h)

Hersov, Robert & Kim
15 Thurloe Sq
London SW7
0207-584 0764(h)
0207-439 5184(w)
0374 810898 (p)
011442075907552 Robert's w

Heseltine, Mr & Mrs
Thenford House
Thenford
Nr Banbury Oxon
0295 711765 (h)

Heseltine, Mr & Mrs
30 Chapel Street
London SW1
0295 712 012
0295 712 013

Heseltine, Ms Annabel
Husband: Peter Butler
4 Palace Gardens Terrace
London, England W8 4RP
0777 442 0913(p)
0207 727 9907
0207 727 9907 (h)
01295 712774(c)

Heseltine, Rupert
001 212 532 9200(w)
001 212 744 8613(h)
0207-221 6201 (h)
071-351 5776

Hicks India
David Flintwood
Hibiscus Hill
PO Box 225
Harbour Island
Bahamas
001 242 333 2180
001 242 333 2180(h
001 242 333 2060(f
0208-878 0111

Hill, Anthony
105 Oxford Gardens
London W10
0208-960 1982 (h)
0207-283 8577 (w)
Clifton Castle
Ripon N Yorks
0765 89326 (h)

Himmelstein, Howard
ZYZZX
212-620-0949

Hirsch, Jeff
Photo Care
136 W. 21st Street
bet 6th/7th
212 741 2990
917 842 5755 Scott (p)
201 493 7647 Scott (w)

**Hissom, Robert &
Andrea**
6a Herbert Cresent
Knightsbridge, London
0207- 584 8070(h)
01428 656744
Email: rdhiss@aol.com
001 303-920-4680
0207-589 8555
001 713 739 0750 (w)
001 713 956 5613(h)
001 713 965 5613
07836 360 460 (p)

Hoffman, Dustin
001 212 207 8127(w)

Hoffman, Hetty
0207- 373 4203 (h)
& Brocas Ellisfield
Nr Basingstoke, Hants
0256 83279 (c)
0207-373 4203 (h)

& Brocas   Ellisfield
Nr Basingstoke, Hants
0256 83279 (c)
0207—589 1435

Hoffman, Jessica
185 Fiddlers Hill Road
Edgewater, Maryland 21037
001 410 798-8590

Holland-Martin, Ben
Radnor Walk
London SW3
0207-351 3631 (h)

Hollond, Mr & Mrs James
Bea and James
European Financial Products Ld
45 Rutland Gate.(h)
London SW7 1PB
0207-584 4466(h)
07802 757520 (p)
Email:
b@hollond.com/james@holla
(Hm)Donhead Lodge
Donhead St. Andrew
Nr. Shaftesbury
Dorest, SP7 9EB
0207 439 9061 (w)
07802 757 520 (car)
077860 66671 (other)
0207 201 9258 (wf)

Horne Adam & Tierney
14 Eaton Terrace
London SW1 W8EZ

0207-730 4068 (h)
07768 258 126 (p)
Email:
adam@caledonpartners.com
(Hm)Broadmoore Farmhouse
home)
Near Sherbourne and Clapto
on
the hill, Bourton on the Water
Gloucestershire, 6L54 2LQ
0207 758 2871 Ivana Bastian
(assistant)
0207 758 2876 (w)
01451 820 403 2nd home
0207 758 2871 (wf)

Hovenian, Nina
001 212 996 1687(h)

Hovnanian, Shaunt
Hovanian Group
520 Naversink River Road
Red Bank, NJ 07701 (h)
Ste 12 Dag Hammarskjold Blvd
Freehold, NJ 07728
908-462-8200
908-462-2789
908-530-8511 Sally
908-741-0076 (h) Vahkn - the
dad
917-763-6444 MB
212-996-1687 Nina

Howard J. Kaplan
1717 N. Bayshore Drive
Suite 2000
Miami FL 33132
(305) 539-5115

305 466 0677 (h)
Email: hk@kaplangroup.com
(Hm)(home)
20023 NE 19 Place
North Miami Bea, FL 33179
305 466 9954 (hf)
305 466 9954 (hf)

Howegego Lucy (Johnnson)
0410 841808(p)
0207-903 5310
0207-242 3136

Hsu, Peter
001 212 734 6007(h)

Hunt, Laura
1 E. 62nd, Apt 3C, 10021
001 212 644 1991(h)
001 212 355 3822(w)
Email: LBHunt@aol.com
(Hm)3525 Turtle Creek Blvd. (h)
Apt. 12B
Dallas
TX 75219
001 214 526 4404 TX (h)
001 917 969 9442 NY (p)
001 970 925 2300 Aspen
214 876 6150 TX (p)

Hunter Gordon, Kit & Georgina
31 Alexander Street
London W2,

0207-229 7566 (h)

Hunter, Carlyn & Laurie
9 Mallard SL
London, England SW3 6DT
0207-376 7652
0207-584 4168 (h)
001 307 733 7149

Huntsman, Jon & Mary Kaye
1369 Military Way
Salt Lake City, Utah 84103
001 801 364 0998 (w)

Hurd, Nick & Kim
Hartley Court
Three Mile Cross
Reading Berkshire
0207 792 5354(h)
0781 804 8464
Email:
nhurd@nhurd.homechoice.co
(Hm)24 Chepstow Place
W24TA
0208-995 3031 (w)
0207-792 5354(h)
0993 841828 (np)

Hurley, Liz
Simian Films
3 Cromwell Place
London SW7 2JE
0207-589 6822(w)

Hurst, Anne
212 744 3485
631 537 7668

Hurst, Robert J.
Vice Chairman
Goldman, Sachs & Co.
85 Broad Street
New York, NY 10004
212 902 5262(w)
212 346 2850FAX
Email: RJHURST950@aol.com
(Hm)950 Fifth Avenue
New York, NY 10021
Hamptons Phone

Hussain, Ayla
CEO
Sundari
379 West Broadway
Suite 404
New York, NY 10012
212 343 0600 (o)
212 343 1671 (f)
Email: ayla@sundari.cim

Hussey Simon
27 Holywood Rd
London SW10 9 HT
0207-352 2310(h)
0207-567 4726(w)

Hutley, Henry
29 Lansdowne Crescent
London W11
0486 32345 (h)

0207-727 8782 (h)

Hutley, Lulu & Edward
33 Edna Street, London SW11
Slades Farm, Thorncombe Rd,
Br
Near Surrey GS OLT
0207- 385 3735 (Lw)
0207- 408 1455 (Ew)
0860 508995 (car)
0207- 585 0208 (h)
0483 892000 (w)
0483 208693(h)
0207- 493 4211 (h)

Hutley, Mr & Mrs
Wintershall
Nr Bramley
Guilford Surrey
0483 892167 (h)

Hutton, Lauren
212 254-6980
614-0787 boyfriend Luca

Hymes Ivan
(Eddie's irv friend)
00 35 3 87234 1489

Inca
8 Gramercy Park South
Apt #3D
(around corner of 20th & Park)
New York, NY

212 475 2180
917 561 6744 (p)

Ind, Charlie
6 Upper Cheyne Row
London W3,
0207-351 4117 (h)
0207-753 5353 (w)

Inzerillo, Gerard J.
211 Madison Avenue (h)
Apt 18A
New York, NY 10016
001 212 79 1514
001 917 306 0895 (p)
Email: jerry.inzerillo@kerzner.c
(Hm)Kerzner International New
York
730 Fifth Avenue
5th Floor
New York, NY 10019
001 212 792 2030 wildfire
212 659 5180 (w-direct)
212 659 5200 (w-main)
212 659 5202 (Asts. Carolie,
Justine)
917 922 4947 (p)

Ireland, George
K1 Top Albany Piccadily
London W1V 9RQ
0207-287 5114 (h)
0207-822 2498 (w)

Irvine, Eddie
0786 660 7693 (p)

011 305 776 9000(p)
Email: edirv1@cs.com
(Hm)820 West Toledo
001 305 531 5370(h)
0793 9500000 (p)
00 353 868298626 Alan pilot
alannee1@cs.com Alan pilot
email

Isamel Abdullah
96 62 671 2203 (w)
96 65 535 8000 (p)

Isham, Chris
001 212 496 5842(w)

Jackson, Michael
Samuel Gen (Attorney)
240 Central Park South
New York, NY 10019
1 212 974 1117 (w)
1 212 374 0577 (wf)
Email:
samgenlaw@netscape.com

Jacobson, Julian
0207-589 2237 (h)

Jagger Mick
212 245 6055
0208-877 3100(o)

Jagger, Hattl
Percy Lodge (h)
15 Christ Church Road
London, England SWi47AB
0797 072 8005 (p)
0208-878 0111(h)
Email: harriettjagger@hotmail.co
(Hm)B.B.C. Worldwide
80 Wood Lane
London
W12 U.K.
0208-392 9171(hf)

jake
011 34 669 467 504

Jameel, Mohammed
00 966 2 628 3931
001 214 740 9191
Email: MJ3200@aol.com

James, Susie
212 Piccadilly
London W1V 9LD
0207-229 4648(w)
0208-960 9987(h)
Email: susiejames@123send.net

Janklow, Linda
Lincoln Center Theatre
150 West 65th Street
New York, New York 10023
001 212 362-7600
001 212 873-0761 f

Jarecki, Nancy & An-drew
hit the ground running films
200 West 57th St (w) Andrew
Room 1304
New York, NY 10019
212 581 3173 (w)
212 586 3059 (wf)
Email: anjarecki@aol.com
(Hm)131 E 66thSt
4D
NY NY 10021
39 06 69200457, 00 39 06
699211
212 717 14009 Nancy
212 717 3900 Andrew

Jarecki, Nick
Falconwood
565 Fifth Avenue
3rd floor
New York, NY 10017
01 212 984 1470(w)
01 212 593 0434(h)
Email: njarecki@mail.com
01 917 359 1554 cell

Jason (canada)
001 514 989 9797
001 514 979 6010(p)

Javier
001 646 734 7618
Email: javier@meites.com

Jeffries, Tim
74 Cornwall Gardens
London SW 7
6 East 68th Street
New York, NY
0207-937 4002 (h)
0207-499 9494 (w)
001 212 772 2113 (h)
001 212 925 8831(h
0777 1767715

Johnson Richard & Nadine
32 Perry Street
New York, NY 10014
001 212 228 5555(w)
001 212 675 5965(h)
001 516 286 5647(c)
212 982 9939 work fax

Johnson, Lucy
2 Chester Street
London SW1X 7BB
0207-235 2088 (h)
0207-378 7070 (w)

Jones Ann & Mick
001 212 799 7424(h)

Josephson, Barry & Jackie
(Barry w)
Hollywood, CA 90038
310 369 7497 (b-w)

310 969 0898 (b-f)
Email:
jmarcus@montecitopic.com(
(Hm)972 Palisades Beach Road
Santa Monica, CA 90403 (h)
818 560 0606 Main #
310 383 5969 (bp)
310 434 9640 (h)
310 344 3718 (Car)
800 235 2168 (b-beeper)
310 383 5969 (bp)
310 567 7648 (jp)
310 247 9880 (jw)
760 345 8142 jackie's parents in country
Barry email
barryjosephson@palm.net
212 226 4090 (w) until Jan 2004

Karella, Kalliope
& Michael Rena
11b,31 East 72
New York, NY 10021
001 212 288 0438 (h)
001 212 303 5916 (w)
001 917 453 4503 (p)

Kastner, Ron
0207-235-2337
07930-561-888
001917-539-9601, 001
212-977-345

Katz, Anton & Robin Plant
200 E. 66th st.
C2004
New York, NY 10021

212 754 0070 (h)
253 484 4258 (f)
Email: nkatz@nyc.rr.com
917 400 3613 (robin p)
917 400 2613 (anton p)
212 284 2502 (anton w)

Katzenellenbogen, Mark
Capetown, South Africa
001 27 21 4613601 w
001 2783 375 9908 p

Keeling, Sarah
0410-657-887

Kegan, Rory
17 Redcliffe Place
London SW10
0207-349 0414(h)
0956 312754
0207- 790 3346 (h)
0207-790 3346 (h)

Keidan, Amanda
Amanda Keidan Jewelry
750 Third Avenue
6th floor
New York, NY 10017
212 922 2003 (w)
212 922 5537 (p)

Keidan, Jon
212 210 0066
917 626 5880

Email: jon@keidanmgmt.com

Keller Georgie
001 760 324 0046
07712 421842
(Hm)0171—589 6929

Kellett Fraysse, Caroline
Jeanmarc FRaysse
56 Christchurch St
London SW3 4AR
0207-795 0323
07958 401436
Email: kellettfraysse@btinternet

Kelmenson, Leo-Arthur and Gayl
Bozell, Jacobs, Kenyonn & Eckh
40 West 23rd St
New York, NY
10010-5201
212 727-5279(w)
212 988 7273

Kennedy Cuomo, Andrew & Kerry

1344 Kirby Road
McLean, VA 22101
001 202 333 1880 (w

Kennedy Jr, Ted
Box 447 Hyanannis Port
Mass 02647 USA
001 508 775 7177 (h)
001 508 548 1400 (w) ext 2216

Kennedy, Bobby & Mary
326 S. Bedford Road
Mount Kisco, NY 10549
914-241-2313(h)
914 422 4343 (w)
Email: mpostman@law.pace.edu
(Hm)Pace Environmental Litiga-
tion
Clinic
78 North Broadway
White Plains, NY 10603
914 422 4437 (wf)
914 234 3275(h)
914 241 4616 (hf)
914 804 0058 (Ro)
914 715 2004 (Mp)
917 885 4411 Emergency Contact
Kerry Cuomo

Kennedy, Ethel
Hickory Hill
1147 Chainbridge Road
Mclean Virginia 22101 USA
001 305 865 4875 (h)

Kennedy, Jo
73 Bigelow St
Brighton Mass 02135 USA
001 202 225 5111 (h)

Kennedy, Senator Edward
636 Chainbridge Road
McLean, VA 22101
001 703-524-0733 Home

Kersner, Sol
Capetown, S.A.
011 27 21 790 1109 (
011 27 1465 73000
809 363 3000/3916

Khayat, Antoine, Jana & George
47 Perrymead Street
London SW6 3SN
0207-731 6170 (h)

Kidd Jemma
001 646 229 2502(p)
001 646 638 3178(h)

King, Abby
10 Smeaton Road
London, SW18 5JH
020 7642 9813(h)
07944 57 4202(p)
Email: abyrufflesking@hotmail.co
(Hm)Berrimais
Middle Lypiatt
Nr Bisley
Gloucestgershir, GL6 7LN
0207 734 5522 (hf)
020 7734 6565 (w)

Kirwin Taylor, Charlie & Helen
21 Redcliffe Square
London SW1
0207-370 3889 (h)
0207-623 8000 (w)

Kirwin Taylor, Peter
001 212 888 0020

Kissinger, Dr. Henry A
350 Park Ave
435 East 52nd Street
NY NY 10022
001 212 759 7919
& Suite 1021
1800 K Street NW
Washington DC 2000 6
001 202 872 0300

Klee, Rupert & Charlotte de
29 Kensington Palace Gardens
London W8
0207-221 7853 (h)
0207-408 1455 (w)
0860 360643

Klesch Johnathan
0385 372672
Email: johnathan@klesch.co.uk

Koch, David
001 212 832 1036 (h)
001 212 682-5755 (w)

Kohl Astrid
5 Rue Bonaparte
Paris 75006
00 33 1 4326 5757(h)
00 33 1 4633 6128(f)
Email: astrid@astridkohl.com
001 212 744 1600
00 49 171 3326239 (p)

Kotic Boby
001 310 255 2202
001 310 738 6668(p)
Email: BKotick@activision.com

Kotze, Alex Von
27 Rosary Gardens
London SW7
0207-491 4366 (w)

Kravetz, Anna
001 212 288 2815

Krooth Caryn
001 323 882 6328(h)

Kudrow, Alistar
011 331 538 94762(w)
011 3342527234(h)

Lal Dalamal
7 York Gate
(h)
London NW1 4QG,
Email: laldalamal@aol.com
(Hm)Akron House
86A Allen Avenue
(w)
Ikeja, Lagos, Nigeria
0207 935 7072 (h)
0207 935 0305 (hf)
2341 493 6178 (w)
2341 493 6291 (w)
2341 493 6293 (w)
2341 493 6310 (w)
2341 493 6311 (w)
234 802 302 7153 (w) direct line
234 261 7258 (wf)
44 7710 056624 (UK p)

Lalaunis, Demetra
47 East 64th Street
NY NY 10021
001 212 265 0600 (h)

Lambert, Christopher
001 213 557 1401 (h)
001 213 276 4337 (w)
00 331 4723 0184

Lambert, David
212 864 1535 (h)
917 748 3946 (p)
561 863 4140

Lambert, Edward
ESL Partners
115 East Putnam Avenue
Greenwich
Conneticut 06830
001 203 622 4293 (h)
001-203-861 4600
001 212 886 5640 Cath(h)
001 212 727 13361 Cath(w)

Lambos Duff & John
001 212 807 9185(h)
001 212 761 8094(w)
Email: lambosj@ms.com
(Hm)001 860 542 1616(h)

Lang, Caroline
400 East 52nd Apt 9c
NY 10022 USA
001 212 832 7189 (h)
001 212 702 9518 (w)
00 33 1 4277 7132 (h)

Lange Dieter
0207-872 1000(w)
0207-872 1013(f)
Email: dlange@wilmer.com
00 39 55 409796(h)
00 39 55 409807(f)
001 39 55 499546 (enid h)

cell 07 785 996600
asst. (h) 0208-673 5090(renata)

Larsen Janet
30 Rutland gate
london SW7
0207-581 7073

Laurie, Jonathan
28 Chesham Place
London SW1
0207-235 6691 (h)
0207-709 4222 (w)

Laviada, Laura D.B. de
52 55 5540 7444
525 540 5803 (f)
Email: llaviada@hotmail.com
(Hm)52 55 5415 3366(p)
52 55 5540 7444(h)
00 525 261 2717
001 212 717 9055
001 858 735 6494(p
001 305 935 7202(p
41 795045812 euro cell

Lawford Christopher & Jean
1150 Monument Street
Pacific Palisades
310-505-9940 portable
212 790 0519
310 456 6633 CA office
310-505-9940 Portable
310 230 8533 home office

Lawton Paul
07946 584700
0207-577 1835 (w)

Lazar, Christophe & marie
L'orongerie
95590 Presles
00 33 1 3470 0656(h)
00 33 61178 0384(p)
Email: christophelazar@aol.com
00 33 1 4562 8566 (h)
0207-351 2576 (h)
0207-491 7408 (w)
00 32 2 358 4033 (p)

Le Bon, Simon & Jasmine
397 Upper Richmond Road
London SW155TZ
0208-878-5858 (h)

Le Fur, Jean-Yves
104 Rue de l'Universite
7eme
00 33 4705 4601
00 33 4705 4602
001 331 0752 6726

Le Marq, Willie
55 E. 76th St.
New York
10022 (h)
001 212 403 3507(w)

212 734 6968(h)

Lea, Piers
16 Talbot Road
London W11
0207-727 4677 (h)
0734-33260 (c)
0207-792 8480 (w)

Leeds, Jeffrey
570 Park Ave 8A
NY, NY 10021
001 212 835 2000(w)
001 212 754 5813(h)
001 212 835 2020 Fax
 Leeds@LeedsGroup.com

Lefcourt, Jerry
212 737 0400

Lester, Dominick
50 East 78th St,
12c
New York
NY 10021
001 212 821 2843 (w)
001 212 628 7855 (h)
001 917 721 6861 (p)

Levine, Philip
Baron Corporation
305 673 9500 (w)
001 305 775 0659 (p)
Email: philip@baron-corp.com

(Hm)1425 North View Drive (w)
Miami Beach, FL 33140
011 305-531-9911 (h)
01305.672.2494f, 011
305.672.249
001 305 491 0005 (wp)
001 305 450 3255 Dina's cell
305 491 1998 Roy-Driver
305 496 5141 Victoria (p)-House-
keeper
305 338 5578 Sonia(p) Housekeeper
305 613 7623 Jerry (p)
305 534 1188 Jerry home
305 673 9944 (wf)

Liman, Doug
001 917 733 3165
001 212 809 3202
Email: dliman@hypnotic.com

Lindeman-Barnet, Sloan & Roger
001 212 754 2144(w)
001 561 790 4516
Email: slindem406@aol.com
(Hm)001 203 629 8821
001 561 655 3011 George
 001 516 726 6894
917 453 5097 (p) Sloan
001 212 826 3773 Fax
001 646 206 2410 Roger's cell
001 631 287 2233 (Rparents)
001 212 605 0811 Roger (w)
001 917 592 3179
011 874 762 463283 The Adela
Boat
011 561 655 2926 (sloane direct)

2

Lindemann, Adam & Elizabeth
730 Park Avenue, apt 10A
New York, NY 10021
212 794 4542 (h)
917 374 1753 (p)
Email: elind794@aol.com
001 212 794 4542 (h)
001 212 980 8861 (w)
001 917 734 9714

Lindemann, George(Sr.)&Freida
60 Blossom Way
Palm Beach, FL 33480
001 561 835 0557
001 561 655 3011

Lindsay, Alex & Jaclyn
Studio 5
Necklnger Mills
162 Abbey Street
London, SE1 2AN
0207-252 0569(h)
07812 169415(p)
Email: alindsay@deeplight.co.uk
0870 139 2516 (f)

Lindsey, Ludovic
12 McGregar Rd
London W11.
0207-221 5353 (h)

Lindsley, Blake
6024 Bonsall Drive
Malibu, CA 90265
001 310 472 3820
001 310 699 5180 (p)

Linley David
0207-730 7300(w)

Liogos, Babis
001 212 986 4850 (w)
00 33 1 607 24200
001 212 888 2000

Lister, Paul
0207-431-1340 (w)
0207-835-1098 (h)

Livanos, Arriette
001 212 265 2300
001 212 980 6863 (h)

Lo Cascio Robert
CEO
Live Wire
462 7th Ave 2nd Fl.
New York, NY 10018
212 609 4230
212 609 4220 (f)
Email: robert@liveperson.co

Loeb, Alex
71 Horatio
NY, NY
001 212 752 9043
001 212 627 9675 (h)

Lonsdale Richard
Email: rlh@rlh.com

Lorenzoti, Eva Vivre
125 East 72
NY NY 10021
001 212 739 6221(w)
001 212 879 6420(h)
917 385 8157 (p)

Lorimer, John & Lottie
33 Chidding Stone Street
London, SW6 3TQ
0207-736 1454 (h)
070 500 99678 (p)
Email: lottelorimer@hotmail.com
0207-376 3055 (w)
0207-351 3557 (h)
00 31 16 445 9705
00 33142 724068

Louthan Guy J.
323 876 0345 (CA.)
07788 748 314
Email: highlandfilms@earthlink.n

Love, Courtney
9536 Heather Rd
Beverly Hills, California 90210
310 666 1945 (p)Dana ⬅
310 275 4205 (h)Dana
001 310 666 1945 (p) Dana
001 310 275 4205 (h) Dana

Lowell Ivana
265 East 66th St
NY NY 10021
001 212 988 4829

Loyd Mark
197 Knightsbridge 7th floor
London SW7 1RB
0207-584 3333(w)
07771 547199(p)

Lucas, Colin
01865 270 243

Mack, Carol & Earl
The Mack Company
370 West Passaic Street
Rochelle Park, NJ 07662
201 346 5400
201 368 0349 (f)
(Hm)860 United Nations Plaza
Apt. 35B
New York, NY 10017
212 387 7003 private
212-750-8007 (hF)
212 755 2518 NY Home

Macmilan, Dave & Bella
5 Stanley Crescent
London W11
0207-373.6070 (w)
0976 243637(bp)
0207—861 8000(h)

Magaziner, Ira C.
617 774 0110 (w)
617 774 0220 (wf)
Email: ira@sjsadvisors.com

Maguire, Jennifer
140 W. 86th Street   (h)
New York, New York 10023
001 212 496 2664(h)
Email: jennifer.maguire@turner.c
001 917 539 9608(p)
212 941 2015 (w)
212 941 2015 (direct line)
212 941 3941 (Elsa Hurley)
212 941 3959 (wf)

Mahler, Giovanni
00 41 91 227904 (Lugano)

Mahoney, Sean
666 Greenwich Street, #1004
NY, NY 10014
001 212 902 2961 (h)
001 212 727 3777 (w)

Mailer, Michael
28 Old Fulton St. #7H
Brooklyn Height, NY 11201
001 718 834 0020
001 212 343 7916(w)
Email: mmailr@bigelmailer.com
(Hm)443 Greenwich Street, Suite
3A
New York, NY 10013

Mailman Josh
001 212 262 4782

Malek, Harry & Didi
8 Ennismore Mews
London SW7 1AN
0207-584 1576 (h)
0207-584 9161 (w)

Malenga (Mandela) Machel
00 0829908000(SA)
07958776607
Email: rissi@yahoo.com

Malina, Marjorie
00 33 1 46053266 (h)

Malkin Shelly & Tony
107 Doublin Road
Greenwich, CT 06830
001 203 629 5772

Mallinckrodt, Mr Philip
8 Graham Terrace
London SW1
0207-516 1944(w)
0207-30 4166 (h)
0207-516-3719 (l)

Manconi, John
48 Albermenaire Street
0207-409 0466
0207-352 4662 (h)
0207-409 2217 office fax
0207- 352 3021 home fax
00 41 22 341 4680 Geneva office
00 41 22 341 4675 Geneva office fax
01784 431 562 Wisteria Cottage

Mandelson, Peter
80 Archel Road
London, W14 9QP UK
+44 207 610 2574(h)
+44 7860 419 934(p)
Email: pe-
ter@mandelson.demon.co.
(Hm)The Right Honorable Peter Mand
Member of Parliament
House of Commons
London, England SW1 A0AA
07 977 001 444 Reinaldo (hf)
07641 120 391 (b)
01144 207 219 2449 Peter's direct line
0207 460 4195 home
+44 207 219 4607 (w)

+44 207 219 2632 (w)
01429 766 713 (country h)
011442072194525 work fax

Manfredini Alessandro
117 Walton Street
London SW3 2HP, England
0207- 460 6600(w)
0385 322730

Mangope Eddie
Las Arcadas Leopard Park
Monabat Ho 2867
P.O. Box 245
Buhrmansdrie
00 27 183861212
00 27 183814044

Manners, Eddie
49 Ladbroke rd
London W11
0207-355 2121(w)
0717-727 4260(h)
edmanners@aol.com

Manners, Miss Lucy
19 Kersley St
London SW11 4PR
07831 527770
0207-622 3030 (w)
0207-223 6696 (h)
0207- 373 6008 (l)
0831 527770 Alice

Manners, Terssa
28 Brynmaer Rd
London SW11
0207-498 6755
0956 477184

Manzano, Jose Luis & Alejandra
001 202 337 1133 (
00 541 826 0917 (h)
001 305 586 5329
00 54 61 298411
00 54 1150 0571 64

Mappin, John
30 Southacre
Hyde park cross
London W2
001 310 854 5478(h)
03706 71650

Margolis, Eric
Chairman
Jamieson Laboratories
2 St. Clair Ave. West # (w)
#1600
Toronto, Canada M4V 1L5
416 960 0052(w)
416 809 0506 (p)
Email:
margolis@foreigncorrespon
(Hm)63 St Clair Ave W.
#1001
Toronto
Canada, M4V 2Y9
416 323 0078 (h)
416 960 1769 (wf)

416 960 4228 Grainne Jones (assistant)

Marks, Stephen & Alisa
23 The Boltons
London, SW10 9S0 UK
+44 207 259 2266 (h)
+44 207 259 2211 (hf
Email:
stephen@frenchconnection.
(Hm)341 Further Lane
East Hampton, NY 11934
631 329 5984 hamptons
631 329 9904 hamptons fax
+44 207 399 7677 (w)
+44 207 399 7684 (wf)

Marocco, Manilo & Pia
57 D Cadogan Sq
London SW1 OHY
0207-912 1580(hf)
0207- 349 8828(w)
Email: pia@marocco.co.uk
0207 734 98828 (w)
07776 253 561 (p)
07785 737 673 Pia (p)
0207- 259 6380 (h)
0207- 349 9377 (wf)

Marsh, Jeremy
Swalles Farm 8 Giraffes Rd W14
Hyde Lane
Ecchins Well
Newbury Berks
0208 392 6821(w)
01635-299966(h)
Email: jeremy.marsh@telster.co.u
(Hm)Fulmam Village

Apt 213
No 4 Farm Lane
London, SWG 1DG
01635 299 933 (h/)
07785 317 999 (p)
07799 658 128 (car)
020 8392 6820 (direct)
0208 392 6842 (wf)
Ast. Tash Courage natasha.cour-
age@telstar.co.uk

Marterler Astrid

350 East 52nd
NY NY 10022
001 212 753 0003(h)
001 212 753 1111(w)
001 917 734 0404 (p)

Martins Peter
Director
NYC Ballet
212 870 5655

Marzotto, Matteo
Valentino
39 02 62492 600
39 02 62492 571 (f)

Mason, Christopher

330 East 59th St
New York, NY 10021
001 212 675 0989(h)
001 212 517 6632 (h)

Massimo Parisi
Baltic Models
01139 335 360 895(p)
0113902 58316 269(f)
Email: pbmodels@tin.it
011372 646 4386 Estonia
011372 646 4387 Estonia (f)
011370 866 9537 Lithuania (p)

Mattsson, Carolina

Vanadisgatan 9
42676 V. Frolunda
Gothenberg, Sweden
011 46 3113 1594 (h)
011 46 7074 92995(p)
011 46 737 854 490 (p) Father
011 47 760 100 (w) Mom-Dr. Sylvia Mattsson

Mavroleon Caitlin

0207-225 0350
07831 575541
001 347 742 5116

Mavroleon, Basil & Carina

001 212 223 0090 (h)
001 212 510 8902 (w)
0207-233 9767 London

Mavroleon, Carlos

143 Beaufort St.
London, SW10
0207-351 5695

Mavroleon, Manoll
32 Princess court
88 Brompton Road
London SW3 1E5
0207-589-6059

Mavroleon, Mr Bluey
La Gordanne
1168 Perray
Switzerland

**Mavroleon, Nicholas &
Barbara**
001 213-476-6885 h
001 331 42 669025 w

**Maxwell & Laurens, Ms
Anne**
Holve
11 Oakeshott Ave.
Highgate
London
N6 6NT
0965 441882(p)
0207-681 9127(h)
0207-482 1248(w)
0207-482 1248 Laurens practice
and fax
0207-681 0127

Maxwell Malina, Christine
18 Les Jardins du Montaiguet
Pont des trois Sautets
France, 13590 Meyreuil

00 33 4 4238 6529(h)
00 33 442913784(w)
Email:
christine@christinesworld
(Hm)95 Hiller Drive
Oakland, CA 54618
00 33 620724063
001 510 548 7035 (h)
001 415 732 6170 Global track-
ing #
001 510 841 8556 (hf)
001 334 42933242 (f)
001 510 381 8865
00 334 42 93 32 42 Home fax
00 334 42 66 81 07 Office fax
00 33 619787391 (zavier p)
011 33 680 45 9447 (rodger p)

Maxwell, Debbie
0207 736 3570(h)
07967 681 607(p)

**Maxwell, Dr & Mrs
Philip**
26 Florence St
Hendon
London,
NW4 1QH
0208-203 0710(h)
0208- 202 0722(w)
(Hm)07803 245697(p)
07803 245697 (p)

Maxwell, E.
11 Lochmore House
Cundy Street
London
SW1W 9JX,

Email: drmaxwell@btinternet.com
(Hm)Montagnac sur Lede
Fraytet dels Boscs
Lot et Garone   47150
France,
00 33 55 336 5179 Guy and Anne
Thonelle
00 33 5 533 63096 (f)
00 33 5 533 63091 (h)
07798 774189 (p)
0207-259 9795 (h)
0207- 730 9289 (f)
see notes email
 01491 652780(h)
 01491 652781(f)
01865-726297 (Opi)

Maxwell, Ian & Tara

18 Hyde Park Gate (h)
Flat 3
London
SW7 5DH,
0207- 591 0416(h)
0207- 584 4883(hf)
Email:
imaxwell@telemonde.com/ir
(Hm)Telemonde Networks Ltd (w)
40 Portman Square
London
W1H 6LT,
0207 467 5851 Direct (w)
0207 935 0922 Direct (wf)
0786 778 0865 (p)
0207 486 6300 (w)
0207 487 4001 (w)
0207 486 9300 (wf)
0207 487 4001 (wf)
07979 755 493 Tara (p)

Maxwell, Isabel

1775 Green Street
San Francisco, CA 94123
001 650 864 2377asst
001 650 864 2277(d)
Email:
maxwell@commtouch.com
001 415 771 4650 (h)
001 415 298 0009 (p)
001 415 771 4678 (hf)
017881 622653(p)
001 415 203 5613 Isabelle's car
07881 622 653
001 415 420 0308 Alexander
Djerassi
001 650 747 0608 Dale Djerassi
2nd email
magician@mentalmagic.zzn.com

Maxwell, Kevin and Pandora

Telemonde Inc.
Moulsford Manor
Moulsford, near Wallingford
Oxon
OX1 9HU,
01491-651247 (h)
01491-652263 (hf)
Email:
kmaxwell@telemonde.com
(Hm)230 Park Avenue
Suite 1000
NYC 10169
07990 525855 (gsm)
001 917 862 9935 (p)
001 212 683 4999 (w)
0207 467 5850 Direct (w)
07979 597899 Pandora (p)
001 646 435 5645 (w) NY
001 646 435 5595 (wf) NY
07887 525855 Ade driver
0207 486 6300/4900 (w)

0207- 487 4001 (wf)
0207- 486 9300 (wf)
01491 651 782 (h)
07880 792422 (Tilly p)

Maxwell, Marcella
13 Penn Road
London, N7
0207-609 1877 (h)

Mayhew, Mr John
Home Farm Lartington
DL12 9BW
Teesdale 50571
35 Lennox Gardens
London SW1X 0DF
0207-584 1544 (h)
0207-379 0258 (w)
0207-836 5314 (w)

Mazandi, Yassi
47 Cheyne Walk
London SW3 5LP
001 917 453 6633(p)
0207-351 7333 (h)
001 212 751 0365 (h)
001 212 751 0270 (h)
001 310 475 8987
0207-351 1030 (h)

Mazzoti, Mateo
00 39 335 1331 3333

MC & Allenor
Lime close
Drayton Abingdon
Oxfordshire
OX14 4HU
01235 531231(h)
0207-622 8414(h)
Email:
mcldesign@compuserve.com
(Hm)30 Prairie Street
London SW8 3PP
0207- 6228414,
0831 861 463 mobile

McAlpine Alistair & Romilly
c/o The porters
Gritti Palace Hotel
San Marco
Venice 30124
011 390 415236541(h)
00 39 41 5210040(f)
0207-723 9309(w)
0860 203310(car)

McDonald, John
001 212 966 2727 (w)

McFarland, Anthony
007 095 242 2723 (h)
007 095 960 2633 (w)

McKenzie, Raymond
Lazard Freres & Co,
65 East 76th Street

New York, NY 10021
212-489-7339
212-632-6973
001 212 288 1385 (h)

561 655 0114 WPB
212 715 2810 work fax
212 715 2801 Todd Work DI-
RECT

Mclancy, Cas
0207-730 2779 (h)
07831 400034
Email: cazyan@compuserve.com
001 917 293 7321

Mclane, Shannon
Cose Belle
001 212 988 4210

Mendoza, Neil
14a Nevern Mansions
Warwick Road
London SW5.
927 685 6583 (p)
212 784 9608 (h)
(Hm)99 Jane Street #7F
New York, NY 10014-7221
0207-373 9593 (h)
0207-734 2303 (w)
212 414 1710 (f)

Mcleod Jock & Pru
4 Lansdowne Cres
London W11.
0207-243 8010(h)
0207-234 8023(h)

Menzies, Kate
32b Queensgate Mews
London SW7.
0207-584 9397 (h)
0207-581 0384/5 (w

Meister, Todd
The Regency Hotel
540 Park Avenue
New York, NY 10021
212 476 9236 w
212-476 9236(w)
Email: tmeister@priderockfunds.c
(Hm)8 South Lake Trail
West Palm Beach, FL 33480
212 441 1660 (Bob w)
212 476 9236 (w)
917 568 8427 Katrina
917 716 9199 (p)
212 476 9245 Cami Neiss
212 759 4100 Regency

Merison, Guy & Caroline
001 212 628 5661

Merivale-Austen, Bruce
35 Moore St.
Chelsea
London SW3.
0207-581 4026
0207-867 3978 (w)

Mermagon, Mr Jonathan
19 Weatherby Gardens
London SW5 0JP
0207-373 1938 (h)
0207-351 6755 (w)
001 202 244 1411

001 561 891 2399 (jo
001 917 783 4078 (Jus

Metcalf Justin
0207-591 8807(w)
0207-591 8800(h)

Metz Robin
Noml's
001 212 644 8211
001 917 566 0466

Metcalf Melanie & Julian
High Lodge
Blenheim Park
Woodstock
Oxon OX20 1QA
07977-273-659 (p)

Meyer, Tony
644 Broadway #8W
at Bleeker
New York NY 10012
001 212 771 8616 (h)
001 212 317 8000(w)
001 917 975 9100 (p)

Metcalfe Julian & Melanie
Alexander House
7 North Terrace
London SW 3
0207-827 6300(w)
(Hm)High Lodge
Blenheim Park
Combe Whitney
Oxon, OX8 8NE
01993 898828 (h)

**Micklethwait, Fev &
John**
38 Sussex St
London, SWl V4RH
0790 9974829ph)
0207-630 0658 (h)
Email:
JohnMicklethwait@econo
(Hm)0797 1691689(fp)
0207-821 9687(f)
001 212 508 5344

Milani, Gianluca
Via Cenisio 47
20154 Milan Italy
00 39 2 3493065 (h)
0337 294298 (porta ble)
00 39 2 76001413 (w)

Metcalfe, Justin & Joane
204 Sunset Rd
Palm Beach
FLA
001 561 804 6646(h)

Milford Haven George and Clare

Great Trippets Farm
Milland, Nr. Liphook, Hampshi
GU30 7JX UK
01428 741350 (h)
01428 741301 (hf)
(Hm)12 Soudan Road
London SW11 4HH UK
020 7409 0451 (wf)
020 7499 9080 (w)
020 7720 4031 (2nd home)
020 7617 5867 (2nd home fax)

Milford Haven, Sarah

31, Victoria Road
London, WB
0207 938 4794(h)
0831 099099
 00 33 93 410073

Miller, Nicole & Kim Taipale

100 Hudson Street (h)
#10E
New York, NY 10013
001 212 719 9200 (w)
001 212 431 8200 (h)
Email: nicimil@aol.com
(Hm)525 7th Ave, 20th floor
New York
10018
001 212 391 4327 (wf)
001 212 334 5064 (hf)
001 917 513 7400 (p)

Mills, Cheryl

01 202 258 5666(p)
Email: cdmonline@hotmail.com

Minot, Carie & Bell, George

001 516 671 0338

Minot, Susan

50 West 9th Street #2D
New York, NY 10011
001 212 420 1072

Mischer, Kevin

001 310 850 8796(p)
001 818 777 8796(w)
(Hm)001 310 456 8477(h)

Modafferi, Daniela

Via S.Marta 11
Milan, Italy
00 39 2 86451573 (h)
00 39 2 8572 (w)
00 39 2 857 2236 (dir)
00 39 81 575 2934 (p)
00 41 82 43363 (S t M)

Moncada Cico

0410 352999

Monckton, Rosa
Asprey & Gerad Ltd.
Cox's Mill (home)
Dallington, East Sussex TN21
9JG
0207 493 6767(w)
01 435 831 075(h)
Email: rosa@gpo.sonnet.co.uk
011441435 831075 Private
01435 831076 Dominic's
44 77 99 8822 33 portable
0207 331 2680 Asprey Fax
+44 1435 831075 (hf)
44 7774 67 9135 car
44 1435 831075 Emerg

Money Kryle, Mr Charlie & Kit
102 Albert Palace Mansionsma
Louline Gdns
Londond SW11 4DH
0207-350 2067(h)
0207- 321 0177 (w)
0207-508 8964(w)

Montemayor, Cesar
001 212 769 9760 (h)
001 212 751 9600 (o)
011 331 45491611 Paris (h)
00 528 368 0068(w)
00 528 338 9242(h)

Monti Riccardo
00 39 335 71 64427

Moore Deborah
73 Eccelston Sq
flat 1
London SW1
0207-834 9067(h)
0777 1884133(o)
001 310 456 47777 Jeffrey

Moore, Julliet &Chris
136 East 79th Street #7B
New York, NY 10021
001 212 737 2244

Moore, Mr Geoffrey
22 Eaton Square
London SW1W 9DE
0207-235 8305 (h)
00 33 93 227198 (S France)
001 301 456 47777 (h)

Morris Stephen
Capita Advisors, Inc
10 East 63rd St
New York
NY
10021
001 212 813 0347(w)
0207-584 6252
07801 163399
07765 007 007

Morris, Nick & Lucy
1 Airlie Gardens
London W8
0207-792 8734 (h)

0207-584 8764 (w)
0207-839 9060 (lw)

Mortimer, Gigi & Averell
President
Arden Asset Management, Inc.
2 East 67th St.
New York, NY 10021
1 212 772 7590 (h)
1 212 751 5252(aw)
Email:
amortimer@ardenasset.com
(Hm)350 Park Ave, 29th Foor
New York, N.Y. 10022
1 212 772 3113 (hf)
212 751 5252 (w)

Morton, Peter
001 310 854 3366(w)
001 213 273 4036 (h)
001 213 276 1182 (w)

Morton, Robert
Producer Letterman s
001 212 541 6364(w)
001 310 457 0594(h)
001 310 888 3200 (o)

Mruvka Alan
001 310 274 5227(w)
001 310 990 1171(p)
Email: amruvka@yahoo.com
(Hm)001 310 274 5227(h)

Munro, Donald
970 Chestnut Street #10
SF Ca 94109
001 415 567 5401 (h)
001 415 627 2615 (w)

Murdoch, Rupert
001 310 203-1226
001 212 852-7100

Murray Phillpson Kate
0207-371 2571
07973 176369

Murray Phillpson, Mr & Mrs
The Cottage
Blasten
Nr Market Harborough Leics
0858 892333 (h)

Murray Threlpland Tertious/Cia
01722 421155
01593 731202

Murray, Jean Pierre
001 213 550 0516 (h)
00 33 1 4720 0233
00 33 94 97 0197 (St Trop)

Nadler Emánuel
001 212 758 5430

Nagel Adam
001 212 873 8622
0207-242 9636

Nagel William
0207-242 9636

Nardi, Dott M Jacope
0335 683 1385
Email: janardi@tinoit
00 39 02 2364726 (h)
00 39 02 8360678 (w)

Nastasse Ille & Alex
44 East 67th Street
Apt. 9D
NY, NY 10021
001 212 472 2543
00 401 210 2232(H)
OO 401 230 0484(h)

Negrete, Jelltza
903 Park Avenue
3C
New York, NY
001 212-744-8771
001 917 783 7753

Neil Andrew
55 Onslow Gdns
London SW7 3QF
0207-581 1655
Email: afneil@aol.com

Neil, Andrew
235 E 49th St #118
NY NY10017
001 212 888 9060
001 212 556 8555 (w)

Newman, Hetty
3 Pelly Place
London, England
SW3 5DJ,
0207-351-4544

Newman, Mr & Mrs John
Compton Park
Compton Chamberlayne
Wiltshire
0207-370 0769 (h)
0207-930 3007 (w)
07270 294 (h)

Ng, Clive
652 Broadway
5th Floor
New York, NY 10012
212 598 0203
0207-235-9686(o)
0207-259-5599 (w)

Niarchos, Constantine
33 Grosvenor Square
London SW1
0207-370 7648 (h)
0207-629 8400 (w)
00 41 82344108/36 938 (St M)

Nickerson, William & Jayne
131b Portland Road
London W1
0207-221 1605 (h)

Nishio, Yoshi
400 S.McCadden Pl.
LA, CA 90020
001 213 934 0714 (h)
0207—6291187(h)
0207—493 7086(f)
0207—6373429(w)

Noel Alix
812 Park Ave
10021
001 203 661 0993(h)
001 203 661 0505(w)

Noel, Hon Thomas
24 Lennox Gardens
London SW1X 0DQ
0207-589 1841 (h)
The Grange Farm

Exton Oakham Leice stershire
LE15 8BN
0780 86488 (h)

Noel, Vanessa
12 East 86th St. #535
New York, NY 10028
212 906 0054
212 906 0058 (f)
001 212 517 5133 (h)
001 212 737 0115 (w)

Noha, Cecilia
001 212 683 4649

Noonan, Tim
001 212 446 3661

Nuttall, Harry
Chairman
RNR International Ltd
15 Sloane Court West (h)
London, SW3
0207-823 4308
0207-590 6262(w)
Email: mrsport@aol.com
(Hm)17 Queens's Gate Place
Mews(w)
London
SW7 5BG
UK
07768 004 328 (p)

O'Donnell, Mr Carletto
13 West Eaton Place
London SW1,
0207-235 0153 (h)
0207-495 4939 (w)
0860 353056
& 655 Park Avenue
New York, NY
001 212 517 7507 (h)
001 809 326 5925 (h)

234 1 775 2565 (p)
234 803 40 00 442 GSM

Olsen, Camille
917 859 9923
917 693 9935

O'Neill, Louis
230 E. 15th Street
NY 10003
00 1 917 539 8889(p)
00 1 212 473 7277(h)
Email: loneill@stanfordalumni.or
(Hm)001 212 335 9117 (w)

Omar, Ralph
13 Cliveden Place
London SW1 8LAA
0207-730 8077 (h)
6F 6 Sloane Square
London SW1
0207-730 4253 (f)
0207-730 4382 (w)

Oates, Simon
0207-724 1010 (w)

Ong BS & Chritina
Como Holdings 2nd floor
Pemberton House
15 Wrights Lane
London
W85 SLL,
0207-368 8888(w)

Oates, Tom
72a Sydney Street
London SW3
0207-243 0141 (h)
0207-280 2199 (w)

Ong Melissa
001 817 373 4028(p)

Ojora, Yinka
0207 722 3252(w)
07831 556 778(p)
Email: yinkaojora@aol.com
0207 722 4370 work fax
234 1 269 0054 Nigeria (w)
234 1 269 0055 Nigeria (wf)

Oppenheim, Mr Laurie
17 Avenue Duquesne
Paris 75007
00 33 144 53 50 00
00 331 4763 2014(h)
0207-223 8642 (h)

00 33 93 5252 (S Tropez)
00 33 1 4551 6306 (h)

Oppenheim, Ms Marella
16 Bolton Gardens
London SW5 0AJ
0207-373 1213 (h)

Orchard (Vaughn-Edward), Katie
Orchard End
Fittleton
Salisbury
Wiltshire, England SP4 9QA
0207 905 1329 (Sw)
0772 029 6237(Sp)
Email:
vaughanedwards@ukgateway.
(Hm)Alexander Mann
9-11 Fulwood Place
London, WC1V 6HG
0208 947 0027 Parents
0198 067 0311 (h) try this # first
0780 175 4736 (Kp)
0208 968 4832 (h)Tim
0198 067 0900 (f)

Orlando, Fabrice
011729 7250
06 0938 2893

Osbourne Rachel
19 shile Hall Gdns
London, W4 3B5
0208-994 9018(h)

Oswald, William & Arabella
Buckton Park
Leintwardine
Craven Arms
Herefordshire, UK SY7 0JU
001 547 540 405
001 547 540 495(f)
Email:
williamoswald@asysytems.c
(Hm)(2nd home)
6 St. Olaves Court
9-11 St. Petersburgh Place
London, W2 HJY England
01547 54001 (wf)
01547 540490 (w direct line)
01547 54000 (w)
020 7229 0773 (2nd home phone)

Otto, Beo & Edvige
00 331 4747 1398 (M
00 331 4011 2525 (C

Owen Edmunds, Tom & Kate
The Coach House
Talycoed Court
Nr Monmouth Gwen NPS 4HR
0207-322 3418 (w)
0207-259 2081 (h)
0207-727 9742

Oxenberg Christina marc Yaggi
102 W 86 #3R
NY NY 10024
001 917 208 9962
Email: oxenberg@earthlink.net

Paini, Nicole
12 Stanhope Mews South
London SW7
0207-516 1735
0207-259 2081 (h)
0207-322 3418 (w)

Palau, Marcia
98 Cheyne Walk
London SW10
0207-351 4553
0207-225 3474 (h)

Palmer Tomkinson Tara
0207-244 6856(h)
0468 893371(p)
01256 389331(c)

Palumbo, Mr James
Flat number 5
78 Onslow Gardens
London, SW7 3QB
0207-378 6528(w)
0378 160176(p)
0207-244 8353 (h)

Palumbo, Peter
2 Astell Street
London SW3
0207-351 7371

Panah-Izadi, Nader & Brigitte
241 Boulevard St. Germain
Paris
5 The Boulton
London SW10
0207-244 6362 (h)
00 33 1 4550 3511 (ph)

Pank, Ms Victoria & Alby Carto
22 Thames Quay
Chelsea Harbour
London, SW10
0207-352 8889
0585 336319
0207- 581 0174 (w)
0860 320811
071-736 6333(h)

Parker Jackie
001 678 296 0042
001 505 242 4272
Email: jackie@jackieparker.net

Parsons Carolina
19 14 527 4505
Email: carolinaparsons@aol.com

Paschen, Elise
001 212 254 9628
001 212 769 2711 (h)

Pashcow, Joel
Atlantic Realty Trust
747 Third Ave. - 10th Floor(w)
NY, 10017
860 UN Plaza (h)
#19A, NY 10017
212 702 8566 (w)
212 355 3080 (wf)
Email: thejoel18@aol.com
(Hm)27 St. George Place (h)
Palm Beach Gardens, FL, 33418
21 Fir Drive (h)
Great Neck, NY 11024
561 301 7133 Denny-Boat Capt.
212 702 8566 (w)
212 355 3080 (wf)
917 842 8811 emergency
561 691 9745 Line 1(h)
561 691 4915 Line 2 (h)
561 691 6867 (hf)
212 308 4595 UN Plaza (h)
212 750 2453 UN Plaza (f)
516 466 4950 Great Neck (h)
516 466 4954 Line 2 Great Neck
516 466 9856 Great Neck (f)
917 842 8611 (p)
561 309 0587 (p)
917 860 6159 (car)
212 570 1016 Carter
516 487 6465 Father's home

Pashcow, Stacey
(married name Gardi)
215 W 75th street,
Apt 12C
New York, NY 10023

212 501 7983 (h)
212-456-5927(w)
917 921 8002 portable
917-520-7294 car phone

Pastrana, Andres
Ex President of Colu
Casa de Narino
Carrera #8A N7/26
Bogata, Columbia South Amer-
ica
00 571 562 9300
00 34 636 869257
Email: APA98@aol.com
(Hm)Castello 64 Piso 6
Madrid, Espana
28001,
917 443 0195 (p)
212-317-8915 (NY)
91 7810051 (spain)

Patricof, Alan & Susan
830 Park Avenue
Apt 11C
New York, NY 10021
212 777 6211 (w)

Paulson, John
001 212 982 9875 (h)
001 212 350 5751 (w)

Pavoncelli, Cosima & Riccardo
28 Thurloe Square
London, SW7 2SD
0207-589-7677(h)

3

0207-589-9998
Email: cosima_pavoncelli@ya-
hoo.c

Pearson, Hon Charles
14 Markham Square
London SW3 4UY
0207-225 0096 (h)
00 41 26 75542 (V erbier)
079 85 655

Pease, Simon & Clem
Underley Grange
Kirkby Lansdale
Carnforth
LA6 2LE
0468-36242 (h)

Pedrini Lorenzo
Next Model agancy
001 917 297 9980
00 33 53451300(w)
01 53 45 13 01 Office Fax
0663 00 8741

Pedrini Tito
001 212 888 3355(w)
001 212 688 2472(h)
Email: 001 917 545 7277(p)

Pekeler, Marcus
0041 794 015 377

Peltz, Harlan
117 East 57th
New York, NY 10022
001 212 486 2826(h)
001 212 622 7300(w)
Email:
harlanp@youthstream.com
001 516 283 5053/4
001 917 971 4012 (p)

Pennell, Mark
00 61 39 787 3592
00 61 04111 89293(p)
00 61 3 9670 1505(w)
00 61 3 9690 3291(h)

Perelman, Ronald
Revlon
35 East 62nd Street
New York, NY 10021
212-572-5060
212-572-8401

Petangi, Helsius
00 41 7922 0202

Peters, John
Peters Entertainment
4000 Warner Blvd.
Bldg. # 15
Burbank, CA 91522
001 818-954-4960 (w)
001 818-954-4976
001 818 954 4983 (f)

Peterson, Holly
212 472 1142 (h)

Peterson, Riki
001 212 721 7217 (h)
001 212 644 4188 (w)
001 212 362 9867 (h)

Pham Linh-Dan + Andrew
111 West 57th suite 1105
NY NY^ 10019
001 646 456 0744
Email: linhdan@hotmail.com

Picasso, Olivier & Alice
35 rue Marbeuf
75008 Paris France
00 33 6 08 68 69 70
00 33 1 4703 6969(w)
00 33 1 4284 1010 (h)
00 331 67 03 69 69 (w)

Picciotto Michael
0207-584 4726
00 41 22 7003715
0207—839 22 21(w)
0370 468461
00 41 22 9193203

Pickering, Jane & William (Nic
20 Stonce Road
London W12 8BV
0207-499 9080(w)
0208-749 9970(h)

Pignatelli, Frederico
468 W Broadway #6H.
NY, NY 10012
001 917 860 3200 (p)
001 212 529 3000 (h)
001 310 888 1111(h
001 212 691 5959(w)
001 212 206 7600
00 39 348 5811000 (p)

Pigozzi Jean
1 West 67th
NY NY 10023
001 212 721 0355(h)
00   41 22 312 197
00 331 4634-6555 Paris
00 33 4936 13370 Antibes
001 242 333 2895 Bahamas or
333 2620
001 917 446 7368
001 917 414 5147
0493-613 370

Pittman, Bob & Veronique
President & CEO
AOL Networks
150 Columbus Avenue (h)
Apt. 17-C
New York

NY 10023
001 212 336 5944(h)
001 210 824 0466(p)
Email: bpittc21@aol.com or vchoa
(Hm)75 Rockerfella Plaza
29th Floor
New York
10019,
001 212 484 6780 (w)
001 212 956 2668 (wf)
Pittman @ AOL.com e.mail
001 212 580 56 69 (veronique h)
001 914 767 9233 (h)

Pittman, Sandy

001 805 693 1212 (w)
Email: sandhill@mindspring.com

Plepler, Richard

755 Park Ave(h)
1100 Ave of the Americas
Room 1046, 10036(w)
001 212 772 2174(h)
001 212 512 1960(w)
001 917 833 5047(p)

Plouvier, Diane & Denis

46 Villa Chaptal
LeVallois-Perret
Paris, France 92300
00 33 1 3485 9207/5
00 33 1 4758 0619(h)
(Hm)(W) Porthault
6 Rue Collange
Levallois Perret France
92300,
00 33 1 4737 1400(w)
00 33 0860165638 cell

011 336 61 575164 Denny's cell
33147377320 FAX

Podolsky, Jeffrey

New York Editor
Tatler
150 East 72nd St
Suite 2C
NY, NY 10021
212 988 4912 (w)
212 988 7115 (wf)
917 533 5580 (p)

Polk, George

001 212 529 2424 (h)

Polli, Edoardo

Legler S.p.A.
Corso Manzoni, 1
Capriate S. Gervasio
24040 Crespi d'Adda (BG)Italia
02 909341
02 90934579 (f)
00 39 335 237219 (p)

Polu Emmanuelle

00 331 4326 4092(p)
Email: epolu@group-etc.com
00 33 0615 381 870 (p)

Polu Isabelle

07801 881017(p)
0207 831 6317
Email: isapolu@microsoft.com

Polu, Clary
79 rue de Rennes
Paris, France 75006
01 45 44 00 34
06 13 27 61 83
Email: clary@caramail.fr

Porrin Ivanisevic
001 212 579 9323(w)
001 212 579 9523 (h)
 001 917 593 4191

Porter, Pliny
Fireworks Pictures
1170 Eventide Place
Beverly Hills, CA 90210
001 310 276 8120(w)
001 310 435 8015(p)
Email:
plinyporter@mindspring.co
310 276 8130 (f)

Porthault Emmanuele
00 33 607362020

Porthault, Mr & Mrs
77 bis rue Charles Laffitte
Neuilly 92200 France
00 33 1 4722 3215 (h)
00 33 1 34859205 (c)

Porthault, Pascal
3 Place du General Catroux
75017 Paris France
00 33 1 4738 6479 (h)

Porthault, Remi & Isabel
43 Avenue Charles de Gaulle
Neuilly Sur Seine, P. France
00 33 1 4737 1400 (w)

Poster, Meryl
Sr. V.P. Production
Miramax Films
375 Greenwich Street
#3
New York, N.Y. 10013
001 212 941 3828 (w)
001 212 941 2099 (f)
(Hm)25 E. 86th St.
#5c
New York, NY 10028
 Amy- Assistant
001 212 439 6187 (h)

Potter, Muffie
01 917 691 2626(p)
01 212 737 3223(h)

Prestin, Electra
001 212 879 4214

Prevost, Catherine

20 Egerton Gdns
London SW3
0207-584-5240 (h)
001 212 628 6423

Price, Charles H. II
One West Armour Blvd.
Kansas City, Missouri 64111
001 816 932 0175
001 816 931 2720
001 816 931 5585

Price, Judy
Avenue
950 3rd Ave, 5th fl.(w)
New York, NY
001 212 541 9465

Princess Firyal
1 East 66th St.
New York
NY
10021,
001 212 879 3900
0207 235 2143
(Hm)34 Chapel St.
London
SW1

Pritzker, Nick
Hyatt Fevelopment Corp.
200 West Madison (w)
Chicago, IL 60606
312-750-8401 (w)
312-593-8401(p)
Email: npritzker@earthlink.net

(Hm)1518 N. Astor Street
Chicago, IL 60606
312 750 8347 (Mary Ryan)
312 664 2599 (h)
312 664 0889 (hf)

Pritzker, Thomas
Numero Uno
200 W. Madison
Suite 3800
Chicago, IL 60606
001 312 750 8101 (o)
001 312 920 2395(f)
Email: tomp@interacess.com
(Hm)2430 North Lakeview #7N
(h)
Chicago, IL 60614
07881 507181
312 420 8101 (p)
773 327 1313 (h)
312 787 5153 (hf)
847 362 1802 (farm)
312 787 5132 (h)
847 362 2087 (hf)
312 750 8101 (w)
312 920 2395 (wf)
312 750 8451 Emergency contact
312 750 8400 Main Office Number

Propp Rodney
Birkman friend
001 212 421 1117(w)
Email: propppbros@aol.com

Prunier Christy & David Doss
315 Riverside dr #15D
NY NY 10025
001 212 864 0424
001 917 648 5003

Pucci, Laudomia
Husband: Alessandro Castellano
Via de Pucci 6
5100 Florence, Italy
0039335 615 3240 (p)
Email: laopucci@tin.it
00.39 55 2618431 (w) Florence
00 39 55 290619 (h) Florence
00 39 6 32650295 (h) Rome
00 39 55 280 451 (f) Florence
1 212 355 2800 (h)
1 212 752 4777 (w)

Puig Marc
President Fashion Di
Travessera de Gracia 9
Barcelona 08021
Spain
34 93 400 71 41 (w)
34 93 400 70 15 (f)
Email: pincortede@wanadoo.es

Puig Tarla
Esperanza No. 15
Barcelona 08017
Spain

Puopolo, Sonia
617 510 9292
305 860 8086
Email: soniatila@yahoo.com
305 860 1060

Puttnam, David
Kingsmead Mil
Little Somerford
Nr. Chippenham
Wiltshire Sanis su n
Malmesbury 4431
0207-529 0500 (w)

Pymont, Chris
4 Crane Court
London EC4
0207-353 6210 (h)
0494 814615 (h)
0207-404 4800 (w)

Quartucci, Alan
001 212 421 0043(w)
001 212 414 0472(por
001 516 287 1588
001 518 584 9175 Country
001 318 584 9175 Saratoga
001 407 842 8448 Florida
001 407 758 5101(p)

Quinn, Topper
001 212 779 4882
0207-493 2223 (h)
001 212 779 4882

Rachline, Nicholas
001 516 537 0123
0207-589 4463
00 33 1 4555 9399
44(0)777 5913913 uk cell

Radziwill Carole
29 King St
Apt 2F
New York, New York 10014
0790 327 1605(p)
0207-229 3368(temp
Email: radziwill@aol.com
(Hm)001 917 992 6415(p)
001 212 463 8015

Rankin, Mr Gavin
52 Bassett Road
London, W10 6JL
0208-968 6266 (h)
0207-925 0555 (w)
0207-493 5088 (w)

Rappaport Don
001 908 874 4300(w)
845 373 8586 (h)

Rattazzi Isabel
001 212 988 0963
001 917 854 8380

Raynes, Patty
001 212 988 1133
001 212 980 1669 (w)
001 561 798 2000 Florida

Reardan, Kate
Albyn House
239 New King's Road
London SW6 4XG
0207 370 5818
0207-731 5092 (h)
0207-499 9080 (w)
0207-499 2138 (w)

Reynal Michael
00 54 1 312 6301(w)
001 561 833 6446(mum

Reynal, Miquel
Montivideo 1336
Buenos Aires
Argentina
00 54 1 424918 (h)
00 54 1 4401805 (w)

Reza, Ali
55 Eresby House
Rutlan Gate
London, United Kingdom
SW71BG
0207-589-5997 (h)
0207-584-3800 (w)
Email: alireza@freestream.com
001 212 750 1260 (h)
001 203 790 6800

0207-584 7757 (f)
07979242424 (p) Ali

Ritblat, Nick Rebecca Willis
37 Queens Grove
London NW8 6HN
0207-586 9707

Ritson Thomas Rupert
0770 3593252

Rivers, Joan
Melissa Rivers
1 E 62nd St
NY, NY 10021
1 310 454 6179(h)
1 212 826 4211(w)

Robert, Joseph & Jill
1650 Tysons Blvd.
Mclaine, VA 22102
703 624 1810(p)
00 703 714 8024 (w)
00 703 506 0560 (h)
703 714-8103 w-fax

Roberts Deb
001 917 693 5794

Robilant, Mr Edmondo di Maya
5 Woodborough Road
London SW15 6PX
0208-788-7800(h)
0207-409 1540(w)
(Hm)0410 921192(mp)
0370 471410(ep)
0207-409 1540 (w)
0207-373 1543 (h)

Robin
917 856 7477 (p)

Robinski Kasia/Pod
46 Sutherland Place
London, W2 5BY UK
0207 792 5366 (h)
0207 792 5367 (h)
Email:
rodneyhodges/kasiarobinsk
07815 153 857 (p)

Robinson, Jo & Lisa Shields
001 631 537 3934(h)
001 212 301 2305(w)
011 212 434 9677(w)
001 561 832 0551(parents)
001 516 324 9503
001 917 854 1224()

Rocksavage David
0207-408 0418(w)

Roedy, Bill
MTV Europe
24 Hanover House – Wood Hi St.
St. Johns, NW87DX
0207-478 6000 (w)
0207-383 4250 (w)

Rolfe, Gail
46-48 Gertrud Street
London SW10
0207-351 1836 (h)
0207-938 6000 (w)

Ronson, Lisa
54 Grosvenor Street
London, W1X OEU
0207- 493 3577
0207- 493 3524 (f)
212 412 2200 Lisa's work

Ronson, Mr & Mrs Gerald
Carrington Chase
54 Winnington Road
Hampstead, London N2 OTY
07785-975-607Gail p
0207-487-2970 (f)
0208-458 9309 (h)
0207-486 4477 (w)
0836 202207
00 87 11440333 (b oat)

Rose Wendy & Jo
001 212 633 9270 (h)

001 212 720 3200 Jo (w)

**Rose, Charlie &
Burder, Amanda**
119 E 71ST. Street
New York, NY 10021
212-940-1600 (w)
212-249-4645 (h)

Rosen, Andrew
001 212 556 0614
001 212 496 6644
001 917 861 4035(p

Rosen, Denis & Sylvia
78 Twyford Ave
Fortis Green N2
0208-883 5377 (h)
01797 226486(c)
0207—267 6991(h)

**Rosencrantz, Ms
Claudia**
11 Pottery Lane
London W11 4LY
0207-607 1401 (h)
0207-261 3733 (w)

Rosenfeld Donald
11 East 68th St
7G
NY NY 10021
001 212 535 5379

001 212 462 4101
(Hm)001 917 523 0446(p)

Rosenstein, Rob
001 212 416 4082 (w
001 212 249 8150 (h

Rosenthal, Jane
Tribeca Productions
375 Greenwich Street 8th floor
New York, NY 10013 (w)
212 941 4040(w)
212 941 4044(wf)
 001 516 537 6274
212 877 7042 (h)

Roth, Peter Thomas & Noreen
Karbra Co.
52 E 73rd st (h)
New York, NY 10021
212-581-5800 (w)
212-737 7303 P.(h)
Email:
proth@peterthomasroth.com
(Hm)Peter Thomas Roth Labs
LLC
630 5th Avenue, Suite 1406 (w)
New York, NY 10111
212-753-0663 Parents (h)
212-737 7303 N. (h)
917 608 1701 (p)
212 737 2074 (hf)
212 581 5810 (wf)
917 608 1702 N (p)
212 736 9300 (other office)

Rothchild Jessica
07710 579799
0207-243 4525

Rothchild, Hannah
5 Clifton Villas
London
W92 PH
London, UK
0207-289 0035(h)
0207-493 8111(w)
0207-286 9784 (private fax)

Rothenburg, Rich
001 212 893 5300(w)
001 917 239 7424(p)
(Hm)001 212 744 9341(h)
01 646 436 3283 cell

Rotherwick, Tania & Robin
Orc Software Ltd
21 Ansdell Street
London W8 5BN
0207-937 9999(h)
07887-985 801
Email: tania.thorn-
ton@omgroup.co
(Hm)
Cornbury Park,
Charlbury,
OX7 3EH,
01865 858730 (h)
0207-942 0949 (w)
0207-722 1240 diana (h)
0207-393 1642 diana (w)
01608-811 600 Country

Rothschild, Edouard de
18 rue Jean Goujon
Paris 75008 France
00 33 1 4074 4022 (w)
00 33 1 4225 4177 (h)

Rothschild, Evelyn de
New Court
St. Swithin's Lane
London, EC4P 4DU
011 44 1712805302
011 44 171 220 7108f

Roumugere Caroline
001 212 228 0832
Email: 105157,3276@compuser
e.co

Royle, Hon Lucinda
47 Cadogan Place
London SW1,
0207-235 0323 (h)

Rucellai Natalie
Catherine's friend
00 39 55 2011294
00 39 55 2011292
00 39 33691 4322 (p)
00 39 55 237 4731 (h)
011 39 335 385 945
00 39 55 231 3488
39 335 385945 Natalie's cell

Rudnick, Della
001 212 582 8111(h)
001 212 556 2721(w)
001 407 833 8111

Russel, Michelle
235 East 83rd St.
NY, NY 10028
001 212 772 7812(h)
001 212 224 3871(w)

Rust, Marina & Ian
33 E. 70th Street (h)
#2N
New York, NY 10021
212 535 8566(h)
Email: mmrust@aol.com or
Ian.con
(Hm)Ian-office
Lazard Freres
30 Rockefeller Plaza
001 212 632 2650 Ian (w)
001 917 679 3705 Ian (p)
207 734 2260 Maine
212 632 2650 Ian work

Rustow, Tim
128 East 61st St
NY NY 10021
001 646 613 0271(h)
917 302 0908 cellular

Rutalnd Duke and Duchess
Belvoir Castle
NR. Grantham
Lincolnshire
NG32 1PE
01476 870246(h)
0476 870246 (p)
01476 870262(w)

Ruttenberg, Eric & Perri
1 Beekman Place (h)
NY NY 10022
001 212 317 0809(h)
001 212 552 0382(Pw)
Email: eruttenberg@tinicum.com o
(Hm)Tinicum Inc.
800 Third Ave.
NYC 10022
001 917 456 0668
001 917 680 0602 (Perri)
001 212 317 0811 (hf)
001 212 446 9301 (Ew)

Ryder, Mr Nicholas
74 Cornwall Gardens
London SW7
0207-623 2070 (h)

Sacco Amy
001 917 518 0101
Email: amy@lot61.com

Sachs, Jeffrey
001 212 750 1363(h)

001 212 754 6750(w)

Saffra, Edmund
001-212-355-5250 (h
001-212-525-6427 (w

Safro Wayne
Cute S afican (heide
001 917 533 6190
001 212 382 8480

Said, Wafic
00 33 1 4503 1616 (h)
00 33 1 4501 5051 (w)
00 93 303 050 (h)
00 93 304 450 (w)

Sainsbury, Mr Jamie
18 Tedworth Square
London SW3 4DR
0207-352 7566 (h)

Salama, Eric
1 212 632 2332 (w)
1 917 561 6525 (p)
Email: esalama@wpp.com
07785 234 505 (p)
0207-408 2204 (main office w)
0207-656 5700 (w)

Saltzman, Elizabeth

35 Ladbroke Grdns
W11 2PX
0207-243 5258
0771 4503818
Email: elizabeth_saltzman@vf.com
001 212 737 4810
001 917 971 5875 Car
001 914 354 7033 (p)
001 212 880 8968 (w)
001 212 988 8889 (h)
001 212 286 6150
001 207 235 0818 (h)
0771 4503818

Samuels, Mia

ABC Prime Time
001 212 580 6194 (w)

Sandelmar Jon & Corrie

635 Park Ave
New York, NY
212 861 8008

Sangster, Guy & Fi

19 Crescent Grove
London, England SW47AF
Email: sangster@saqnet.co.uk
0207-498 9558 (h)
0207-498 9298 (w)

Sangster, Mr Ben

13 Fernshaw Road
London SW10 0TG
0207-352 0453 (h)

Santo Domingo, Julio Mario

14 Promenade Saint Antoine
1204 Geneva
001 917 859 9090
Email: jmsd@alphageneva.ch
00 41 22 781 0870 (h)
00 41 21 9030 (w)

Santo, Mr & Mrs M Espirito

Rua Inglaterra 31
2765 Estoril
Portugal
0207-373 5233 (h)

Saud Prince Solman

703 288 8770 (h)
202 409 3866 (p)

Scerbo, Randall

321 East 22nd Street
Apartment 6B
1 212 260 9749 (h)
1 917 520 1443 (p)
Email: 1 646 336 9823

Schiatti, Gianmarco

00 39 337 701 472 (p)
00 39 2 877 781 (w)
00 39 2 4819 4728 (h)
00 33 1 4221 3201 (h)

Schifter, Helen & Tim
784 Park Ave
NYC
10021-3553
212 535 8281
917 882 5775(p)
917 856 9290 Tim Schifter P
646 226 4696 Helen P
516 537 7744 2nd home

Sebag Montefiroe Simon & Santa
0207-353-4675
0207-498 7292

Seilern Christine
302 W12th St
#5c
NY NY 10014
001 212 633 1609(h)
001 212 924 5060(w)

Sejournet, Isabel de
11 Gedhow Gardens
London SW7.
0207-370 7621 (h)

Shabtai, Benny
001 212 355 3350
001 917 972 5080(p)

Shad, Brenda
212 777 1122
Email: brenda.schad@verizon.net

Shearer Andre & Angie
001 212 877 5666(h)
001 212 906 9100(w)

Shore Chris and Maura
1040 Park Ave 10F
NY NY 10028

Shriver, Bobby
Suite 1850
100 East 42nd Street
New York NY 10017 USA
001 212 830 9109 (h)
001 301 444 9609 (w)
1095 North Ocean B lv
Florida USA
001 405 842 4278 (h)
Special Olympics P roductions
Inc
Room 220
1440 South Sepulve da Blvd
Los Angeles CA 90 025-3492
001 619 294 7402 (w)
001 310 478 8886 (fax)

Shriver, Maria
001 818 840 4813
001 818 840 4275 (f)

Shuster Susie
001 212 556 8572(w)
001 212 877 9371(h)

Siegal, Peggy
125 East 74th(h)
#4c
NYC 10021
212-570-9804(h)
212-570-0084(hF)
212-966-5000(w)
212-966-4277(wF)
Email: peggysiegal@aol.com
(Hm)270 Lafayette St.
Suite 404
NYC 10012
917-783-4113(p)
201-615-1837(ca

Siegel, William (Bill)
Chris-Craft Industries
767 5th Avenue 46th fl.
New York, NY 10153
212 421 0200 (w)
212 759 4100 (h)
Email: bsiegel@chriscraft.net, w
(Hm)The Regency Hotel (h)
540 Park Ave.
New York
NY, 10021
917 741 2189 (p)
212 759 7653 (wf)

Sieghart, William
75 Oxford Gardens
London W10
0208-968 8352 (h)

Silver Ron
001 914 723 5712
001 212 838 4900(h)
001 212 869 8545(w)
001 212 838 4900

Silverman, Nancy & Henry
4 East 72nd Street
11th Floor
New York, NY 10021
001 212-535-3232(h)
212-472-7601(hF)
Email:
henry.silverman@cendant.c
(Hm)9 West 57th St
NYC 10019
212-421-6080(w)
212-421-9813(wF
212-265-1232(wF
917-861-2227 (p)
917-991-1383 Car phone
888-993-9545 Boat phone

Simon, Bren
MBS Associates, LLC
10110 Ditch Rd. (w)
Carmel
IN
46032,
001 317 726 0665(h)
001 317 844 9467(w)
Email: tasha310@aol.com
(Hm)8545 Olde Mill Run (h)
Indianapolis
IN
46260,

001 317 726 0741 (hf)
001 317 844 9450 (wf)
970 920 2113

Simpson (Caruth), Sophie
Email:
simpson@artistsindependen
0207-373 0124 (h)

Sindi, Rena & Sami
813 Park Avenue, 10th Floor
New York
New York
10021
01 212 734 3236

Slayton Bobby
001 310 995 0493(p)
001 818 995 3913(h)

Smith Osborne
19 Sitwell Gdns
London W4
0208-609 2177

Smith Peterson, Noona
00 392 7200 4527

Smith, James
Aegis Trust
UK Head Office
P.O. Box 2002
Newark
Nottinghamshire, NG22 9ZG UK
Email: office@aegistrust.org
(p) 44 (0) 1623 836978
(f) 44 (0) 1623 862950

Snyder, Maria
466 Washington Street Suite 4E
New York, NY 10013
001 212 247 3679(h)
001 212 274 9577 (h)

Soames, Rupert & Milly
Chief Executive(Bank
Misys

The Wilderness Upper
Winchendon Aylesbury Bucks
01296 651225(h)
0208-879 1188(w)
Email:
rupert.soames@misys.co.uk
(Hm)Misys Plc
Burleigh House
Chapel Oak
Worcestershire, WR11 5SH
00 33 1 4887 3326 (h)
00 33 1 4080 5403 (w)
0208-486 1813 (w)Direct
0208-879 7885 (wf)
01844-299 540 (h)
01844 299 543 (hf)
07831-487 487 (p)

Sobrino, Esperanza
Acquavella Galleries
55 E 65th St 7D
NY,NY 10021
18 E 79th
NY, NY
001 212 439 6737(h)
001 212 734 6300
001 212 734 6300 (w)

Solomon, Andrew
The New York Times
18 West 10th St.
New York, NY 10011-8702
212 477 3595 (w)
212 477 2223 (f)
Email: aws@awsolomon.com
(Hm)154 Kensington Park Rd
London, United Kingdom W11
2ER
0207 221 5673
0207-727 3533 (f)

Soros Peter
30 Ennismore Gdns
London SW7
001 212 628 8455
001 917 882 1224(p)
0831 720772
0207—235 3355
011 212 397 5515(w Sharon
0207-584-0851(f)
001 508 257 6335

Soros, Peter
900 Park Ave
New York, New York 10021
0207-823 4564(h)

001 212 891 3750(h)
001 212 891 3750 (h)

Soto, Fernando de
81 Nunez de Balboa
Madrid 28006 Spain
00 34 1 575 9595 (h)
00 34 1 275 6396 (w)

Soto, Jaime & Marina de
34 Cadogan Sq
London SW1
0207-584-7910 (h)

South, Hamilton
001 212 686 2241 (h)
001 212 880 7623 (w)
001 212 529 5533 (regan)

Souza, Carlos
Valentino
0335 372103
00 39 (0) 6 3612346
011 39 2 6739361 (w)
011 39 2 654 5223 (h)

Spacey, Kevin
Trigger Street Productions
755 La Cienega Boulevard
Los Angeles, CA 90089
310 360 1612 (w)
212 841 5443 (h)

Squire, Hugo
38 Evelyn Gardens
London, SW7
0207-244 0496

St. Bris, Edward
25 Faubourg St Honore
75008 Paris
France
00 33 1 4265 0318 (h)
00 33 1 4266 9225 (w)
00 33 607 885 386

Stanburry Caroline
0207-373 1555(h)
Email: ccstanbury@aol.com
01794 301 393 country home
0468 636 555 mobile
07956-114 877 Lisa (p)
0207-370 7506 Lisa (h)
001 310 860 8979 Rachael
Hunter

Stark, Koo
0207-727 0977
001 203 855 8823

Starzewski Thomas
78a Queensgate
London SW7
0207-244 7257(h)
0207-235 0112(w)

Steenkamp, Chris
082-567-9801
082-928-9235
054-451-0081 work
054 451-0082 Office Fax

Steiner Jeffrey
001 212 308 6700(w)

Steinkampf, Chris & Nina
Box 30
Rooiead Augrabies
Cape Province, 8874
00 27 82 5679801(p)
00 27 54 451 9400(w)
00 27 28 314 1352 beach house

Stengel, Andrew
24 Fifth Ave #723 NY 10011(h)
001 212 219 4556(w)
001 212 254 8665(h)
Email: an-
drew.stengel@miramax.co
001 917 270 6505 (p)

Stengel, Rick & Mary
225 West 86th Street Apt. 611
New York, NY 10024
001 212 724 0317
001 212 522 2709 (w)
001 212 721 6224 Mayn

Stern, Allison & Leonard

925 Fifth Avenue(h)
NY, NY 10021
001 212 744 2342(h)
001 874 630 330610
Email: scratchams@aol.com (Allis
(Hm)667 Madison Avenue
NYC 10021
954-536-9764 boat
212-772-7352 (hF)
212-308-3336 Leonard(w)
212-838-8845 Leonard (wF)
631-537-1645 Hamptons
631-537-1645 Hamptons fax
631-537-8083 Hamptons fax 2
001 284 496 8636 (boat)
00 814 331 904515 (boat)

Stevens Michael

001 917 940 7564
0790 0000111

Stopford-Sackville, Char-
lie &

Shona McKinney
91 Albert Bridge Road
London SW11 4PF,
01832 731014
07973 316624
Email: charlie@stopfordsackville
0207—924 7532(h)
0207—627 5077(sw)
0973 316624
00 34 71 634190
01832733202(drayton)

Stracher Kate

0207-371 2571

Sundlun, Stuart

961 Lexington Avenue
New York, NY 10021
001 212 396 4911 (h)
001 212 535 1743 (f)
001 212 535 0838(w)

Sunley, Mr James & Amanda

45 Bury Walk
London SW3
0207-499 8842

Sutherland Harry

0207-223 1073
07931 282 731

Svenlinson, Peter

33 Redburn Street
London SW3,
004670 778 8123
071-499 9990(w)
0385 326000
0790 069 1461

Swire Sophie

1 Lennox Grdn Mews
London SW1 XODP
0207-795 0064(w)

07973 348520(p)
Email: sophiaswire@yahoo.com
0973 348520(p)

Swire, Hugo
4 Beechmore Road
London SW11,
0207-627 3237 (h)
0207-839 3321(w)

Swire, Jenny
0207-499-9080(w)

Swire, Mark
2 Lennox Gardens Mews
London
SW1X 0DP
0207 589 0888 (w)
07768 875 808 (p)
Email: markswire@mspuk.com
(Hm)Mark Swire Properties Ltd.
87-89 Walton Street
London, SW3 2HP
07768 875 808 (p)
0207 589 0888 (w)
0207 589 2777 (wf)
0207 584 5285 (h)

Sykes, Lucy Ewen
001 212 242 3136(h)
001 212 649 5020(w)
Email: lsykes@hurst.com
001 646 325 7224 (p)

Taaffe, Paul
Hill & Knowlton
212 885 0500
Email: ptaaffe@hillandknowlton.c

Tabet, Karim and Cristina
65th Street Neighbors
114 East 65th Street
New York, NY 10021
212 737 9773 (h)
212 772 6008 (h)
212 821 2841 Karim (w)

Taki
35 Cadogan Square
London SW3,
0207-235 6462 (h)

Talbot Williams, Simon
44 Anselm Rd
London SW6,
0207-386 8681 (h)
0207-499 6291 (w)
0836 239924

Tang, Mr David, & Lucy Wastnag
dwct@hongkong.com
DWC Tang Development Ltd
76 Eaton Place, London, SW1
1112 Jardine House, Central
Hong Kong
07831 193 860(Lp)
00 852 252 56320(w)

Email:
lucywastnag@compuserve.co
(Hm)LG/F No 8 (h)
Clovelly Path
Hong Kong
0207-493 8272 (w)
0836 282596 (car)
00 852 286 83291 (p)
00 852 2792 3787 (w)
00 852 2810 1804 (wf)
00 852 252 56320 (w)
00 852 2810 1804 (f)
0207-352 0486 (h)
001 201 463 9788 (dp)
00 852 9467 2268 (dp)
011 44 831 193 860 ans. service
00852 90812888 (lp)
852 2425 3290 home
852 2524 0112 home fax

Tate, Rupert
5 Inworth Street
London SW11,
0207-280 2923 (h)
0207-228 5035 (w)

Taubman, Alfred
200 East Long Lake
Bloomfield Hills, Michigan 48304
810-258-7201(w)
810-258-7476
(Hm)7 - 12 5th Avenue
New York
NY
810-855-3700 (h)
212-541-6400 (w)
561-832-0700

Taubman, Bobby
001' 810 258-7213 (w
001 810 644 7775(h)
 001 212 541 6400(w)

Tavoulareas, Mr Billy & Nicket
Somerlese
Courtney Avenue
Highgate London N6 4LP
0208-340 6417 (h)
0208-348 0267 (h)
0207-439 9721 (w)

Tavoulareas, Peter
7 Prince Albert Road
London NW1
0207-284 0425 (h)
0207-439 9721 (w)

Tayler, Emmy
011 44 1865-559181 (h)
01144 7956 509 659(Laura sis.)
07956 248 584 (p)
323 650 7588(h)
Email: emtayler@att.net
(Hm)1017 N. Laurel Ave
apt. #1
West Hollywood, CA 90048
001 323 821 3699 (p)
001 561- 373 4880 Kyle Work
No. Only

Taylor, Felicia
784 Park Avenue #10A
001 212 517 0085
001 212 664 2600 (w)
001 917 562-0022 voice mail
202 483 0817/5437 John
917 975 7735 (p)
561 833 9856
561 833 4464 private line
917 834 4993 car phone
07799 644 851 UK cell

Taylor, Pamela
001 212 527-4068 (w
001 212 527-4068 (f

Taylor, Sebastian
15 West Halkin St.
London SW1,
001 917 846 4161
212-750-3835 (h)
235 4472
0207-245-6816 Fax

Taymor, Julie & Eliot
Lah Inc. & Zarathustra Music
874 Broadway #1001/1005
New York, NY 10003
212 475 4829 private
212-505-8507 pvtfax
Email: Lohinc@earthlink.net
(Hm)26 North Redoubt Road
Garrison, NJ 10524
917 846 0467 Eliot portable
212 505 1452 Assistant Jules
212 505 3572 Jules fax
917 689 1659 Julie portable
212 505 8032 (h)

212 674 1018 (h)
845 424 4329 (h)

Tennenbaum, Harry
010 212 722 3055

Teodorani-Fabbri, Eduardo
CNH Global N.V.
Opus Landmark Building
100 Sth. Saunders Road
Lake Forest
IL, 60045
11447803 956782(p)
Email: eduar-
do.teodorani@cnh.com
(Hm)Flat 51 - Royal Court House
162 Sloane Street
London, SWIX 9BS UK
001 847 735 9200(w
011447803956782 Eduardo cell
0208- 479 8851
44 1268 292 629 wf
847 955 3380 fax
44 1268 295383 Karen Bird-Lon-
don office
011 44 207 8234768 h
+390115090662 IFI corp
+44 207 823 4768 (h)
+39 06 678 0783 (h)

Theilmann, Baroness Francesca
011 541 815 2409
011 541 815 3193

Theodoli Catherine
001 305 931 4292(w
001 212 439 1712
Email: ktheodoli@aol.com

Tholstrup, Moegens
6 Fawcett St
London
SW10 9HE
0207-351 6429(h)
07785 250 990 (p)
Email: mtholstrup@cs.com
0207-584 7215 (w)
0033 49 497 7837 (St. Trop.)
0041 27 771 8551 (Verbier)

Tholstrup, Paola
11 Sheffield Terrace
London, W87NG
0207-727 9211
07889 437 363 (p)

Thompson, Barnaby
001 212 265 7621 (w)

Tisch, David
212 752 0560 (w)
917 385 3377 (p)
Email: david.tisch@edb.com

Tisch, Merryl and Jimmy
9 East 79th Street

NY, NY 10021
001 212 879 9414

Tish, Anne & Andrew
Regency Hotel
540 Park Ave. 10021
One Park Ave. #18th Floor
New York, NY 10016
001 212 545 3456

Titopupolo Sonia
001 212 706 2457(h)

Todhunter, Emily Olypitus
23 Warwick Sq
London SW1V 2AB
0207-828 4343(h)
0207-828 5353(f)
Email:
emily@todhunterearle.com
0207-221 8006
0468-473 793

Tolédo Ignacio, Alvarez de
00 33 1 6458 9451(h)
00 33 1 4413 0343(w)
001 212 688 5127
00 33 07614287 (p)
001 305 582 9171
001 305 864 8080
+44 795 183 5245

Tollman, Bea
011 207 235 9251

Tollman, Brett
485 Park Avenue
New York - NY 10022
001 212 838 4950 (h)
001 203 868 0720 (country)
001 914 745 2177

Tollman, Mr. & Mrs.
485 Park Avenue
New York, NY 10022
001 212 888 6048 (h)
001 407 859 0999

Tollman, Syrie & Gavin
21 East 93rd Street
New York, NY 10128
001 212 996 2417 (h)
001 212 489 8970 (gw)
001 212 606 7516 (sw)

Tollman, Wyne
641 Fifth Ave. #34E
NY NY 10022
001 212 355 0083
001 212 245 6952 (h)

Toub, Veronica (Busson)
570 Park Avenue
New York, NY 10021 USA

(Hm)5 Rue Lalo
Paris
France
75016
001 212 888 0764 (h v)
001 212 472 8757 (h a)
00 33 1 4500 0519 (h)
00 33 1 4500 3341 (h)
001 917 88121455/3

Treacy Philip
69 Elizabeth St.
London
England
SW1 W9PJ
0207 259 9605
0207 824 8794 (h)
(Hm)07939 528663 Stefan)

Trump Blaine & Robert
167 E 61 St
New York, NY 10021

Trump, Ivana
001 212 319 4500
0207-823 1172 (h)
001 212 759 4770 (w)

Trump, Ivanka
0777 565 1554
001 917 446 2617

Trump, Robert & Blaine
Trump Management, Inc.
2611 W. 2nd Street
Brooklyn, NY 11223
718 743-4400
(Hm)167 E. 61st Street
Apt. 36 C
New York, NY 10021
212 838-6693 home
001 914 677 8455

Tucker, Chris
213 386 0084 (h)
800 976 1285 (b)
310 815 1651 Rylyn-her home
(his assistant)
310 593 2990 offic Rylyn (his assistant)
310 801 5489 (Rylyn's Portable)
310 593 2997 (f)

Turlington, Christy
379 W. Broadway (w)
Suite 404
NY, 10012
001 212 343 0550(w)
001 212 343 1671(f)

Turnbull, Governor Charles
Governor of USVI
340 693 4300
340 714 1114

Turner, Jenny
7A Burstock Road
London SW15
0207-245 6447 (h)

Turner, Miles Creswell
28 Edgeley Road
London SW4,
0207-622 6721 (h)
00 34 1 248 7822 (h) (Madrid)
00 34 1 419 9749 (w)

Tyssen, (Chessy) Francesca
00 43 6643 406080

Urbiola Jorge
00 34 91 390 0331(w)
00 34 629 917403
Email: jurbiola@presidencia.gog.

Vahabzadeh, Iraj and Linda
15 W. 53 St. #44
NY, NY 10019
001 212 247 7289

Van Hauen Sophie
Charlotte Morgan
62 Frith St. 1st Fl.
London, WIV 5TA
0207- 734 7511(w)

0207- 734 6114 (f)
01836 66 0684 (P)

Van, William Straubenzee
10/33 Granley Gard
London SW7
0207-835 1749

Varsavsky Martin
Email: martin@ya.com

Velasquez Patricia
001 917 406 4418
Email: sisily@aol.com

Verdin, Julia
142 N. Kings Road
Los Angeles, CA
001 310 502 9771 (p)
001 323 848 2900 (w)
001 323 848 2900 (h

Verdin-Mulot, Annie & JP
1 Rue Richpanse
Paris, France 75008
Email: annemarieverdin@yahoo.fr
(Hm)1 Rue Chevalier St. George
Paris, France 75008
00 33 1 4296 0107 (h)
00 33 6 7483 2827 (jpp)
00 33 1 4221 6858 (jw)

00 33 6 0802 0089 (ap)
00 33 1 4296 0107 (jpw)
00 33 3 2360 9016 Puisieux
6A93B door code

Veronis, Jane
900 Park Ave.
NY, NY 10021
212 570 0555
917 865 4006
001 212 410 4490 (h)
001 212 371 1330 (w)

Villani, Carmine S.
President
Milestone Capital LTD.
00 393 332 3678 (p)
001 212 279 7900
0207- 977 1250
00 39 02 365 18600

Villeneuve, Jacques
00 33 680 869 850

Vittadini, Emanuele A.
5 Rue du Pont de Lodi
Paris, France 75006
+33 620 87 71 74 (p)
00 39 335 6341277 (p)
Email: malele1@iol.it
(Hm)emanuele.vittadini@iol.it
Emanuele.VITTADINI@arc-intl.co
001 516 726 4695 (h)
001 516 726 4695 S Hampton
011 39 2 89 40 64 Milan
011 39 2 58 11 19 Milan

00 33 620 87 71 74 (p world phone)

Vittorelli, Dott. Marco
Via Korilska 4
Milan 20154   Italy
00 39 335211481
00 39 02 86451476 (h)
00 39 02 381971 (w)
00 33 94 822454 (St Tro)
00 33 92 059802 (MC)
001 212 752 0866/9 pierre
00 39 33 52 11481 (p)

Vittoz Martine
00 33 1 3962 7905(h)
00 33 1 3493 0422(w)
0033 (0)13962 9592 Direct line

Vittoz, Patrick
10 York Road
Heaton Moor
Stockport
Cheshire, SK4 4PQ
161 432 0394 (h)
0161 4432 464 (w)
Email: vittoz@mail.exploit.com
0161 431 6140 (f)
07966 147 656 (p)
05533 67301 Cazel

Vittoz, Vonnic
00 33 1 396 22375
00 33 53 364763
06 13 58 76 12 (p)

Vivian Smith, Charles
40 Eaton Mews North
London, SW1X8AS
Email: charles.viviansmith@peopl
0207-235 2248 (f)
07785 900437 (p)
0207-235 2305 Parents

Von Habsburg, Francesca
004366 434 06080(p)
Email: francesca@habsburg.com

Von Hase, Bettina
Nine AM Limited
36 Pembridge Villas
London W11,
Email: bettina@nineam.co.uk
0207-221 7075 (h)
0207 221 8245 (f)
07768 270 518 (p)

Wachtmeister, Eric
136 East 65th St W 90
New York, NY 10021
Viking Internet, Strandvagen
5b, First Floor, Stockholm 11451
Email: erik@vikinginternet.com
011 33 0762 4110 European portable
001 917 873 7315(p)
011 46 708 260600 (p)

Wagner David
001 212 783 7143

Wainright, Rupert
001 213 876 3199 (h)
001 213 653 7665 (w)
001 213 308 2796 (car)

Waksal, Sam

150 Thompson Street
7th Floor
New York, NY 10012
001 212 777 3379 (h
001 212 645 1405 (w

Wallace, Mike
60 Minutes-CBS
524 West 57th Street
New York, NY 10019
001 212 975 4321
001 212 757 6975 F

Walters, Barbara
944 Fifth Avenue
New York, NY 10021
001 212-456-2020

Ward, Kevin
001 212 627 9675
001 212 340 9134 (h)
001 303 925 3234 (h)

Warner, Ozzie
001 212 340 9134 (h)
001 303 925 3234

Warnford-Davis, Ms Mandy
6 Claxton Grove
London W6
0207-370 5025 (h)
0207-248 4282 (w)

Wasserman, Casey & Laura
722 Rexford Drive
Beverly Hills, CA 90210
310 788 7733 (w)
310 275 1011 (h)
Email: laura: lzw@avengerent.co
310 980 8990 (p) Laura
310 441 6890 (w) Laura
310 801 1816(cp)

Wassong David
Partner
Soros Private Equity Partners
201 East 69th St. Apt# PHJ
New York
NY 10021
001 212 288 7114(h)
001 212 333 9780(w)
Email:
david_wassong@sfmny.com
001 917 744 3438 (p)
001 212 262 6300
001 212 376 1709 (f)
001 212 288 1316 Mrs. Lisa
Wassong

00 917 539 6359 Lisa's cell
(Mom)

London SW3,
0207-622 9933 (w)
0207-351 0042

Wastnage, Lucy
3 B Rose Garden
9 Magazine Gap Road
Hong Kong
001 852 5 9081 2888p
001 852 5 2868 3291
Email:
lucywastnage@compuserve.c
(Hm)The Garden House
153 Old Church Street
London SW3 6EB
001 0171 352 0486
001 0831 193 860 portable

Weimberg, Jason
Untitled Entertainment
20 Fifth Avenue
Apartment 2E
New York
NY, 10011
001 310 860 1515 (w)
001 310 863 1531 (p)
Email: jwuntitled@aol.com
(Hm)Untitled Entertainment
9255 Sunset Blvd.
Suite 1111
Beverly Hills, CA 90069

Waterman, Felicity
1982 N. Navyandie
Los Angeles, CA 90027
001 213 913 1569 (h)
001 213 999 4578 (w)

Weinstein, Bob
001 212 941 4030 (o)

Watson, Victoria
265a New Kings Road
London SW6,
0207-731 4973 (h)

Weintraub, Harriet
920 5th Avenue
New York, NY 10021
212 935 1033 (w)
212 734 5013 (h)
212 935 1426 office fax

Webb, Veronica
001 917 929 3193 (p)

Westheimer, Ruth Dr.
001 212 861 9000

Weidenfeld, Lord
Flat 23 9 Chelsea Embankment

Weymouth, Mrs Lally
001 212 570 0040 (w)
001 212 288 1082 (h)

White Somers
19 Est 80th St
NY NY, 10021
001 212 861 6073(h)
212 757 0915ext. 201

White Victoria
001 310 440 29869(f)

White, Michael
0207 734 7707
0207 734 7727 (f)
07 836 202 175

White, O'Gara, Victoria
112 Price Lane
Bellevue
Idaho
83313
268 788 6335
Email: vwhite3145@aol.com

Whitworth, Alan & Wendy
16 Field Way
Cambridge CB1 8RW
07774-781-676(p)
Email:
wendy@whitsend.demon.co.u
0223 249918 (h)
0223 24 6887 (f)
07947 141580 (2nd p)

Wial, Jim
William Morission Agency
01 310 859 4200(w)

Wienberg Anouska and Mark
0207-602 5811(w)

Wiesel Dr Eli and Marion
001 212 371 7029

Wigram Liionel and Lydia
011 818 753 8442(h)
011 818 954 24 12(w)

Wigram, Lionel
329 N. Palm
Beverly Hills, CA 90210
001 818 753 8442(h)
001 818 954 2412(w)

Williams Alexandra & Nick
Home Farm
Thenford
Nr Banbury Oxfordshire
OX172Bx,

Williams-Ellis, David & Serena
4 Walham Yard
London SW61JA, England
0207-381 9339
0207-381 9330
01768 898071 office

Willis, Rebecca
Flat 1
99 Talbot Road
W11 2AT
011 44 71-229 1127
0207-499 9080 x2111

Wilmot-Sitwell, Alex & Fi
27 Sibella Road
London SW1
0207-352 9377 (h)
0207-672 5086 (w)
00 21 418 1813 (f)
00 27 21 794 2354 Home

Wilson, Carter
303 East 83rd Street
New York, NY
001 212 570 1016

Windisch Grazot, Manfred
00 39 66 87 2292 (h)
00 39 68 08 8515 (w)

Windsor-Taylor, Tim & Helen
4 Carpeners Close
Kinnerton St
London SW1
0207-235 1574(h)
0207-409 3344(w)

Winn, Steve
702 733 4123(w)
702 204 1000(p)
212 753 1711(h)

Winston, Elizabeth
Travis Ranch, Kenney
TX 77452
001 979 865 2911
001 713 705 7917(p)
Email: ewinston@ix.netcom.com
011 979 865 1391 (f)

Wipple, George
Journalist - Fox
001 212 949 0202

Wolper Carol
308 North Sycomore Ave
Apt 306
LA 90036
001 323 934 7018(h)
Email: cigarettegirl@earthlink.n

Wong, Andy
0777 618 8883 (p)

Wong, Theodore
138 Pavillon Road
London, SWix Oax England
01 212 984 8888(w)
01 212 334 8181(h)
Email: ted_wong@tigerfund.com
917 363 3333 cell

Woodall, Trinny
14 Thurloe Street
London, SW7
0207-581 8675

Woods Emily & Carrie
001 212 941 4023(w)
001 212 647 0195(h)
001 212 886 2525(w)

Woodward, Alexa
001 212 966 0090
001 323 464 6964(h)
001 323 356 3388 (p)

Woodward, Shaun & Camilla
70 Ladbroke Road
London W11,
01608-659 617 (oxf.)
0207-233 2216

Email: woodwards@msn.com
(Hm)0773 3106633
07919 596707 (saun p)

Worcester, Marq & Marc of
(Bunter & Tracey)
28 Halsey Street
London SW3 2BT
0207-584 6592 (h)
0454 221 8491 The Cottage
Badminton The Cottage
GL91DG Avon

Wyatt Jim
001 310 359 4200

Wyatt, Steve & Cate
40138 Main St.
Waterford
VA
20197
0207-243 2810 (h)
001 703 244 2328
Email: sbwoil@aol.com
00 33 93 761064 S Fra
001 703 549 9291 (h)
001 202 466 0599 (w)
223 5337

Yamani, Mai
72 Eaton Terrace
London SW1,
0207-730 3493 (h)

7

Yariv Zghoul
00 65 98 209149
917 378 4485
Email:
yariv@synergyventures.com

Yates Andrew (piggy)
0208-743 2090
0207-938 7275(w)
07976 423137 (p)

Young Toby
6 Hopgood St.
London
W12 7JU
001 212 229 1050
Email: tyoung@infohouse.com
0208-743 6665(h)
0208-743 2695(f)
07946-519253(m)

Younger, Tracy & Lee, Greg
0207-589 3124(h)

Yugoslavia Dimitri
Phillipps
400 E. 52nd Street (h)
3 W. 57th Street(w)
New York, NY 10022
001 212 980 9484(h)
001 917 216 1616 (p)
Email: dkarageorge@phillipsny.co
001 561 659 4826 (ph)
001 212 940 1282 work

Yugoslavia, Prince Michel of
Access International Advisors
509 Madison Ave
22nd Floor
New York
NY 10022
001 212 223 7167 (w)
001 212 223 3463 (f)
Email: mdy@aiagroup.com
001 917 415 4849 (p)
001 212 214 0698 Voicemail

Yugoslavia, Serge de
0777 914 9260
0039 338 591 7025

Zacks Gordon
R G Barry Corp
001 614 864 8069

Zales, Alexi
001 917 864 8865
001 212 226 8747

Zangrillo Paige & Bob
1419 Crystal Lake Road
Aspen CO 81611
001 970 925 3812

Zawauri, Waleed
30 Wilton Cres
London, England SW1
0207-235 0121
Sultanate of Oman P.O. Box 879,
Muscat 113

Zecher Bibi and Adrian
(Julia Walters)
Executive Assistant
00 65 646446743(h)
00 65 64646745(hf)
Email:
jwalters@maharesorts.com
(Hm)00 65 7333460(w)
00 65 65 7333465(wf)

Zeff Mark
212 580 7090 x 201
Email: mzeff@zeffdesign.com

Zeiler, John
3 Lincoln Center
New York, NY 10023
001 212 799 9600(h)
0207-376 3733 (h)
001 212 799 9600 (w)
001 212 941 6336

Zevi, Dino & Rosi
8 Lennox Gdns
London SW1,
0207-584 8661 (h)
0207-495 8867

Zilkha, Bettina
Apt. 16A
50 East 79th St.
New York
NY 10021
001 917 825 8761(p)
001 212 585 2011(h)
Email: Bettinalz@aol.com

Zipp, Brian
160 E. 72nd St. #3A, 10021(h)
01 212 879 8240 (h)
01 212 332 1113(w)
Email: bzipp@zippcaptial.com
0101 203 868 9787
portable 01 917 626 5800
0101 212 772 7057 Home Fax

65TH STREET

Dionne, Ryan
the chef
301 East 66th Street
#8c
New York, NY 10021
1 609 915 9311 (p)
1 212 535 7374 (h)
1 888 533 9632 (b)

Geffert, Scott
413 South Maple Ave.
Glen Rock NJ
07452
001 201 493 7647(h)
001 917 842 5755 (p)
Email: scott@cdiny.com

(Hm)PO Box 4495
Grand Central Station
NYC, NY
10163-4495,
201 493 7640 (h)
917 842 5754 Howie cell

Joseph & Florina Rueda
917 690 8794 (Jp)
917 499 7936 (Fp)
301 793 1695 (Fp)

Kellen, Sarah
301 East 66th Street
Apt 10N
New York, N.Y. 10021
917 855 3363 (p)
212 517 7580 (h)
Email:
sarahlynnelle@hotmail.com

Kelly, Brian
67 Kayuga Rd.
Putnam Valley
NY 10579
845 526 3716, (h,f)
914 804 6719(p)

Maxwell, Ghislaine
116 East 65th St
New York, NY 10021
Email: gmax1@mindspring.com
212 737 0335 Voicemail (Pass-
word 5356831)
212 879 8204 (wf)
212 879 2670 JE Line 3

212 879 8013 Guest Modem
371432863 Resale Number
212 202 4941 New E-fax
1 800 335 4685 AT&T World
Connect
917 690 8794 Joseph (p)
917 499 7936 Florina (p)
800 335 4685 World connect
chip SIM
917 842 5755 Scott cell
201 493 7647 Scott (h)
866 782 3274 Scott (w/Howie)
916 843 4685 AT&T World Con-
nect(outside US)
212 879 9366 GM Line 1
212 879 2058 GM Line 2
212 879 9459 (h))
212 535 7871 JE Line 2
212 535 5612 JE Line 1
212 535 6831 Guest
212 472 6991 Staff
212 535 3030 (w) Line 1
212 535 6833 (w) Line 2
212 535 4384 (w) Line 3
212 535 5611 (w) Line 4
212 535 6837 Spare office
212 249 8510 71st St
212 717 4672 71st St (f)
917 520 3106 (p)try first
917 497 4880 (p)
01144 7785 771552 GSM#
917 494 9690 Tahoe-Line 1(621)
917 855 6931 Tahoe-Line 2
561 346 7141 PB Merc.
1 877 358 9350 Flight Options
212 744 5611 Tahoe Garage
1 888 387 4383 Etrieve
959084 Etrieve Mailbox#
9366 Etrieve security code
212 535 8817 Rich's Security

Mitrovich, Andrea
Ballerina
153 West 75th St #4B
NYC, NY 10023
917 957 5341p
Email: andrea_mitrovich@ya-
hoo.co

Police
Serg - RObert Goldberg
19th Precinct
917 363 3879
212 452 0600,

Rueda, Joseph & Florena
116 East 65th Street
New York, NY 10021
Joseph 917 690 8794
Florina 917 499 7936

Tahoe, Kinney Garage
301 East 66th
212 744 5511(George)

AMERICA(A)

**Antiques - Resale Num-
ber**
13-3647756

Arizona
206 East 60th Street
001 212 838 0440

Aspen Club
303-925-8900

Au Bar
58th Street
Between Madison & Park

Avis International
800-331-2112

Bel Air Hotel
General Manager
Frank Bowling
701 Stone Canyon Road
Los Angeles, CA 90077
310-472-1211
310-476-5890
310 472 1211 Reservations
Manager Marc

Beverly Hills Hotel
9641 Sunset Blvd.
Beverly Hills, CA 90210
310-276-2251
310-271-0319
310 887 2887 fax

Beverly Wilshire
001 310 275 5200

Bice
54th (Madison/Fifth)
001 212 688 1999

Bilboquet
0101 212 751 3036

Bond Street
6 Bond St
777 2500

Carlyle
35 E. 76th Street
001 212 744 1600

Christies- New York
GM's Acct# 2074367
JE's Acct# 20745
20 Rockefeller Plaza
New York, NY 10020
001 212 636 2000 (f)
212 636 2010
212 546 1036 Michael
212-636-2511 Sharon Kim
212 546 1002 Natasha
0207-389 2865 (bidno)
212 546 1122 Patrick Cooney
0207-581 7611 S. Ken
0207-639 9060 St. James

0370 917 323 (p)Franka Mercati
0207-589 4181 (h)Franka
212 546 1195 Carol Magill
212 636 2515 Maria Loss - Client
Services
212 702 2627 Kim Solow
212 636 2389 Sarah Charnon

Cipriani Downtown
376 West Broadway
New York, NY 10012
212 343 0999

Coffee Shop
162 Union West
162 Union West

Cohen Gibby
Polly Gym
428 East 75th Street (bet 1st
176 E. 71st St Penthouse
001 212 570 0616(h)
Email: Gibby-Cohen@nyc.rr.com
(Hm)Patti-Cohen@nyc.rr.com
001 212 628 6969(gym)

Cook
Henry Meer
001 212 924 6160(h)
0101 212 677 4100

Dawat Haute Cuisine of India

210 East 58th Street
New York
0101 212 355 7555

Delmonico's
Rosa/account under NYSG
320 Park Avenue
New York, NY 10022
212-317-8777

Doyle's

175 East 87th
001 212 427 2730

Elaine

577 Second Avenue #61
NY, NY
001 212 779 9645

Electrolysis
988 1215

Elio's Restaurent
2nd avenue between 84th and 85
212 772 2242

Essex House
160 Central Park South
New York, New York 10019
212-247-0300

Estia
308 E 86th
NY, NY
628 9100

Exercise-New York
1 212 228 2655 (h) Kristin Mcgee
1 646 498 8095 (p) Kristin Mcgee
1 212 996 1127 (h) Magali
1 917 553 0136 (p) Magali
646 338 4491 Jessica Benton (p)
212 737 5947 Jessica Benton (h)
781 820 6694 Jennifer(ballerina)

Four Seasons
212-758-5700

Four Seasons Hotel
57 East 57th Street
212 758 5700

Four Seasons Restaurant
99 E. 52nd (Park/Lex.)
New York, NY 10022
212-754-9494
212-754-1077

London
SW1X 7PA

Myers of Westwick
Pork Pies, Pork Sauages
634 Hudson Street
New York,, NY
212 691-4194

Nicolas
001 212 249 9850

Opia
antoine Blech
917 751 4551
212 688 3939

Peninsula Hotel
mathew bartle (mgr)
9882 South Santa Monica Blvd
Beverly Hills
Los Angeles, CA 90212
310 551 2888
310 788 2319 (f)

Peninsula Hotel
700 Fifth Avenue
New York, NY 10019
212-247-2200
212-903-3949

Pierre Hotel
2 East 61st Street
New York, NY 10021
212-838-8000

Plaza
001 212 759 3000

Plaza Athenee Hotel

Trust House 40
37 East 64th Street
New York, NY 10021
212-734-9100

Province Restaurant
between Mcdougal & Prince

Ritz Carlton
001 212 757 1900

Royalton
44 West 44th St.
(between 5th & 6th)
212-869-4400

Sette Mezzo

969 Lexington
New York

0101 212 472 0400

Shoes-Repair
Shoe Service Plus
15 West 55th Street
001 212 262 4823

Shutters on the Beach
1 Pico Blvd.
Santa Monica, CA 90405
310 458 0030 (t)
310 458 4589 (f)
800-334-9000

Sotheby's
JE Acct# 3011 4352
GM Acct# 3062 4014
1334 York Ave
NY, NY 10021
001 212 606 7000
0207-493 8080
(Hm)34-35 New Bond Street
London
W1A 2AA
001 212 606 7423 Sully
001 212 606 7683 Sotheby's
Realestate-Meredith
0207 293 5000 UK
212 431 2424 Real Estate-Steve
Mcguire

St Regis Hotel
2 East 55th St
betn 5th/Mad
New York, NY 10022
001 212 753 4500

Stanhope Hotel
212 774 1234

Sunset Marquee
0101 213 657 1333

Tao Restaurant
42 E. 58th Street
bet. Madison/Park
001 212 888 2288

Taylor, The
300 East 82nd Street
001 212 535 8940

The Great American Health Bar
35 West 57th Street
New York
0101 212 355 5177

The Lowell
0101 212 838 1400

The Westbury
0101 212 535 2000

Tickets
For shows and games
212-643-1274 Premiere Tickets
212 590 2531 NYC Con-
cierge/Johanna London

Tribeca Grill
001 212 941 3900

Two Bunch Palm
0101 619 329 8791

Waldorf Astoria
0101 212 355 3000

Westbury hotel
212 535 2000

BRAZIL

Cecilia Szajman
55 11 30 34 3771 (h)
55 11 55 06 9553 (l)

Ganero, Mario Sr.
Brasilinvest
Av. Brigadeiro Faria Lima,1485
Torre Norte - 19 Andar
Sao Paulo, Brazil
CEP 01451-904.
01155113813.7011(w)
01155113813.7110 (f)
Email:
mgamero@brasilinvest.com
01133493761330 house in
France
01133621051972 cell in France

Riccardo
#1 Polo player
00 55 11 9937 8688

ENTERTAIN-
MENT (E)

Annabels
071-629 1096

Aspinals
071-629 4400

Bibendum
581 5817

Clermont Club
071-493 5587

Daphne
589 4257

Foxtrot Oscar
352 7179

Harrys Bar
408 0844
408 0844

Marks Club
212-499-2936

Nam long
373 1926

Nikitas
352 63 26

Patisserie Valerie
0207-823 9971

San Lorezo
584 1074

Scalinis
225 23 01

Tramp
071-734 3174

FINANCE (F)

Bear Stearns
Ira Zicherman
245 Park Avenue
New York, NY 10167
001 212 272 4189
acct # 042 33431

Centurion
1877 877 0987
3715 659 404 44006 Card number
10/04 Expiry date

Chemical Bank
Vice President
James A. Growney
Madison Ave. & 52nd St.
New York, NY
212-935-9935
212-688-6355
Barbara Parsley Wire Dept.
425-0800 Sel-Bus
090-44-3348 Select/800-821-2088
Stop payment no. 935-9935
212-980-8573

Colonial Bank
Cristina Bello
125 Worth Avenue
Palm Beach, Fl 33480
561 627 1776 (w)
561 833 0943 (f)
Leonor

Nat West
Rob Bowran (Sharon Mulvany)
Personal Accts. Executive Dept
121 High Street
Oxford, OX14YU
01865 79 0053
01865 20 5157 (f)
Email: www.natwest.com
(Hm)32 Cornmarket Street OX1 3HQ
08201994 Current Account
01865 79 88 18 Main number

Natwest Bank
1865 790053
1865 205157 (f)

PB National
Dottle Wilson
ck acct # 0110056698
mm acct# 0110019334
001 561 653 5352

FRANCE (FR)

Alaïa, Azzedine
7 Rue De Moussy

Paris, France 75004
00 33 1 4272 1919

ATT Acess
0 800 99 0011,

Bristol Hotel
112 Rue du Faubourg St. Honore
75008 Paris, France
011 33 153 43 43 00
53 43 43 01(f)
Email: clientservices@hotel-bris
331 698 99475 Jean marie home
33(0)611999322 Jeanmarie port

Cab Blue
4936 1010

Cabaret (night club)
Contact Frank
68 rue Pierre Charnet

Car rental
Avis/St Tropez
Mr. Baccati
00 33 04 93 21 48 90

Chateau de la Messardier
011 33 4945 676000

Chez Denise
00 33 1 4236 2182

Chez L'Ami Louis
32, Rue du Vert-Bois
Paris, France 75003
33 1 48 87 77 48
Ferme Lundi & Mardi

Epstein, Jeffrey
French Apartment
22 Avenue Foch
Apartment 2DD
Paris, France 75116
331 441 70210
331 441 70211(f)
(Hm)1 Rue Chalgrine/Staff Entrance
BA135
B298
01 47 37 18 18 Ambasador Car Co.
0153 43 4300 Jean Marie (w)
01 698 99475 Jean Marie (h)
06 11 999 322 Jean Marie (g)
061 30 14 377 (p) Valdson Cotrin
0 148 27 85 33 (h) Valdson Cotrin
01 40 67 18 82 staff line
01 45 00 44 78 Mr. Cornu/garage
06 77 81 5521 car phone
06 8072 7282 Evelyn
06 10786479 Mr. Coulaux(p)
0607 269 785 Experton(p)
0144 014 401 Experton (w)
331 441 702 19 guest line
331 44 86 4552 Ms. Guerin
01 45 00 88 90 Ms. Peres(conc.)
01 45 00 30 79 Ms. Peres
06 09 592 853 Ms. Peres (p)
331 44 01 4401 Mr. Stephane

Coulaux
06 12 14 37 56 Mr Santos

Epstein, Jeffrey (G)
French Apartment
22 Avenue Foch
Apartment 2DD
Paris, France 75116
331 441 70210
331 441 70211(f)
Email:
epsteinj@wanadoo.fr(Valds
(Hm)1 Rue Chalgrine/Staff Entrance
BA135
B298
01 47 37 18 18 Ambasador Car Co.
01 53 43 43 00 Jean Marie @ Bristol
01 698 99 475 Jean Marie @ home
06 11999322 Jean Marie cell
01133 61 30 14 377 (p) Valdson Cotrin
01133 148 27 85 33 (h) Valdson Cotrin
01 40 67 18 82 staff line
01 45 00 44 78 Mr. Cornu/garage
06 77 81 5521 car phone
Evelyn 0680 727282
331 441 702 19 guest line
01 45 00 88 90 Ms. Peres(conc.)
01 45 00 30 79 Ms. Peres
06 09 592 853 Ms. Peres (p)
01 45 27 65 05 Ms. Roule/Kitchen appliances
01 42 64 50 21 Mr. Pascal(cable tv)
06 62 31 88 55 Mr Pascal cell(cable tv)
01 43 87 49 30 Mr Karim or Lazno (stereo)

06 09 65 65 55 Mr. Karin or Lazno cell(stereo
01 48 71 23 23 Mr. Tourteau(videophone)
06 62 96 04 67 Mr. Tourteau cell(videophone)
01 40 60 93 93 Mr. Belistan(alarm)
06 09 21 15 15 Mr. Belstan cell (alarm)
01 42 71 99 93 Mr. Domenichini(electricity)
06 07 34 50 84 Mr. Domenichini cell (electric
01 42 39 11 90 Mr.Lafond(a/c, heat, plumbing)
06 07 80 25 51 Mr. Lafond cell(a/c,heat,plumb
06 08 03 42 71 Mr. Pasquer cell(a/c,heat,plum
06 12 14 37 56 Mr Santos

Experton, Marie Joseph
Berlioz & Co.
Avenue Louise 113
1050 Brussels
011 32 25 38 22 34
011 32 2538 22 46FAX
Email: mjexperton@skynet.be
011 32 474 95 0073 Belgian Cellular
011 33 607 26 9785 French Cellular
01133144014401 Berlioz France(w)
01133144159415 Berlioz France Fax

Gerard
33 (0) 609 515 909

Hotel Crillon
10 Place de la Concorde
Paris, France 75008
331 44 71 1500

Hotel Raffael
4428 0028

Junot, Philippe
509 Madison Avenue
New York, NY
212 223 7167 (w)
212 223 3463 (wf)
Email: pjunot@aiagroup.com
(Hm)15 avenue Matignon
75008 Paris
France
+33 145 042611 Paris
+33 616 60 6000 (p)
+34 952 77 8425 (Spain)
+34 95 277 0294 (Spain fax)
+34 699 212 298 (Spain p)
917 250 6416 (p)
212 223 7167
011 44 370272428 portable
212 223 3463 New York f

L'Amijean
Rue de Varene
7eme
Rue de Varene

L'Arc
Rue Pulsite
33 1 4500 4500

6eme

L'Arpege
00 33 1 4551 4733

La Merlot
Rue de la cherche midi

La Poste
00 33 1 4280 6616
9 rue Peronaid

Lagardere, Betty
34 Rue Barbet de Jouy
75007 Paris
01 40 69 17 25
06 85 755 555
06 85 754 444
01 53 593 575
01 53 593 574 (f)

Lawyers
01 4401 4401 Stephane Coulaux
(w)
06 1078 6479 Stephane Coulaux
(p)
01 4401 4401 Geraldine Talavera
(w)

Le Telegraphe
00 33 14015 0665
Rue Lille

Le Voltaire

Madame Lemercier
00 33 1 4329 44b5 (4)
00 33E 160460293 (h)

Maid
01 48 49 07 50 Faiza
(Jeanmarie'sBurlet's)
06 16 79 25 49 Faiza's cell
01 45 39 28 93 Anne-France

Massage - Paris
Claudia Hadida 0494791726(St
T
331 4262 3091 Debbie/ Paris
331 4299 8800 Marie Francois
331 4763 3301 Rosemary
336 8280 5320 Alexandria
336 7043 8359 Carolina
336 7043 8359 Caroline
336 1409 3317 Debra Wakshal
336 0740 4991 Isabelle
336 6091 5535 Stephan(better
than Gypsy!)
331 4244 5033 Bastien-foot
massage
3314266 2422 Bastien-foot
massage
334.9487 2631 Deborah
336 6063 3127 Francois
336 1117 5286 Su-
zanne(Nicole's contact)
336 6098 3802 Corine-thai
(Nicole's contact)
336 6261 7962 Karine (Nicole's

contact)
3314766 3727 Karine (Nicole's
contact)
336 6520 0066 Deborah (p)
0661100404 (p) Laetitia
0682940794 Magdall
336 606 33172 Francois
011 336 6760 8207 Donna
011 331 4658 1508 Donna
011 336 1109 9059 Yelena
01133609635180 Nadia
06 2247 4450 Deborah
0609635180 Nadia
0662384798 Sonya (speak little
English)
0666033635 Tanya (speaks NO
English)
01133624604141 Nadia (USE
THIS as of 4-9-03)

Miele, Mr & Mrs
00 33 9301 3359 (h)
00 33 9306 1179 (c)
00 33 9306 1273 (c)
00 33 9301 2196 (fax)

Ott Cynthia and Claude
22 Avenue Foch, Apt 2DD
Paris, France 75116
011 331 4502 7300(h)
011 33674 003080 (cp
Email: 011 33 686 558377 (claude
01133 153 05 70 83 (w)direct
01133 153 05 70 98 (f)

Pinto, Alberto
Hotel de la Victoire (w)
11 Rue d'Aboukir

75002
Paris, FRANCE
011 331 401 30000(w)
011 331 4418 7575(h)
Email: alberto.pinto@albertopint
(Hm)Alberto Pinto (h)
61 Quai D'Orsay
1st Floor
Paris, France 75007
011 331 4753 8421 (h) Linda
001 809 362 4335 Nassau
001 809 362 4336 Nassau
011 331 4013 7580 (f)
011 33 60 770 2913 (p) Linda
011 33 6077 31338 (p)Alberto
011331 45 51 03 33 Serge
Boquet
011336 07 17 07 24 Serge
Boquet 3/2000
011 33 67 800 4392 (p)Serge
011 33 680010222 Car
011 33 140 137 596 Linda dir.
011 331 401 37642 Linda &
Alberto pvt fax
alberto.pinto@albertopinto.com
linda.pinto@albertopinto
serge.boquet@albertopinto
delphine.rateau@albertopinto
jean.huguen@albertopinto
011331 45 51 45 58 Danielle
01133 609 18 11 26 (p) Jean
01133 609 78 68 26 Yves
01133 662 62 71 36 Chantal
pascal.laparra@albertopinto
+33 144 187 575 Paris h
01121239933939 Pinto in
Morrocco
011 212 39 93 7171 Morrocco
fax
+33 144 1875 71 (hf)
+33 140 13 0000 (w)
+33 140 1375 98 Direct
01133680598876 Nissan' s cell
infographie.pinto@albertopinto

Plaza Athenee - Paris
25 Avenue Montaigne
Paris, France 75008
33 1536 766 65
33 1536 766 66 (f)

Restaurant-takeouts
Sushi 01 56 26 00 55

Restaurants
Entrecote
15 rue Marbeauf
0149520717

Ritz - Paris
15, Place Vendome Cedex 01
Paris, France 75041
331-4316-3030
331-4316-3178(f)
331-4286-0091 Direct Fax Reservations

River Cafe
00 33 1 4093 5020
146 quai de Stalin grad

Tante Louise
41 Rue Boissy d'anglais
00 331 4265 0685

Taxi Bleus
01 49 36 10 10

Taxis
00 331 420 24202
00 331 49 361010
00 331 420 39999
00 331 420 06789

Taxis Bleus
0149 36 10 10

Vieira Cotrin, Valdson
21 Rue Voltaire
Paris
St. Dennis
Paris, 93200
014827 8533 (h)
06130 14377
(Hm)1 Rue Chalgrin (Ave.Foch Apt)
Room 4041 Floor 6
Paris France
0613 011 763 Maria (p) girlfriend
0144 778 840 Maria (w)

HOTELS (HT)

Berkeley Hotel
0207 235 6000

Blakes
071-370 6701

Carlton Tower
071-235 5411

Claridges
Brook Street
Mayfair, London W1A 2JQ
44 207 629 8860
44 207 499 2210 (f)

Cliveden House
London,
011441717306466
062-866-8561

Connaught
071-499 7070

Dorchester
071-629 8888

Lanesborough Hotel
General Manager
Geoffrey Gelardi
1 Lanesborough Place
Hyde Park Corner, LONDON
SW1X 7TA UK
44 207 259 5599
44 207 259 5606 (f)

4471-333-7633 Private fax. 8/2

Ritz
071 493 8181

Savoy
071-836 4343

The Barcley Hotel
London,
0207-235-6000

Waterside Inn
0628 20691

ISLAND(I)

Air Center Helicopter
340-775-7335 Nicholas & Tina
(o)
340-774-0976 home
340-690-1012/11 cell

Christopher Taxi
340-690-1581 (cell)
340-777-5092 (home)

Cox, Madison
Madison Cox Design, Inc.
220 West 19th Street
9th Floor
New York, NY 10011
212 242 4631(w)
212 807 8081(f)
Email: mc@madisoncox.com
917 495 9399 (p)
01121263526382 Moroco p

Epstein, Jeffrey
LSJ
6100 Red Hook Quarters B-3
St. Thomas, USVI 00802
340 774 1611 staff 1
340 777 9181 Offic(f)
Email: cathmile@yahoo.com
(Hm)manager@littlestjeff.com
340 774 1611 staff 1
340 775 7335 Air Center Helicopter
340 690 1012 Nicolas (p)
340 777 5334 Gretchen(h)
340 774 0056 JE 1
340 714 0805 JE 2
340 714 0806 JE 3
340 774 3578 JE 4
340 771 2680 JE (p)
340 777 4414 JE Study (f)
340 714 2552 GM
340 771 2679 GM (p)
340 771 2024 Miles (p)
340 771 4897 Cathy (p)
340 714 0807 Staff 2
340 771 1523 Cell Backup 1
340 771 3828 Cell Backup 2
340 771 2032 Boscoe Hague(p)
340 777 0669 Boscoe (b)
340 771 1339 Bruce White(p)
340 771 6264 Tim Cook
340 775 6454 Amer. Yacht Harb.
340 776 5970 Amer. Yacht Harb.(f)

340 774 4265 Cottage(f)
340 771 2678 Guest (p)
340 714 0808 Spare (unused)

Epstein, Jeffrey
Financial Trust Company
6100 Red Hook Quarter
Suite B-3
St. Thomas, USVI 00802
340 775 2525
340 775 2528 (f)
340 775 0093 Leon (h)
340 690 0241 Leon (p)
340 690 3623 Leon (b)
340 775 6971 Dale (h)
340 777 6157 Cecile (h)
340 775 6265 Jeanne (h)
340 775 2770 Lorette (h)
340 774 9599 Jermaine (h)
340 776 1351 Jamie (h)
340 775 6057 Daphne (h)
340 714 3955 Kim (h)
340 690 1443 Cecile portable
340 771 6086 Leon car

Hoffman, Paul
Paul Hoffman, P.C.
41-42-Kongens Gade
P.O. Box 870
St. Thomas, USVI
00804-0870
340-774-2266 (w)
340-774-3318 (h)
Email: PaulhoffmanPC@ATT.net,
ph
(Hm)Estate Havens
P.O Box 870
St. Thomas, VI 00804
340-690-6688 (p)
340-774-2030 (f)
617 547 7907 Boston h

340 774 3318 (h)
340 776 8309 (hf)

Massage A - Island
340-693-9040 Grapevine Salon
(Lynn & Karen)
340-693-8378 Lynn & Karen Gray
(h)
340-776-2414 Muffie Landt
340-777-7049 Zeno (h)
340-626-2913 Zeno (p)
340-693-7617 Kevin Raynold
340 693 9040w Gretchen Rhodes
340 777 5334 Gretchen Rhodes
home
310 435 4725 Gretchen's cell

Moseley, Brian
340 774 5310
340 776 4090(f)
Email: bmoseley@viaccess.net
cell

Roberts, Theresa
6501 Red Hook Plaza
Suite 201 PMB 540
St. Thomas, USVI 00802-1306
340-777-3030
340-776-5835FAX
Email:
TSRarchitects@compuserve.
340 513 4007 (p)

Romualdez, Daniel
architect
119 West 23rd Street

Suite 909
NY, NY 10011
212 989 8429 o
212 989 8986 f
Email: dan-
iel@danielromualdezarc
(hm)130 East 67th
212 647 7019 Fionna's fax
212 989 1781 xt 34 Fiona's dire
line
917 650 8429 (p)
212 989 1781x27 Jennifer

Sanchez, Carlos
Pedro Antonio Dealarcon 41
4th floor
Granada, 18004 Spain
00 34 958 250466 (w)
00 34 958 250454(wf)
Email:
estudio@carlosanchez.net
00 34 609 380840 (p)
00 34 958 225521 (f)
00 34 958 250454 (wf)

Tropical Shipping
Point Pleasant, F3
St. Thomas, USVI 00802
340-776-8767
340-776-1860 (f)

Water Taxi
340-775-6501

ISRAEL

Eshed, Elisa
00-972-53-830-540(p)
00-972-25-666-156(h)
Email: esheda@itc.mof.gov.il

Evani Duud Efrat
00 972 51 522022(p)
00 9723 895569
Email: efratd@intgov.il

Gil Avi
00 972 66 311240
Email: gil_avi@netvision.net.il

Gutman, Arik
972 5 (0) 335786 (p)
011 972 3 641 7830f

Gutman, Arik
00-972-50-335-786(p)
00-972-3-642-1649(o)

Jerusalem Hyatt
00-972-2-533-1234

Neima, Yakhof
Hovevei Zion #8
Jerusulam, Isarel
00-972-50-997-755(p)
00-972-23692-2020(o)
00-972-23692-2032f
0097 23 691 6271 (w)
0097 23 691 6630 (f)
0097 22 283 697 (h)
001 212 977 4000
001 917 817 6832 (p)

Olmert, Ehud
00 97 2 6296014(f)
00 97 2 2 6297997
00972 (2)229 6014

ITALY (I)

Torne di Pisa

Via Mercato 26
87 48 77

Train Info
010 39 2 80231

JEFFREY (J)

301 East 66th St.
Front Desk
301 East 66th Street
New York, NY 10021

Apt. for Models

212 879 5540
917 857 4546 And.pgr
917 545 6300 Guest cell
212 744 3122 8D
917 242 0111pager Yokosta Caba
- cleaning lady
718 466 0373 (h) Yokosta Caba
212 472 4606 2G (Morrison)
212 472 4420 2G (fax)
212 988 8164 3F- (Anna
Macedo/Guest)
212 628 3213 3F - (Guest)
212 861 9072 4M (guest)
917 432 1502 4M (not used)
212 585 3170 5P (L&J)
212 628 3931 7J (ans/fax)
212 628 3952 7J -
(Jean-Luc/Guest)
212 517 7580 8A (Brent)
212 452 1565 8C (guest)
212 249 4958 10N (Sarah)
212 249 5755 10N (Sarah)
212 517 7779 10B (Dave)
212 737 7975 11P - (guest)
212 737 9536 12C (Larry V)
212 737 9536 12C (h)
212 517 5380 14G - (guest)
917 603 2296 Natty

212 318 3201 (w)
516 287 3553 (h)
 516 287 2921 (Cath.)
212 318 3400 (wf)
203-629-5216 (Conn. h)
203-629-5216 (f)
212-888-1520 (h)
212-935-1990 (hf)

All
212 242 5782 (h)
347 256 7078 (p)
212 334 7480 (w)

Adler, Frederick (Fred) & Cath
Fulbright & Jawokski
666 Fifth Ave. (w)
New York
NY
10103,
561 659 1520 (h)
561 561 659 1010(hf)
Email: cgadler1520@aol.com
(Hm)1520 S. Ocean Blvd.
Palm Beach
FL
33480,

Andersson, Eva
1010 Fifth Ave. Apt 10A
New York, NY 10028
212 288 4844 (h)
212 396 1843(hf)
Email: evadubin@hotmail.com
(Hm)Skraddarstigen 1
450 34 Fiskebackskil
Sweden
561 804 9293 (h)
XXXXX XXXXXX
212 664 6941 (w)NBC
+46 70 566 0463 Mr. Anderson's
cell
917 562 3265 (p)
914 669 4651 N.Salem
631 283 5282 Hamptons
011 46 5232 2113 Sweden
011 46 5232 2116 Sweden(f)
646 271 1304 Lulu
917 613 0291 Lulu (p)
914 669 8157 NS fax
44 777 159 6557
914 669 8157 North Salem f
011 46 5227 0397 Parents (win-
ter)

212 751 4583 (w) Glenn
917 887 6349 (car)

C/O Martha Grimes
P.O. Box 2795
Aspen, CO 81612
303-920-3776

Archer, Bill
230 Alumwood Drive (h)
Westerville, OH 43081
Three Limited Parkway
Columbus, OH 43230
614-415-7194(w)
614-415-7194 (wf)
Email:
warcher@limitedbrands.com
(Hm)Three Limited Parkway
Columbus, OH 43230
614-895-2733 (h&f)
888-620-3515 Beeper
614 746 1445 car
614-370-3225 (p)
614-370-7002 Mobile
614-895-2733 Home Fax
614 415 7186 Sherry Castle
614 939 3070 emergency
614 415 7171 (wf)

Aslanian, Linda
225 E. 57th St., 11J (h)
New York, NY 10022
212 758 5700 w
917 373 4083p
(Hm)Four Seasons Hotel(w)
58 E. 58th Street
212 582 6605 (f)
212 754 4432
212 758 5700 work(1-9-03)

Bandar Prince
sec. Cas Elliot

Bannenberg, Jon
Jon Bannenberg Limited
6 Burnsall Street
London, England SW33ST
4420-7352 4851
4420-7352 8444

Barak, Ehud
Chairman
Barak & Associates, L.L.C.
917 841 7851
212 202 4032(f)
Email: ehud@barak-associ-
ates.com
01197236869991 office in Israel
484 919 5582 Barak's personal
cell in US
011 972 5570 2222 Barak's cell
01197256205375 Shimrit (assis-
tants cell)
01197236869995 Fax number in
Israel

Barrack, Tom
Colony Capital Inc.

1999 Avenue of the Stars
Suite 1200
Los Angeles, CA 90067
310 282 8820
310 552 7240 direct
Email: tjbarrack@colonyinc.com
310 282 8813 main fax
310 552 7215 assistant Jodie Pitts

011 336 0331 9710 European portable
212 832 0500 NY office
310 720 5900(p)
805 969 5339(h)
bobz.ccap@pacific.net.sg
310 407 7315 direct fax to Tom's assitant
011336 3048 7995 Euro cell
011 39 3356 172044 Italian portable
011 3933 5765 1775 Tracey
011 3933 5617 2011 David Monahan
808 885 8668 David Monahan (Hawaii)

Barrett, Anthony
Ossa Properties
30 East 60th Street
Room 403
New York, NY 10022
212 288 3579 (h)
212 702 8818(w)
Email: ossa1@aol.com
(Hm)27 East 65th (h)
Apt. 2A
New York, NY 10021
718 268 7331 (f)
212 702 8814 (wf)
212 288 3579 Donna Landa - home
718 575 1000 Ossa Prop
908 249 3633 x224 Donna Landa - work
917 612 4137 (p)

Barrett, Jonathan
220 E. 63rd street #PH
New York, NY 10021
212 644 3012 (h)
001 212 816 9519 (w)
Email: J3arrett@aol.com, jbarret
(Hm)Luminus Management
499 8th Ave. 20th fl
New York, NY 10001
917 494 2792 (p)
310 260 4989 (h)
212 615 3424 (w)

212 615 3430 (wf)

Beck, Jerry
Office of Prof. Oper
The Limited, Inc.
4751 Kitzmiller Rd.
New Albany, Ohio 43054 (h)
Two Limited Pky
Columbus, Ohio 43230
614-415-7194
614-415-7171

Benamou, Albert
16 Avenue Matignon
Paris, France 75008
331 45 63 12 21(o)
331 45 63 22 11(f)
Email: benamou@art-culture.com
(Hm)(home)
18 Blvd. Georges Sevrat
92 300 Nevilly Sur Seine
0607011918 cell
0140883637 home

Biddle-Hakim, Sophie
Husband: Gilbert Hakim
Do not send mail to:
249 West 76th Street
Apt 2A
New York, NY 10023
212 873 2344 (h)
(Hm)Send mail to:
1349 Comstock Ave
Westwood, CA 90024
401 423 0495 Parents/ Rhode Island
310 463 5759 (p)
310 553 5218 (h)

Bjorlin, Nadia
3 Longboat
Newport Coast, CA 92657
949 500 5555 (p)

413 637 9745
818 404 7575 (p)

310 286 0279 (wf)
310 722 9948 (p)

Black, Leon
Apollo Management, L.P.
1301 Avenue of the Americas (w
38th Floor
between 52nd and 53rd
New York, NY 10019
212-515-3205 (w)
212-515-3261 (wf)
Email: black@nyc.apollolp.com
(Hm)Residence
760 Park Avenue
(Entrance on 72)
New York, NY 10021
212 288 5578 (h)
631 283 4650 (h)
914 234 9685 Bedford
212 794 0227 (hf)

Brown, Coco
Brown Companies
461 Park Ave., South
New York
NY
10016.
212-683-4400
212-685-0011 (f)
(Hm)59 East 90th
New York
NY 10028
212-289 55 53 (h)
646 281 8158 (p)
631 537 3714 Country

Borden, David
President
Victoria International Corp.
187 West Brookline St.
Boston
MA
02118.
617-247-4100 (w)
617-247-0038 (wf)
Email: davidaborden@aol.com
617-233-3084 (p)

Buckingham Research
David Keidan
750 Third Avenue 6th Floor
212 922-5525 or 26
212 922 5717(f)
212 922 5543 Bob Crowley

Butler Aviation, Newark
(new name)
Signature Flight Support

Hanger 15
Newark International Airport
Newark, NJ 07114
201-624-1660

Bovino, Kelly
120 Hart Avenue
Santa Monica, CA 90405
310 396 9948(h)
Email: kbovino@aol.com
310 286 0271 ext. 113 (w)

Campos, Michelle
11 Dash Place
Bronx, NY 10463

fixed Soty.

718 884 6586 (h)
646 418 9306 (p)
Email: michelle@naproperty.com

+44 207 730 2808 (hf)
917 353 6522 (p)
917 602 1251 driver
212 548 1388 (w)
212 548 1381 other
212 548 1350 (wf)
0777 484 2756 emergen
Driver Iffy

Cayne, Jimmy
President & CEO
Bear Stearns
383 Madison Avenue
New York, NY 10167
212-272-6439(w)
212-272-7808(wf)
Email: patjimma@aol.com,
jcayne@
(Hm)510 Park Avenue Apt 6A
New York, NY 10022
212-832-1707 Home
212-272-2435 Suzette Direct
917-992-4999 (p)
908-222-7177 h - NJ
212-826-6369 (hf)
908-222-7773 2nd Home Fax
212 272 7808 Suzette's fax
917 992 4999 Pat Cayne
732 229 2574 (hf)

Daniel
011 537 879 17 82

Davison, Dayle
Citibank
153 E 53 St.
18th flr
New York, New York 1002
001 212 559 3366(w)
001 212 559-0889(f)
666-8875 Home
559 6083 Geoff VonKuhn

Chou, Silas
80 Chester Square
London, SW1W 9DU
917 353 6522 (p)
+44 207 758 8686 (w)
Email:
silas.chou@aspucy-gavvavd
(Hm)(work)
A&G UK LTD
8 Grafton Street
London, W1S 4EL UK
+44 207 730 2838 (h)
+852 2371 8718 (w HK)
+852 2371 8505 (w HK)
+852 2370 1305 (wf HK)
+852 9499 8708 (p HK)

Delson, George
George Delson & Associate
110 E 59 St. Floor 28(w)
New York, New York 1002
212 909 9680 (w)
212 355 1421 (f)
Email: gvdassoc.com
(Hm)135 East 83rd St. (h)
New York, NY 10021
212 288 1282 (h)
917 834 4716 (p)
917 414 4260 (car)

Derby, Catherine
332 E. 84th St. #1G
New York, NY 10028
646 263 2627 (p)
Email: catherine@naproperty.com

Dershowitz, Alan
*617 661 1965 * firs*
8 Golden Rod Way
Chilmark, MA 02535
617 495 4617 (w)
617 495 7855 (wf)
Email: alder@law.harvard.edu
(Hm)26 Reservoir Street (h)
Cambridge, MA 02138
617 319 9892 (p) New Cell 11-6-02
508 645 9040 Marthas Vineyard
508 645 3774 MV fax
212 573 6885 NY Apartment
617 661 0351 Carolyn Cohen (h)
617 576 1353 (hf)
617 974 7013 (car)
617 661 1965 (h)*First*
000000000000000 (p)
212 573 6885 NEW NY # (12-7-01)

Edelman, Gerald Dr.
Dr.
Neurosciences Research
Neurosciences Research Foun
10640 John Jay Hopkins Dr.
San Diego, CA 92121
858-626-2000
858-626-2099(f)
Email: edelman@nsi.edu
(Hm)7428 High Avenue
La Jolla, CA 92037
858-454-5571 (h)
858-775-7129 (p)
858 454 0532 (hf)

212 861 8218 (h)
858 626 2050 (w-direct)
858 626 2099 (wf)

Engle, Don
570 Park Avenue # 2B
New York, NY 10021
01 212 371 1913(h)
01 212 371 2775(w)

EPSTEIN - PORTA-BLES
800 759 5665 #402 931 8525
2nd Flight phone
646 541 1751 Timeport
319-540-2265 Gulfstream
N909JE (air)
319-540-8265 Gulfstream
N909JE (ground)
319 540 2558 (air)727 N908JE
319 540 8558 (ground)727
N908JE
651 796 5194 (satel-
lite/emerencies) N908JE
917 497 4880 spare 727 p
011 881 6314 54353 satellite -
GM
011 881 6314 54123 satellite -
pilots
917 545 6300 Guest cell

Epstein, Jeffrey
Epstein Interests

Alarm # 64548
457 Madison Avenue - 4th Floor
New York, NY 10022
212-750-9895 ←

212-371-8042
Email: jeffreye@mindspring.com
888 783 3212 JE E-Fax (pin 0120)
917 400 1315 Yuni (p)
718 263 7182 Yuni (h)
203 762 2539 Eric (h)
203 984 6064 Eric (car)
516 791 3744 Jeff S (h)
516 578 7888 Jeff (p)
212 988 3509 Darren (h)
646 246 6434 Darren (p)
212 831 3253 Lauren (h)
917 496 6126 Lauren (p)
212 758 0256 Cimberly (h)
212 486 6609 Lesley (h)
973 650 8447 Lesley (p)
718 230 1767 Helen (h)
212 935 3961 Front Desk
212 935 3960 457 Mad. Switchboard
212 319 8113 Dictaphone
718 787 0327 Al Castricone-457 Manager(h)
917 217 6583 Al Castricone (p)

Epstein, Jeffrey
Michigan Home
Epstein Lodge, PO Box 199,
M 137 Highway (For Fed Ex)
Interlaken, MI 49643
616 276 5295(h)
616 276 7294(f)
616 276 5296 2nd line

Epstein, Mark
Izmo Family of Companies, Inc.
30 Van Dam Street
New York, NY 10013-1214
212- 366-5439 (home)
212-645-6656FAX

212-645-2620 (Work do not try
212-244-5484 King Graphic
Tech., Inc.
917-543 2432 Portable
511 WEST 33 1ST FL King Address
212-229-2057 Mark's assistant-Amanda
212 366 5439 Mark's direct work #
212-645-2517 FAX

Epstein, Mark
55 - 49 Stone Creek
Stone Mountain, GA 30087
770 469 7183
770-356-3295 Cellular

Epstein, Paula
125 Lake Paula Drive
West Palm Beach, FL 33411
561-686-3707
Email: pfepstein@aol.com
561-762-2741 Car
561 689 8966 Golden Lakes
954 792 6447 Joyce Michayluk (nurse)
561 758 6376 Joyce Michayluk (p)
561-308-8684 (p)

Farkas, Andrew
Island Capital
717 5th Ave, 18th Floor
NY, NY 10022
212 593 5700 (w)
212 593 0500 fax

Farkas, Jonathan D.
Live Oak Realty Corp.
52 E. 72nd street
New York, NY 10021-4266
212 772 7400 (h)
917 952 3404 (car)
Email: jrf@aol.com
(Hm)40 E. 75th street
NY, NY 10021
917 699 2654 (p)
631 726 7518 /7583 (h)
631 726 6091 (hf)
212 517 9330 (w)
212 737 4564 (wf)

Federal Express
Acct # 2587-7622-4
Acct #1144-2081-6 JEC
Acct #1814-9779-3 JEE
Acct #1814-9809-9 Zorro
Acct # 2587-7622-4 Max Hotel
New York, NY
800-238-5355
800-654-0920 Automatic Pick-up
800-247-4747 International
212-777-6500 Local Office
800-654-0920 Problems/package
trace
011 33 1 40 85 39 Paris local.
011 27 11 82 35 10 Johannesburg

Foster, Taylor
212 645 6395 (h)
011 336 10523 815(p)
(Hm)Danielle (pastry Dept)
60 E. 65th Street
917 538 5512 cell

Gany, Eric
66 Little Brook Road
Wilton, CT 06897
203 762 2539(h)
203 984 6064 (p)
 Wife - Nancy
718 893 6700 Brother - Victor
941 383 5226 Vacation
203 762 3155 (f)
AFV5232 Frequent Flyer Number

Gell-man Murray
Sante Fe Institute
1399 Hyde Park Road (w)
Sante Fe, NM 87501-8943
505 984 8800 w-main
Email: mgm@santafe.edu
(Hm)1001 Camino Pinones
Santa Fe, NM 87505
1 505 946 3650 (w) direct
1 505 982 0565 (wf)
1 505 989 8781 (h)
1 505 699 3845 (p)
970 925 4135 (h)
970 920 1167 (hf)
505 946 2745 (w olivia)
212 260 2223 NY apt

Gilman, Kenneth
Vice Chairman/CFO
The Limited, Inc.
360 South Columbia Avenue
Columbus, Ohio 43209   (h)
Three Limited Parkway
Columbus, OH 43230
614-415-7222 w
614-415-7185 f
614-252-0089 (h)
212-439-4200 (w)

212-755-3120 (h)
614-252-3317 (hf)
614-370-7222 (p)
614-531-8031 (p)
614-440-8127 (p)
305-932-8501 FL h
614-479-7220 Secretary
614-370-7222 (p)
888-602-5392 Pager
212-439-4203 NY wf
212-755-6360 hf
305-932-8503 FL f

Glick, Howard
Adam's Book Store
2912 M Street N/W
Georgetown, Washington DC
20007
202-337-2665
202-338-5286
703-356-5720 Home

Gold, Bob
9 Wildwood Lane
Westport, CT 06880 (h)
203-222-7360CT
203-226-0755
Email: rginvest@aol.com
203 226 0755 CT
203-222-8250
203-222-8250 Fax at Home
203 984 3335 Cellular

Goodman, Bob
2 Steward Lane   (h)
Englishtown, NJ 07726
120 Francis Street PO Box 8
Manalapan, NJ 07726

732 577 0299 (h1)
732 740 0274 (p)
732 972 4700 (w)
800 909 6565 (w)
561 686 3707 emergency
212 581 8518 (w)
732 577 1953 (h2)

Gray, Vicki
2441 California Street N.W.
Washington D.C., 20008
202-518-2324 (w)
202-437-3155 (p)
Email: victoriagray1@aol.com

Griaznove, Svetlana
208 E. 90th Street, 5W
corner of 3rd
NY, NY 10128
336 1305 1655(p)
917 774 3061p
Email: svetkag@aol.com
011370687583326 mom's home
011 37 06 174 4519 (p)

Guggenheim, Eileen
242 East 19th St(h)
Apt. 4B
NY, NY 10003
212 966 0300 x302
917 669 1637 (p)
407 964 8316 Parent's Home
609 683 0881
212 228 1637 (h)
212 475 9462 (hf)

Harold Mollin
0207-245 6972
Email: HaroldM@mollin.com

Hashemi, Jalila
5 Montrose House
London, SW1 X7DX
447711086252 p)
442072351254
0207-235 1254

Hedberg, Gregory & Margaret
Hirschel & Adler Art Gallery
336 East 69th Street (h)
New York, NY 10021
NY
10021
212-535-8810(w)
212-772-7237(wf)
Email: greg@hirschandadler.com
(Hm)21 East 70th St. (w)
New York
NY
10021
212-472-3783 (h)
212-744-9251 (hl)
508-257-6621 Summer (h)
212-861-5911 (h) 2nd Line
917 612 1083 (p)

Heil, Paula
Millennial Arts
9 East 62nd St. Apt 2
New York, New York 10022 (h)
130 West 56th Street
New York, New York 10019

212-757-2007
212-750 2421
508-645-2803 The Vineyard
317-849-8801 Indiana Home
212-541-7403 Private Line
212-541-5019 Home
917 518 2484 (p)

Hunter, Joey
Director
Modelwire
594 Broadway(w)
Suite 510
New York, NY 10012
212 219 7717(w)
212 219 9960(wf)
Email: joey@modelwire.com
(Hm)238 Mcmanus Rd North
Patterson, New York 12563
646 262 6370 (p)
845 319 3054 (h)

Indyke, Darren K.
2 Kean Court
Livingston, New Jersey
07039
973 597 1165
Email: dkiesq@aol.com
(Hm)53 Kent Clark Road
Lake Harmony, PA 18624
212 249 8992 Parents
646 246 6434 (p)
212 750 0381 (wf)direct to comp.
212 685 3640 Michelle (w)
646 221 7715 Michelle (p)
570 722 3047 Pennsylvania
House
212 202 7666 E-Fax
973 597 1165 New House
8/19/2003
973 439 7222 DKI Graphics

Insurance Office of Central Oh
Herb Wolman
38 Jefferson Avenue
Columbus, OH 43215
614-221-5471 Work
614-221-4776 Fax
614 325 9978(p)
614 221 3437(after hours)
614 855 2463(h)
ext. 204 Dan Cahill
ext. 223 Janice Lichtenstein

Isaacson, Walter
Time Magazine
212-522-1212 work
Email: walter.isaacson@turner.co

James, Randy
Email: randi@randi.org www.ran

Jampanol, Mylene
135 Rue de Sevres
Paris, France 75006
01133673960168(p)
Email:
mylenejampanol@hotmail.co
+33 60388 1316 emergency contact
+33 1 45 49 14 75 (wf)

Jarecki, Gloria
10 Timber Trial

Rye, NY 10580
001 914 967 7220
01 284 494 2354

Jarecki, Henry Dr.
Falconwood Corporation
565 Fifth Avenue (w)
3rd Floor
(between 5th & Madison @ 46th)
New York, NY 10017
212-984-1440 (w)
212 984 1442 (wf)
Email: hj@falconfone.com
(Hm)870 UN Plaza ; Apt 37/38A
(h)
Between (1st & River on 49)
212759-5950desk
New York, NY 10017
340-690-2311/2309 Guyana
212 593 3098 (h)
914-967-7220 Westchester
212 984 1440 (w)
212 984 1442 (wf)
917 974 8076 (p)
888 923 0859/0860 Plane
914 967 8048 Westchester f
212 984 1440 Emergency
914 967 7220 Emergency
212 984 1450 Other

Johananoff, Pamela
14 Rue Maspero
75106
Paris, France
331 4647 8784 (h)
331 4647 8753 (hf)
Email: pamela@johanoff.com
(Hm)4817 Country Club Blvd
Little Rock, AK 72207
501 666 6651 (parents)
336 0711 4988 (p)

331 47 22 49 6184
501 280 3288 emergency contact, home
501 666 5368 home fax
917 7439 383 (US p)

Johnson Lily

917 520 0787,
541 552 7576

Johnson, Elizabeth (Libit)

Trump International Hotel & To
One Central Park West
Penthouse 50 B
New York, NY 10023
212 245 5445 ERJ hou
212 245 5439 ERJ hou
Email: jengatien@aol.com
(Hm)Lighting Tree Farm
543 N. Mabbettsville Rd.
Millbrook, NY 12545
914-677-9351 Country home
914-677 9351 Secretary Anita
212-245-5531 ERJ house
917-282-2302 Elizabeth's Bentley
970-479-7930 Vail
970-479-7945 Vail - Fax
914 677 9390 staff.
914-677-6215 Millbrook house fax
212-586-3463 (wf)
914-677-6800 LTF
212-245-5624 ERJ private
212-707-8954 Anita fax
212-707-8398 ERJ house
917 864 9484 car phone
917 864 8989 car phone
917 733 5757 ERJ's portable

Kerry, Sen. John
Senator

John Kerry for President
101 E. 52nd St, 10th Floor
New York, NY 10022
202-224-2742
202-224-8525
202-224-0214 Direct Line
202-544-1880 Other
202 494 4945 Private line
212 763 4828 Jamie Whitehead (assistant)
212 421 2065 New Work #
(1-13-03)
212 421 2067 New Fax #
(1-13-03)

Kessler, Jack
New Albany Company
4683 Yantes Drive
New Albany, OH 43054 (h)
5906 East Dublin-Granville Rd
New Albany, OH 43054
614-939-8100o
614-939-8025f

Kincaid, Kristina
Victoria's Secret
1114 Sixth Avenue 5th Flr.
New York, NY 10036
330 East 38th Street, #39M(H)
New York, NY
212-403-9284 (w)

Kosslyn, Steve
28 Garfield Street
Cambridge, MA 02138

(Hm)Harvard University
William James Hall #830
33 Kirkland Street
Cambridge, MA 02138
617 495-3932 (w)
617-864-2009 (h)
617 496 3122 (f)
617 953 8156 cell-emergency
only
617 441 8111 hf
617 441 8111 (hf)
617 642 0901 (p)
617 953 8155 other
617 496 3122 (wf)
617 864 8468 emergency contact
(Robin)

Kravis, Henry
Kohlberg Kravis & Roberts
212-230-9403 (w)
212-750-0003 (f)
(Hm)9 West 57th Street 42Fl
New York, NY 10019

Lang, Adam Perry
1 River Place #3508
NY NY 10036
1 212 268 8874 (h)
917 584 4735 (p)

Leach, Robin
Leach Entertainment Enterprise
122 E. 42nd street
Suite 1518
New York, NY 10168
212-557-6900 (w)
212-557 6901 (wf)
Email: roblea@aol.com or
leachr@

(Hm)c/o PMB #260
6130 West Tropicana
Las Vegas, Nevada 89103
809 462 6000 Antiqua
702 221 1470 (h)
702 221 8230 (hf)
702 845 3700 (p)
917 903 0700 (p)
201 222 6004 Nick La Penna

Leese, Nick
House of Orient PTE Ltd.
162 Mount Pleasant Road
Singapore, 1129 (h)
190 Bukit Timah Road
Singapore, 0922
65-253-8636 (w)
65-253-2364 (wf)
Email: nsist@pacific.net.sg
65-253-2364 (hf)
65-253-0417
65-720-4101 Car
65-253-5453 (h)
659-766-0878 (p)
659 468-6122 (h)
65 97660878 (p)

Lopez, (Buklarewicz) Cindy
Karin Models
339 E. 94th Street #C
New York, NY 10128
646 541 9353(p)
917 492 2102(h)
Email: cinleelope@aol.com
(Hm)Karin Models
6 West 14th St., 3rd fl
New York, NY 10011
646 638 3331x226 (w)
732 431 5374 parents

Lundberg, Marc

N.A. Property, Inc.
6525 West Campus Oval
Suite 105
New Albany, Ohio 43054
001 614 794 2544(h)
Email: marcl@naproperty.com
(Hm)6930 Harlem Road
Westerville, OH 43082
614 939 6005 NAPI Direct
614 939 6025 f Marc's fax at na
prop

Luntz, Melinda

345 E. 64th Street (h)
Apt 10D
New York, NY 10021
917 864-5817 (p)
212 706 1667(h)
Email: mluntz@nyc.rr.com
(Hm)Clarkeson Research
Group(w)
19 Townsend Square
Oyster Bay, NY 11771
561 792 2983 Mom in PB
516 624 8823 (wf)
516 624 8825 (w)
561 762 3100 emergency contact
Denise Read

Mast Industries

Pres. John Welch

14/F East Wing
New World Office Building
24 Salisbury Road, Kowloon HK
852-734-4213
852-724-4736
852-813-8223 John Welch Home
852-311-4741 John Welch Fax

852-813-0180 Ron Shulman
(home)

Mast Industries - Milan

Fedorko, Karen
10 Zia Montenapoleome
Milan, Italy 20121
3902-7608-2201
3902-7601-5031

McMillen, C. Thomas

Chairman
8401 Corporate Drive (w)
Suite 230
Landover, MD 20785
301 306 3470 x11(w)
301 306 3479 (wf)
Email:
mcmillen@washcapadvisors.
(Hm)1103 South Carolina Ave
S.E.
Washington, DC 20003
202 251 4471 (p)
202 546 1712 (h)

McMillen, Thomas C.

Chairman, CEO
The Risk Group
8401 Corporate Drive
Suite 550
Landover
MD. 20785
301 306 3470 (w)
301 306 3470 (wf)
Email:
mcmillen@trginsurance.com
202 251 4471 (p)

Meister, Robert
Vice Chairman
Aon-Rollins Hudig Hall
781 Fifth Avenue
New York, NY 10022 (h)
Two World Trade Center, 105th
New York, NY 10048-0090
212-441-1660 Work
212-441-1924 Fax
(Hm)Aon (w)
222 Lakeview Ave., Suite 510
West Palm Beach
FL 33401
212-847-5281 Car
212-573-5650 Kelly
212-355-2800 Home - NY
212-831-7166 Fax - NY
561-694 7635 Work Fax - Palm
Beach
561-655 0114 Home - Palm
Beach
561 253 2520 PB w
561-655 3411 PB hf
917 885 8819 (p)

Merrit, Jerry
001 614 479 7210
001 614 479 7214
001 614 939 7800 (h)

Middleton, Mark
7 Lacelle Court (h)
Little Rock, AR 72223
501 847 0371(w)
Email: mmiddletonus@aol.com
(Hm)22039 I 30
Bryant, AR 72022
501 821 8877 (h)
202 456 6798
800 719 7535 Other

501 821 6800 (w)
501 529 3355 (p)
501 821 8877 (h)
501 821 1881 (priv.)
501 821 1991 (hf)
202 737 9305 Washington office
202 456 2464 Washington fax
501 847 8379 (wf)
501 847 0371 (w)

Minsky, Marvin
MIT
20 Ames Street
4th Floor
617 734 3363h
617 277 0583 (f)
Email: minsky@media.mit.edu
(Hm)111 Ivy Street (h)
Brookline, MA 02446
781 896 5142 Gloria
Rudish-Emergency only
617 730 2335 Gloria Minsky private
617 253 5864 Marvin-office

Mitchell, David
24 East 22nd Street (h)
Apt 7
New York, NY 10010
212-486-4444 (w)
212 358 0911 (wf)
Email: djm@mitchellholdings.com
(Hm)18 E. 50th street, 10th fl(w)
New York, NY 10022
212-358 0911 home
917-362 8787 (p)
917 941 9155 Car phone
212 758 8844 (wf)
1 917 362 8787 (p)
212 758 6622 (w)

Mitchell, Senator George
Piper, Rudnick
901 15th street NW (w)
Suite 700
Washington, DC 20005
202 371 6155 (w)
202 371 6109 (wf)
Email: bchapman@verner.com ;
mkr
(Hm)1965 Broadway (h)
Apt 19B
New York, NY 10023
305 365 2832 Florida
646 505 1352 (hf)
202 329 9466 (p)
646 505 1351 (h)
305 361 7187 Sister Barbara
202 371 6155 (asst Brenda)
202 371 6000 (state)
202 547 9314 DC Home
202 736 4535 DC Fax
646 505 1350 NY (h)
212 857 4292 Heather (f)

Morrison, Larry
11148 Cobblefield Road
Wellington, FL 33467
001 561 798 6544(h)
Email: jetcare@aol.com
(Hm)1514 Perimiter Rd
Suite 105A
(office address)
West Palm Beach, FL 33406
561 317 3082 cell
800 759 8888 PIN# 1158004

Myhrvold, Nathan
Intellectual Ventures
1422 130th Avenue N.E. (w)

Bellevue, Washington 98005
425 467 2307 (w)
425 467 2308(w)
Email: nathanm@intven.com
(Hm)3441 134th Ave. N.E.
Bellevue, WA 98005
(425) 503 5160 (p)
425 936 7333 Sharleen PT Assistant
425 936 2170 Serena FT Assistant
425 881 7828 (h)
425 936 1222 Direct Fax-Use
Instead of Corp
425 936 7329 Corporate Fax Line
(425) 922 4408 Car
800 400 2417 pager
888 493 2791 Pilot Gerry Heinan
866 501 9014 Plane
425-869-5599 Joan Waters (personal asst)
425 467 2309 Claudia Leschuck
(425) 785 7788 p
425 467 2350 (wf)
011 871 331 945111 Boat (sat)
011 881631 425 172 Boat
866 501 9015 Plane
425 260 7319 Claudia - emergency

N.A. Property, Inc.
N. A. Property
P.O. Box 688 (Mailing address)
6525 West Campus Oval
Suite 105
New Albany, OH 43054
614 939 6000
614 939 6025 (f)
5906 Dublin E.Gran Fed Ex Address
Ohio 43054
614 579 9316 Peg portable
614 668 5091 Marc Lundberg

Lesley Wexner

portable
614 927 0878 Paul Burkhardt
614 855 6861 Kathy Kahn
614 794 3607 Carol Snyder
614 764 9847 Peggy Ugland
614 891 5974 Jim Weitthoff
614 939 6005 Marc direct (w)

New Albany Country Club

1 Club Lane
New Albany, Columbus   OH 43054
614-939-8500
614-939-8525 (f)

Newcombe, Timothy W. (Tim)

Newcombe Electronic Systems
2328 Arlington Ave.
Columbus, OH 43221 (h)
9005 Antares Avenue
Columbus, OH 43240
001 614 848 5688
001 614 848 9921
001 614 481 7628 (h)
001 614 361 8625 (c)
001 614 523 6154 Voice Mail
001 614 481 7629 (hf)

Newman, Larry Esq.

& Adelman
211 E. 70th street
Apt 20F
New York, NY 10021
212-833-1185 (w)
212-833-1250 (f)
Email: lnewman@fklaw.com
(Hm)55 West Creek Farms Road
P.O. Box 830
Sand Point, NY 11050
407 622 8828 Florida
212 453 0096
516 883 5697 (h)
212 861 5149 (h)
407 659 9800 Florida
516 883 8823 (hf)
212 833 1100 (w)

Nowak, Martin

781 259 4297 home
Email: martin_nowak@harvard.edu
(Hm)33 Conant Road (h)
Lincoln, MA 01773
781 259 4297 (h)
617 496 3999 (w)
617 496 4629 work fax
617 496 4737 Doreen (assistant)

Oatman, Bob

Protective Operation
R.L. Oatman & Associates, Inc.
600 Fairmount Avenue
Suite 101
Towson, MD 21286
410 494 1126 (w)
410 494 1163(h)
(Hm)Three Limited Parkway.
Columbus, OH 43230
614-221-3281 Hotel-Col
800-759-7243 Beeper - Skypage
271-0645 # Pin Number
410-879-6940 h&f-MD
614-479-7194 Bill Archer
410-440-2226 Mobil Phone-MD
614-329-0251 Mobile Phone-Col
614-899-2742 Home Westerville
614-479-7080 Ohio fax
614-478-9023 Home-Col
614-939-3070 24 hr number
614-479-7188 Sherry Castle's Direct Phone
410 494 1126 Office MD
410 494 1163 Fax MD
443 831 2818 (p)
410 440 9872 Janice Oatman emergency

Ouertani, Selma

16 Villa Di Loureni
Paris, France 75014
331-5380-1971 h
0616248178 p
Email: selmaouertani@yahoo.fr

Ovitz, Michael
Artist Management Group
9465 Wilshire Blvd.
6th Floor
Beverly Hills, CA 90212
310 300 2444(w)
310 300 2455(wf)
Email: michael.ovitz@amg-la.com
(Hm)457 N. Rockingham Ave (h)
Los Angeles, CA 90049
310 300 2444 Hassina/Ovitz' assist
310-251-9900 Portable in NY
212-262-9341 NY Apt.
800-411-3112 Ovitz's pager
310-476-6436 home
310-251-9971 LA cell
310-457-1592 beach
970-923-5750 Aspen
011-954-536-0455 boat ph
011-33609-062—975 boat ph
011-874761-589-147 boat ph
212 262 9340 NY answer.
310 476 5876 (hf)
310 713 3009 Cell as of 1-13-03

Packer, Mark
Canastel's
c/o Motorcycle Equities Inc
888 7th Ave. 34th Floor
New York
NY, 10106
212-399-6000 (w)
212-399-3160(wf)
(Hm)945 5th Avenue # 14E
New York, NY 10021
305-932-2400 Canastel's Miami
917 324 2020 (p)
212 535 9358 (h)

Pagano, Joe
434 East Cooper (w)
Suite 201
Aspen
CO, 81611
970-920-9339(w)
970 274 0323 (p)
970-925-4770 Aspen Home amy
303-925-9081 Aspen Fax

970 920 9339 Office
970 544 0863 JP
970 948 3222 Jeanie p
970 920 6737 Joe temporary # @ Sam's
805-564-4082 Santa Monica
970-920-7931 Office Fax

Perlman, Itzhak
21 West 70th Street
New York, New York 10023
516-324-1941
212-799-5925 NY Apartment/Karin Palmer
212-595-2483 Private Line

Pete
Pilot
561 350 6766

Phillips, Lisa
Monica's friend
1702 Second Ave #1C
New York, NY 10128
917-771-5015 (p)
212 348 5868 (h)
917 207 3601 Anne (Lisa's friend)
212 620 4244 Anne Fisher (Lisa's friend)
732 804 2603 Meredith
917 597 7132 Anna (Lisa's friend)
917 579 4050 Genaveve (Lisa's friend)
505 867 8298 Lisa in New Mexico

PILOT INFORMATION
Hyperion Air or JEGE
1514 Perimeter Road
Suite 105A
West Palm Beach, FL 33406
561 478 6553(w)
561 478 6553(f)
703 419 8440 Washinton-Signature Fl. Supp.
703 661 8450 Washinton-Signature Fl. Supp.

201 288 1880 International Aviation
970 920 2016 Aspen Base Operations
310 568 3700 LA Garrett Aviation
561 233 7242 PB Jet Aviation
561 686 7553 PB Jet Aviation
617 569 5260 Boston Signature Flight
617 569 1606 Boston Signature Flight
505 471 2525 Santa Fe Capital Aviation
614 239 8828 Columbus Pilot Off. Fax
614 237 3747 FBO Lane Aviation
201 624 1660 Newark
340-777-9177 Bohlke International Airways
201-288-1740 Atlantic Aviation-Teterboro
201 288 5040 Million air
561 683 4121 Galaxy
800-942-7738 LAX Garrett Aviation
310-396-6770 Santa Monica - Super Marine
800-447-4452 Van Nuys - Million Air
800-538-9378 Jet West (Van Nyes)
877-759-8724 Sky Trails
718 476 5200 LGA Signature Flight Support
914 428 3730 White Plains Westchester Airpo
718 244 4111 JFK General Aviation

Pivar, Stuart

15 West 67th Street (h)
New York, NY 10023
212-799-1680
212-580-0527
212 875 9664 (hf)
212 299 1680 (h)

Preece Dara

3139 Kingston Court
West Palm Beach, FL 33409

561 704 8946 (p)
561 686 2598h
(Hm)2500 Quantum Lakes Drive #203
Boynton Beach (w)
561 704 8946 cell
561 742 0171 work
561 742 0171 work

Quinn, Thomas H.
Venable Law firm
1201 New York Ave, NW
Suite 1000
Washington, D.C. 20005
202-887-1433
202-466-2198
Email: thquinn@venable.com
(Hm)1201 New York Avenue, NW
Suite 1000
Washington, DC 20005
202-887-1433 Direct line
401-846-4479 Newport Rhode Island
202-337-8683 h-Washington
202 841 5401 cell
202 962 4800 (w)
202 513 4701 (direct)
202 962 8300 (wf)

Ranieri, Lewis S.
Ranieri & Co., Inc.
225 N. Hewlett Avenue
Merrick, NY 11566 (h)
50 Charles Lindberg Blvd, #500
Uniondale, NY 11553
516-745-6644 (w)
516-745-6787/8 (f)
516-379-7433 Home
980-8400 Local w
753-5869/5883 Local f
904 628 2568
352 795 3339 FL
352-628-2568 Lew (h) FL

Razek, Ed

10920 Gorsuch Road (h)
Galena, OH 43021   (h)
Columbus, OH 43230

614 415 6240(w)
614 415 6245(fw)
Email: erazek@limited.com
(Hm)3 Limited Parkway
Columbus, OH 43230
740-965-4382 (h)
614-271-8760 Car
740-965-1339 (hf)
614-531-8760 Car
614-619-7100 Mobile
41-792-229-470 World Cell
212 884 3080 NY office
614 203 7400 (p)

Rockefeller, David
Rockefeller Financial Service
30 Rockefeller Plaza
Room 5600
146 E. 65th St. (h)
New York, NY 10112
212-649-5622 (w)
212-765-6817 (f)
212-661-1180 Trilateral Com
212-472-1474 Home

Rodgers, Dave
7318 Heathley Drive
Lake Worth, FL 33467
561 963 9926(h)
561 969 6631(f)
888-434-9892 Beeper #
212 517 7779 (h)
561 317 5844 (p)
917 842 6117 (p) only in St.
Thomas
1 614 433 7063 david rigg insurance

Rosovsky, Henry
Dean
Harvard University
37 Beechcroft Road
Newton, MA 02458 (h)
Loeb House, 17 Quincy Street
Cambridge, MA 02138
617-495-4151(w)
617-495 9381(wf)
Email: hrosovsky@harvard.edu
617-332-8134 Home

508-349-1794 Cape Home
(Wellfleet, MA)
617-495-1534 Asst. Maureen McCarthy
617 964 3369 (hf)
617 529 6619 (p)

Ross, David
San Fran Museum of Modern Art
151 Third Street
San Francisco, CA 94103-3159
917 892 5151p
917 892 5151p
Email: daross@sfmoma.org
(Hm)51 Telegraph Place
San Francisco, CA 94133
415-538-2680 (wf)
800 609-5744 beeper watch #
415 249 0865 (hf)
415 730 4011 David's (p)
415 357 4015 Daphne (sec)
415 357 4010 Tracy (sec)

Roxton Sporting
Daniel Reynolds
0488 683222
0488 682977 (fax)
Daniel Reynolds
0488 683222
0488 882977 (fax)

Sacks Oliver Dr.
2 Horatio Street #3G
New York, NY 10014
212 633 8373(h)
212 633 8928 (f)
Email: cycad123@aol.com

Schaeffer, Stan
2211 Broadway
Apt
Betn. 78th & 79th
001 212 580 5522 W
011 212 496 8817 F
305 531 2727

Schantz, Jeffrey
1257 Veeder Drive
Hewlett Bay Park, NY
11557
Email: jas@nysgllc.com
516 791 0044 (h)
212 371 0320 (f)
516 791 7214 (hf)
516 578 7888 (cell p)
212 504 8083 E-Fax
1T5R416 AA Frequent Flyer
Number

Schoettle, Douglas A
243 Riverside Dr. Apt. 1005
New York, NY 10025
212 932 0535 (h)
514 292 5804 (Cottage)
242 333 2774 (f) (Bahamas
212 932 1250 (hf)

Shadow, Monty
Abbatia Castello
28060
San Nazzaro Sesia (NO)
Italy
01139 0321 834030(w)
01139 348 3380400(p)
Email: montyshadow@libero.it
011390321834090 work fax
011390262912196 private fax
011390321827000 private line at
home

Shaeffer David
001 212 543 5945(w)
001 212 414 0966(h)
001 917 846 3365 (p)

Snyder, Richard & Laura Yorke
Golden Books Family Entertainm
1020 Fifth Ave. Apt 1A (h)
NY 10028
888 Seventh Avenue (w)

New York, NY 101064100
212-547-6720 (w)
212-452-7878 (h)
Email: Laurayork@yahoo.com
(Hm)Linden Farm (Country home)
34 Boutonville Rd S.
Cross River
NY 10518
914-763-9167 Country
212 547 6720 Gail- Assistant
914 763 9168 Country (f)
212 452 7880 (hf)
212 547 6767 (wf)
917 797 8514 (p)Laura
917 860 9588 (car)

Solomon, Melissa
3520 Kingsbridge Drive
Plano, TX 75075
972 599 7682(h)
Email: melissasolo@cs.com
(Hm)60 Lincoln Center Plaza
Stu Box 621
New York, NY 10023
516 818 6188 Dad's cell (Alan)
631 642 3010 Alan home
631 523 3317 Melissa's cell
646 459 1287 Julliard dorm room
phone

Sowell, Dottie
737 Park Avenue, Apt 8D
New York, NY 10021
212-628-6672
212-628-3930
212-688-2133 Mom
212-847-7681 Car
305 932 4004
917 446 4469 portable

Spector, Warren
President
Bear, Stearns & Co.
383 Madison Avenue (w)
New York, NY 10179
212 272 5719 (w)
212 272 7847 (wf)
Email: wspector@bear.com

(Hm)40 Fifth Avenue (h)
Penthouse A
New York, NY 10011
917 817 8499 (p)
212 529 2823 (h)
508 645 9655 (h) Massachusetts
561 514 0202 (h) Palm Beach

Staley, Jes
JP Morgan
522 5th Ave, 3rd floor
(corner of 44th)
New York, NY 10036
212 837 2375(w)
212-744-0770 (h & f)
Email: jes.staley@jpmorgan.com
(Hm)930 Park Avenue
#6N
NY, NY 10028
917 912 4364 portable
212 837 5003 (wf)
212 744 0770 (hf)
631 283 0188 Hamptons (h&f)

Stark, Caroline
Krista's friend
1100 West Avenue (h)
#326
The Mirador Building
Miami Beach, FL 33139
305 961 6124 w
305 321 4022 p
(Hm)Attn: Personal (w)
1001 Brickell Bay Drive
Suite 110
Miami, FL 33131

Steel, Kim
001 212-517-3063
914 833 5050
415 221 3275 CA
208 727 1835 cell
208 726 1452 Fax number

Stein, Andrew
212 369 3252(h)

212 572 5060
212-339-2708 Work

Stock, Ann
Social Secretary
US Government
The White House
Washington DC, 20500
202-456-2399
202-456-1414

Stone, Linda
P.O. Box 7477
(This is a stable address)
Bellevue, WA 98008
425 882 8080
Email: linda@iocaine.com
(Hm)3226 Cascaida Ave South
(not living here until 6/03)
Seattle, WA 98144
206 760 3226 home
206 760 3227 home & office
425 936 1826 direct line
425 705 8888 Linda Toscano
(asst.)
lindastone@MSn.com another
e-mail
425 703 7094 fax
206 465 3020 p
425 705 6954 Tamara (w)
206 335 6594 Tamara (p)
206 760 3228 (hf)
310 722 9948 Emergency contact
Kelly Bovino

Stroll, Lawrence S.
Chairman
AIHL Investment Group
550 7th Avenue
7th Floor
New York, NY 10018
212 894 9984 (w)
514 487 8173 (h)
Email: claireanne@strollfamilly.
(Hm)7077 Avenue du Parc, Suite
502
Montreal, Quebec
Canada H3N 1X7
514 487 8173 Canada

1 718 288 2171 (cell)
1 514 577 2888 (p)
1 514 487 8173 (h
1 514 278 6000 (w) Montreal
1 514 278 6184 (wf) Montreal
1 212 548 1350 (wf) NY
011 44 207 8810906 (h) London
1 784 456 3439 (h) Moustique
1 784 493 4010 (p) Moustique
1 514 487 8173 (h) Claire Ann
514 953 6009 wife p
011447860923694 John-Stroll's chauffer
212 548 1909 Silas's fax #
212 548 1350 Stroll;s fax
819 425 8825 new country house

Tafoya, Craig
Fraser Yachts
2107 Southeast 18th Street (h)
Fort Lauderdale, FL 33316
954 763 5093 (h)
954 763 9484 (f)
Email: tafoyac@aol.com
(Hm)1800 S.E. 10th Avenue
Suite 400
Fort Lauderdale, FL 33316
954 328 6203 (p)
954 712 0435 (w) direct
954 763 1053 (w)
964 684 1384 Emergency

Tobiason, Larry
Lawrence F. Tobiason Assoc.
6 Hillside Ave.
Winchester, MA 01890 (h)
5722 Freeport Court
Westerville, OH 43081
001 614 855 2310
614 855 1738
001 614 898 0749 (h)
001 617 729 1111 (h)
001 617 729 2519 (h)
001 614 391 4969 (c)

Trossle, Bob
Miller and Raved
914 634 7476(h)

Trump, Donald
The Trump Organization
721 Fifth Avenue
New York, NY 10022
212 832 2000(w)
212 755 3230 (f)
Email: melaniakmelania@aol.com
(Hm)Mar-a-Lago Club
1100 South Ocean Blvd.
Palm Beach, FL 33480
561 833 2466 (h)
561 832 0034 (h)
561 832 2600 (spa)
212 453 7214 (Car)
Howard Willson Houseman
561-832-0079 (h)
212-832-9191 (h)
561 832 2600 Mar-a-lago
212 308 6758 Trump Security
212-715-7220 Norma direct-emergency contact
212 679 6111 Milania
917 584 8222 Milania p
561 832 2669 (hf)

Trust, Marty
Mast Industries, Inc.
601 North County Road (h)
Palm Beach, FL 33480
978 975 6100 (w)
978 975 6116 (w)
Email: mtrust@mast.com
(Hm)100 Old River Road
Andover, MA 01810
561 863 7377 (h)
561 863 6476 (h)
617 426 9543/44 Boston (h)
617 338 1461 Boston (hf)
561 863 7377/6987 (h)
561 863 6476 (hf)
603 490 3660 (Car)NH
888 611 7332 (b)Wife
978 397 3033 (p)
917 699 4247 (b)
561 358 4347 Wife
561 371 4885 Wife
978 683 2788 (wf)

Tuckerman, Steve
Tuckerman Optical Co.
5000 Kitzmiller Road (h&w)
PO box 488
New Albany, OH 43054
614 775 4002 (w)
614 775 4004 (f)
Email:
steveluckerman5000@msn.co
614 775 4000*** (h)
614 775 4004 (hf)
312-649-9182 Chicago h
614-271-3677 Wife's Car
614-206-3600*** (p)
614 370 7373
970 925 8817 Aspen f

Ugland, Peg
7026 Wichita Drive
Dublin, OH 43017
614-764 9847(h)
614-989-0047(p)
Email: pegu@naproperty.com
(Hm)Napi (new) 6525 W. Campus
Oval
Suite 105
New Albany
Ohio, 43054
614-422-0606 Richard Ugland
614-939-6000 w
614-939-6003 w direct
614-939-6025 fax
614-939-6007 F direct

UPS
Account # E10-954
Domestic 800 742 5877
Internatl 800-782-7892
ups)

Valukas, Tony
Jenner & Block
One IBM Plaza
Chicago, Illinois 60611
312-222-9350
312-527-0484
708-866-8348 Home

Visoski, Larry
1131 Pine Point Road
Singer Island, FL 33404
561 842 0345(h/f)
212 737 9536(h)
917 868 6145 (p)
44 778 599 0070 Euro (p)
505 832 2699 (h) Sante Fe
561 543 7513 (p) back-up
614 433 7063 David Rigg
Chief Pilot

Wachner, Linda
Warnaco, Inc.
200 East 65th Street #36S
New York, NY 10021 (h)
90 Park Avenue 26th Flr.
New York, NY 10016
212-370-8204
212-687-6771(f)
331-4742-8132 Paris (w)
310-473-0032 Sepulveda
310-479-0475 Sepulveda (f)
212-370-8204 Direct
212-370-8205 Secretary direct
212-308-1264 (hf)
212-751-3988 (h)
303-925-9029 Aspen (f)
303-920-2027 Aspen (h)
516-287-3178 S. Hampton
516-287-4865 S. Hampton (f)
0607 971 212 Claude-Paris
Driver
917-856-3058 (p)
011-336-0726-5960 (p)

Wahl, Francis
41 22 83 97000 (w)
Bernheim Halperian Ming Ducret
5 Avenue Leon Gaud
1206 Geneva Switzerland (w)
27 Chemin de L'Ermitage (h)
de La Belotte, Vesenaz, Switz
1222
4122-752-5990 (h)
4122-347-6831
41-77-24-0330 Portable
41 22 752 59 94 fax
33 607 167 263 Portable
335 56 22 12 33 Le pyla fax
335 56 22 13 50 Le pyla home

(handwritten)

Wallaert, Alexia

15 Rue Le Sueur
Paris, France 75116
011 33 6608 17425
011 33 66 081 7425 p
(Hm)1 Rue de la Tourelle
Boulogne Billancourt
France
92100
011 33 493646157 Canne
0608471510 mum's p
011 39 055 225 296 Alexia home
in Italy
347 217 0981 NY cell
011331450000207 Fax
011 33 145 0002 07 Cellular

Wasche, Cristalle

10 E 29th St.
Apt #18H
NY, NY 10016
646 232 3311 (p)
212 696 2315 (h)
Email: cristalle@earthlink.net

Wexner - Abigail Plantation

6619 Tallassee Plantation Circ
Albany, GA 31707
229 483 0638
229 483 9843(f)
229-435-5932 Darrell Halstead
229-889-6637 Darrell Pager

Wang, (Becker) Vera

Vera Wang Bridal House, Ltd.
778 Park Avenue (73/74)
New York, NY 10021 (h)
25 East 77th Street
New York, NY 10021
212-879-1700
212-879-1890
(Hm)Showroom (SEND ALL
MAIL)
225 West 39th Street
9th Floor
New York, NY 10018
212-288-9386/9468 Home
212-737-9723 Home Fax
212-628-3400 NY Bridal
516-283-7914 South Hampton
516-287-3090 South Hampton
Fax
212-375-1212 Portable
212-375-0101 Car
331-4727-3789 Paris - Concierge
Msr Femares
331-4553-7876 Paris - Apt
212 575 6400 Showroom
561 655 5676 PB
212 719 1986 showroom fax

Wexner - Flight Dept.

4387 International Gateway
Columbus, OH 43219
614-479-7063
614-239-7043
614-239-8490 Tim Stehly
614 203 9895 Tim Stehly (p)

Wexner, Les

78 Mount Street
London, United Kingdom W1K
2SL
44 20-7499 7711 Home
44 20-7499 8763 Home - fax
4437 427 6744 Range Rover-
London
0831 355 956 Mercedes
011-44-385-323-501 David
Byrne-portable
plane 0385-325-944
4471-499-7711 Home
4471-499-8763 Home - fax
4437-427-6744 Range Rover-
London
0831-355-956 Mercedes
0831 355956(merc)
0374 276744(range rover)
011 44 370 883 954 Mercedes
Mobile Phone
011 44 370 883 955 Range Rover

Mobile Phone
011 44 370 888 011 Bently Mobile
Phone

Wexner, Les

One Ranch Road
Aspen, CO 81611
303-920-4440 Curt Ufkes-Admin
#
970 920 0436 Curt Ufkes - Personal Mobile
970 920 8723 Curt Ufkes - Personal Page
970 920 8586 Curt Ufkes
970 920 8589 Curt Ufkes Page
970-920-1600 Main Line
970 925 8817 Main Fax
970 379 6571 Jeep Cherokee
1991
970 379 5673 Jeep Wrangler
1991
970 379 6570 GMC Pick-Up 1994
970 379 6574 White Range
Rover
303-920-1600
303-925-8817 Fax
970 379 6573 Jeep Grand Cherokee 1993
970 379 7215 Curt Ufkes P.O.V.
#970 379 7215 Curt Ufke's P.O.V.

Wexner, Les

Abigail House
One Whitebarn Road
New Albany, OH 43054
614 939-3000
614 939-3062(f)
614 370 7780 BMW - 750 iL 1996
614-271-3000 Mercedes - 500
SEL (Mrs. B)
614-939-3065 Estate Office
614-939-3061 Abby (w)
614-736-6040 Merc 560SEL '89
614-395-0515 Merc 600SL
614-736-6066 Abby's Jeep
614-371-2042 OPO Jeep
614-271-3646 Jeep reg EKD 479
614-939-3070 Command Center
614-939-3075 Main Gate

614-855-8017 Constuction Gate
614-939-3000 Command Center
614-939-3062 Abigail Hse (f)
614-939-3055 Karl Koon
614-939-3000 House
614 648 1483 Merc 450SEL 1979
614 370 7065 Land Rover 1996
614 619 6066 Porsche 1997
614 370 9810 Lincoln Town Car
1997
614 329 8992 Suburban 1997
614 648 9202 Merc 1997 600S
614-939-3070 Command Center
614-939-3063 Command Center
Fax

Wexner, Les
The Limited Inc.
Three Limited Parkway
Columbus, OH 43230
614-415-5001
614-415-5008 F
Email: dryan@limitedbrands.com,
614-415-5000 Main line
212 439 4222 Daina Ryan
614 415 7000 information
212 650 0477 NY h
614 415 5006 Daina Ryan direct

White House
Main Line (Information)
1600 Pennsylvania Avenue, N.W.
Washington, D.C. 20500
202-456-1414

Whitehead, Jim
301-681-3444 (w)
301-593-5407 (h)

Wolman, Herb
Insurance Office Central Ohio
253 North Columbia Avenue (h)
Bexley, Ohio 43209
38 Jefferson Avenue
Columbus, OH 43215
614-221-5471 Work

614-221-4776 Fax
614-221-5471 Office
614-252-2463 Home Ohio
212-472-3134 Home NY
614-395-4222 Portable
614-221-3437 Office After Hours
  Home 614 855 2463

212 249 1122 (w)
212 249 1113 (w)
717 383 2733 Patricia Hughs
(Mom)
516 883 6498 (f)

Zuckerman, Mort
Boston Properties
599 Lexington Ave, Suite 1800
New York, NY 10022
212 326 4010(w)
212 326 4096 (f)
Email:
mzuckerman@bostonproperti
(Hm)Boston Properties
8 Arlington Street
Boston, MA
212 744 3995 (h)
212 879 4693 (hf)
212 326 4012 Clare Asst.
212 326 4096 Clare (f)
970 920 2983 Aspen (h)
970 920 3141 Aspen (f)
631-324-7086 E. Hampton (h)
631- 329 -5711 East Hampton (f)
202 537 0324 DC (h)
202 537 1435 DC (hf)
202 955 2537 DC (w)
617 859 2612 Bill Wedge (w)
617 859 1555 Bill Wedge (f)
617 859 2600 Boston (w))
917 750 1900 (p)
631 324 7084 (h)
631 329 5711 (hf)
954 648 1281 (boat)
011 39 335 5645933 (boat)

JEFFREY 71ST.

Barnett, Richard
14 Oakland Ave
Port Washington, NY 11050
516 883 4448(h)
116-4497 pin #
Email: rb9east71@aol.com
(Hm)1800 skypage
917 940 6157 (p)

Blachon, Magali
8 Impasse Bourtholle
31100 Toulouse, France
011 33 68 294 0794
Email:
magali.blachon@wanadoo.fr
01133682940794 cell
1 917 553 0136 (p)
1 212 996 1127 (h)
01133 561 41 75 00 Parents

Epstein, Jeffrey
9 East 71st Street
New York, NY 10021
212 772 9416(h)
212 879 0840(f)
Email: jeeproject@yahoo.com
(Hm)Merc Garage
124 East 63rd St.
Account# 047-EP02
1 917 545 6300 Michael (p)
1 917 309 0259 Dennis - Flowers
917 553 0136 Magali (p)
212 772 3733 Rich (f)
212 772 0517 JEE extra line
212 249 8510 GM
212 717 4672 GM (f)
917 860 9177 Merc
917 597 8141 Merc
917 855 6931 Tahoe-JE
917 494 9690 Tahoe-GM
212 772 3853 Staff 1
212 772 0939 Staff 2
212 772 3733 Staff (f)
212 249 1122 Richie Line 1
212 249 1113 Richie Line 2
917 940 6157 Rich (p)
212 535 7374 Ryan(h)
609 915 9311 Ryan (p)
917 856 1285 Lynn (p)
212 517 3215 Lyn & Jojo (h)
917 975 4500 Jojo (p)
212 249 5514 Merc. Garage
212 744 5511 Tahoe-Garage

116 4497 Rich (b)
807 0253 Jojo (b)
130 4666 Lyn (b)

Flowers-Gary Baura
Flowers
001 917 207 2236
212 675 2476 PM only
Email: bauranewyork@yahoo.com

Fontanilla, Lynn & Jojo
aka Rosalyn & Luciano
301 East 66th Street (h)
Apartment 5P
New York, NY 10021
212 517 3215 (h)
800 759 7243 JoJo Skytel pin#
807 0254
800 759 7243 Lynn Skytel pin#
130 4666
917 856 1285 (p) Lynn
917 975 4500 (p) Jojo
212 772 3853 (w) 71

Gaston Steve
310 E. 55th Street #11F
001 212 888 9146(h)
001 917 608 6685(p)

Graces Marketplace
1237 Third Avenue
New York, NY 10021
212-737-0600
Acct # 5002

Hamblin, Sue
41 Meadow Way
Constantia Meadows
7806, Cape Town South Afrl
01127 827 795 782(p)
01127 21 761 8442(h)
Email: suehamblin2003@yahoo.com

Miller, Charles
Miller & Raved
Half moon Bay 609 (h)
Crotin on Hudso, NY 10520
914 235-6555 Work
914-235-5005 W Fax
Email: cmi3540012@aol.com
(Hm)Miller & Raved Inc.
2 Hamilton Avenue
Suite 207
New Rochelle, New York 10801
914-632-3555 Bob
914 271 5579 (h&f)
917 750 4797 (p)
246 419 1345 (h&f)
207 348 2600 (main
917 846 4295 (emerg.)
212 343 1645 +225 (w emergency)
212 965 1069 (h emergency)

Sawyers Tom/Pat (telephones)
Barbara (wife)
133 County Rd 513
Frenchtown, NJ 08825
908-996-6903(o)
908-996-6958 (f)
908 581 2641(ph)
Pin# 5460174 Tom beeper 1 800
759 7243
pin# 4195978 Pat beeper 1800
759 7243
(610) 749-2939 Pat's home
908 581 2641 (Pp)

Tindall, Brent
301 East 66th Street
Apartment 8C
New York, NY 10021
917 601 4143 (p)
212 535 7374 (h)

KENYA (K)

Muthaiga Club
010 254 2 767754/5/6

KINNERTON

Airport Transfers
0207-403-2228

Charlie
0208-994 5458
0956 210252

Chelsea Police Station
0207-741 6212

Coles, Alan
Registered Osteopath
The Brompton Health Clinic
221-223 Old Brompton Rd.
Earls Court SW5 0EA
07802 826 109
(Hm)Courtfield Medical Centre
73 Courtfield Gardens
Earls Court SW5 0NL

Drivers
welcomeminibus@. hotmail.com
020 8866 6644 Les Wallace
07806 324400 Les (p)
0208 866 6644 Les (h)
0797 314 2340 Ray Perkins (p)
0793 132 5729 Walter (p)
0795 632 4328 Walter (p)

Entwistle Isi
0797 0888989
0208- 870 7348

Hair Assocs
Denise
0207-245 0077
0207-235 3231

Harrods Limited
071-730 1234
#87
135 Brompton Road
Knightsbridge, London SW1X7XL
071-730 1234

Harvey Nichols
071-235 7207

Holland & Holland
071-499 4411
212 752 7755 (NY)

Jackson Stops
Jolyn & Benson
0207-581 5881

John Hobbs Ltd.
105/107A Pimlico Road
London, SW1W 8PH
0207-730-8369
0207-730 0437 (fax)

La Famiglia
351 0761

Martin Tim/Debbie Stewart
Grosvenor Estate
0207-408 0988
0207-312 6201(td)

Martine
0207-235 0998(w)
0207-244 6836(h)

Massage - UK (a)
0208 715 6200 Liz
0976 283 625 Liz
0208 747 1268 Annabel
079 7753 5377 Barry cell
016 2848 8654 Barry
0207 924 1897 Joanne Brunt
0402 256 269 Joanne Brunt
31(0) 616 300982 Barry (Amsterdam)
310 821 2799 Barry(LA)
0776 765 5220 Maxine cell
631 329 3869 Maxine NY
07000378737 Lisa dstress
644 GM dstress membership #
077 4768 5190 Bernice Palazo (Stroll's)
0780 262 6109 Alan Coles (osteopath)
0207 251 6109 Felicity (Thai massage)
079 4093 7382 Felicity (p)
0870 225 5007 Unlisted London
Cherie Elling/good unlisted/0870 225 5007

Maxwell, Ghislaine
44 Kinnerton Street
London, England SW1X 8ES
0207-838 9128(f)
0207-838 9129(h)
Email: 2512 '21' #21#
(Hm)fedex package to:Simon Edwards
Alexander Mann Global Markets
Alexander Hse, 9-11 Fulwood Pl
London, England WC1V 6HG

0207-838 9130 2nd Line
0771 423 6573 Range Rover
07785 771552 (p)

Minicabs
0800-654321

Nags Head
Kevin & Valerie
0207-235 1135(w)
0207-931 0789(h)

O'Neil Nessa
0207-235 1209(h)
0831 458686(p)

Oping
01865 726297

Outred, Anthony
533 Kings Road
London, England SW10 0TZ
0207-730 4782
0207-376 3627
0207-736 8756 Home
0208-965-8733 Hedly's Humpers
(Movers)

Police 24 hours
0207-321-8273

Range Rover
0771 4236573

Ray John
001 212 715 7227(w)

Stichcraft
071-629 7919

Tobias, Maxine
Yoga -UK
0207-351 7690
00 631 329 3869
Email: maxinelena@aol.com
07767 655220 (p)
516 329 3869

Unlisted London
Contact: Debbie Nichols
0870 225 5007 (w)

Yara
0207-349 0652

MEDICAL

Birnbaum, Dr
449 East 68th Street
at York
Suite 8, Second floor
NY, NY 10021
212 628 1500
212 288 5760(f)
John Scobell

Burman, Dr.
Vet for Max
52 East 64th Street
New York, NY 10021
212-832-8417

Chiropractor
Dr. Dean
Chiropractor
2067 Broadway between
71st & 72nd.
212 712-2195

Chiropractor
Chiropractor
Calakos, Dr. Dean
370 Columbus Ave.
(between 77th & 78th streets)
1F
NY, NY 10023
212 712 2195

Cope, Bruce
GM Dentist
2 Harcourt House
19A Cavendish Square
London, UK W1M 9AD
0207-580 0648(w)

Dr. Bruno
535 Park Avenue
New York, NY 10021
212 838 3155

Dr. Dean Calakos
370 Columbus Avenue
#1F
New York, NY 10024
212 712 2195

Dr. Farkus
30 East 60th Street
201 Floor
212 355 5145

Dr. Ray, Dr. Kashel
Paula's Dr.'s
561-478-1104

212 717 1688 fax

Dr. Schimoni
212 751 5066 (w)
917 922 7391 (p)

Ear Conning
310 West 72nd Street
NY NY
001 212 580 3333

Gaynor, Dr J R
79 Cadogan Place
London
SW1X 9RP
0207- 351 3454 (h)
0836 236965
0207- 351 6801 (h)
0207-730 3700 (w)

Hirshfield, Dr.
614-864-6016 (f)
614-252-2034 (h)

Ishmail
177 Prince Street
(between Prince & Thompson)
212 353 2038
917 865 0394

Kent, Susan DVM
Park East Animal Hospital
52 East 64th Street
NY, NY 10021
212-832-8417

Krumholtz, Dr. Michael
111 East 80th Street
NY, NY 10021
212 734 5533

Lee, Dr.
614-868-5966
614-457-9585 (h)

Lister Hospital
0207-730 3417
0207-235 2672

Magnani, Dr.
501 Madison Ave. Suite 2101
(btwn 52nd and 53rd St)
New York, NY 10022
212 688 1090
203 629 5608(h)
212 755 3156 fax

Medical
4311440*01 Oxford ID num-
ber(gm)
133 78 4883 Prudential ID num-
ber(gm)dental

MedLink Emergency
001602 239 3627

Meltzer, J. Dr.
903 Park Avenue
New York, NY
212-988-4488
212 535 4796fax

Moskowitz, Dr. Bruce
1411 North Flagler Drive
Suite 9300
WPB, FL 33401
561 833 6116 (w)

561 848 7884 (h)
561 833 6351 (wf)
x21 Melanie
561 833 1628 direct to Moskowitz desk

Oxford Health Plans
800 201 4911
800 444 6222
4311440*01 Member number

Prudential
800 843 3661

Steinburg Dr
NY Hospital 525 E 68th St
001 212 746 4100

Sternberg, Esther Dr.
3610 Uptown Street N.W.
Washington, DC 20008
001 301 402 2773(w)
001 202 237 6020(h)
Email: sternber@bellatlantic.net

Tom, Maggie
0207-486 9272

Victor, Steve Dr.
30 E. 76th St. (P&M) 6fl
NY, NY 10021
212 249 3050 (w)
212 988 5026 (f)
(Hm)845 UN Plaza, apt 32A
New York, NY 10017
001 212 628 5210 (h)
001 516 354 3304
917 913 9029 (car)
516 329 5873 Beach
917 226 1554 (p)
516 625 6222

212 249 1482 (wf)
917 328 8655 emergency

Wyntik, Wayne
Chiropractor
212-249-7790

PB

Babor
561 832 9385

Bard, Dr. Perry
4275 Okeechobee Blvd (w)
Suite H
WPB, FL 33409
561 640 9999 (w) WPB
Email: docbones77@aol.com
(Hm)3636 S.Ocean Blvd
Highland Beach, FL 33487
561 266 5785 (h)
561 302 1844 (p)

Breakers, The
561-655-6611
Account # 17313

Chiropractor
Dr Bard
001 407 640 9999

Cleaners
Francis Peadon
561 833 4486
1 561 820 4642 (w) Bill - husba

witness

Creative Custom Swimwear

Jupiter Town Center Plaza
711 W. Indiantown Rd.
Jupiter
FL 33458
561-747 6424

Devito, Dawn

267 Atlantic Ave.
Palm Beach, Florida 33480
212-750-9198
(Hm)144 Pleasant St.
Watertown
MA
02172,
561 832 4616 Palm Beach Home
617-926 7877 Boston:
401-423-9886 Rhode Island
561-248 3445 (p)

Driver - PB

305 491 1998 Ray

Epstein, Jeffrey

358 El Brillo Way
Palm Beach, FL 33480
Email: jeffreye@mindspring.com
561 309 6415 NY Merc
561 655 7626 JE Line 1
561 655 7629 JE Line 2
561 655 2779 JE Line 3
561 655 3704 JE Line 4
561 655 4870 GM
561 820 8790 (f)
561 655 0995 Main house kitchen
561 804 9849 Main house kitchen (w)
561 379 9390 Armored Merc S500 (front)
561 309 6415 Armored Merc S500 (back)
561 818 8867 Guest Merc S600 (front)
561 758 1672 Guest Merc S600 (back)
561 346 7141 GM Merc SL55

561 762 6380 New Suburban
561 371 1686 Staff Suburban
561 832 0232 Staff House Line 1
561 832 0319 Staff House Line 2
561 832 0414 Staff House Line 3
561 832 4533 Staff House Line 4
561 818 8361 Mike (p)
561 818 8398 Sally (p)
561 369 4354 Jerome Pierre-gardener
→ 561 641 0728 Jerome Pierre-gardener (h) ↗
→ 561 350 1700 Christophe ←
561 686 3707 Paula (h) —
561 308 8684 Paula (p) —
561 762 2741 Paula (car) —
718 449 5440 Fay Goodman —
310 306 1362 Ronnie Carey (h)
310 215 0303 Ronnie Carey (w)
4710157 # Call forwarding

Gaie, Christophe

6102 Wheatley Ct
Boynton Beach
FL 33436
561 350 1700 (p)
561 233 7242 (o)
561 233 7240 (f)

witness

Goldman, Francis

122 Lake Rebecca Drive
Golden Lakes, FL 33411
561 656 4409

Goldsmith, Gerald

220 Wells Road
Palm Beach, FL 33480
561-659-0441 (h)
561-659-7433 (hf)
(Hm)Palm Beach National Bank
125 Worth Ave.
Palm Beach
FL 33480,
772 971 1000 (p)
561 653 5586 (w)
561 650 0866 (wf)
212 319 9404 (w)
212 659 1433 (w)

212308 0519 emerg.

Maronet, Bill
ETC
561-881-8118
Phones

Massage - Florida (a)

561 467 2588 Dawn W-R(b)
561 776 5679 Dawn W-R (h)
561 832 4616 Dawn James
(Devito) (h)
561 554 4272 Cheri Lynch(b)
561 743 3784 Cheri Lynch(h)
561 627 5816 Dawn W-R (w)
561 373 1412 Cheri Lynch(p)
561 758 1011 Alison Chambers
561 799 9176 Jodie
561 222 0864 Jodie (p)
▓▓▓▓▓▓▓▓▓ Johanne (h)
561 589 8116 Alexandra (h)
561 714 0546 Johanna's cell
561 704 0676 Tammy (h)
561 775 9324 Amy Birse(mom p)
561 622 0062 Amy Birse h
561 333 7493 Melissa Hanes-dad
561 670 8562 Vicky (p)
561 745 9574 Vicky (w)
561 967 1496 Lisa
Sturgill Mass/Fac.(Tammy
561 789 3371 Lisa Sturgil (p)
01133 680 240 365 Alexandra
(paris p)
561 655 1849 Amber (mom)
▓▓▓▓▓▓▓▓▓▓▓▓
Raja (h) Gypsy's
girl
561 586 4625 Geri Kay
(h)Mass/Fac.(Tammy)
561 758 5846 Geri (p)
561 309 0079 Dawn WR(p)
561 385 5444 p Janine (red head)
561 624 5679 Melanie(h)
561 212 4702 Melanie (p)
561 351 0944 Melissa Hanes (p)
561 575 9814 Jennifer
561 301 8687 Amber (p)
561 656 5169 Amber (mom)
561 833 7121 Katie Bdhingham ▓▓▓▓
561 471 3984 ▓▓▓▓▓▓▓
boyfriend hse ▓▓▓▓▓▓

561 707 1789 Dominique & Kelly
561 714 9719 Mary Southwell
561 389 6874 ▓▓▓▓▓▓▓▓▓▓▓▓▓
561 379 3177 Amber (mom-p)
561 ▓▓▓ ▓▓▓▓ ▓▓▓▓▓▓▓▓▓▓▓
561 533 7599 Diane Cahill (h)
561 312 1408 Diane Cahill (p)
561 798 6103 Andrea(Tony's
friend)
561 358 9837 Heidi
▓▓▓▓▓▓▓▓▓▓▓▓▓▓▓▓▓▓▓▓▓
440 289 6551 Coleen p
561 514 1158 Cristale
561 358 8259 Cristale
352 281 7032 Michelle Bell
954 525 2084 Hawthornes
954 232 0635 Hawthornes
561 635 6359 Andrea 2nd number
561 373 9042 Amy Birse p
561 841 7858 ▓▓▓▓▓▓ (G
▓▓▓▓▓▓▓▓▓▓▓▓▓▓▓▓▓▓▓▓▓
561 ▓▓▓ ▓▓▓▓ ▓▓▓▓▓▓▓▓
▓▓▓▓▓▓▓▓▓▓▓▓▓▓ (mom)
▓▓▓▓▓▓
561 309 7877 Beth (p)
561 554 3858 Beth
561 889 5900 carolyn (g)
561 832 6968 Carolyn Casey (h)
813 299 4573 Charlotte (18
Worth Ave) p
561 832 5006 Charlotte (w)
561 818 0296 Chelsea (b)
561 748 9105 Chelsea Facials
(brunette-h)
561 373 1412 Cheri Lynch (p)
561 514 2862 Coleen
561 358 8259 Cristale
561 686 2598 Dara Preece (h)
561 742 0171 Dara (w)
561 704 8946 Dara (p)
561 625 0378 Debra (big bond)
(h)
561 339 1988 Debra (p)
561 218 8687 Dina Lombardi
(facialsl)
561 212 8152 Dina (h)
917 922 4359 Gwendolyn (p)
561 822 4932 Gwendolyn Beck
(w)
954 525 2084 Hawthornes

954 452 8582 Heidi Kublick
561 493 8676 Jessie (h)
561 626 5664 Jessie (mom)
561 689 0848 Jill Spina
561 222 0864 Jodie (p)
305 673 6060 Karen Mesa
954 467 0412 Katja (h) gypsy's girl
954 442 3309 Kiery (Lisa P's friend)
561 707 3565 Kristen (carolyn's friend)
561 329 0213 Kyle
561 791 0535 Laura Kline
561 615 8223 Lina (cosmo & co)
561 352 0709 Lina (p)
561 346 2802 Lina (p)
561 627 9966 Maura (h)
561 762 7126 Maura Koons (p)
561 502 8809 Melissa (carolyn's friend) p
561 333 7493 Melissa (h)
561 383 7738 Melissa Hanes (h)
561 351 7248 Nela Estonia (p)
561 301 3101 Nicole
561 848 3073 Sheridon (h)
917 601 2111 Sheridon (p)
561 227 2435 Sheridon (w)
561 881 6998 Symar (b)
561 588 5444 Tammy (facialist)
561 798 6216 Stephanie
561 685 0544 Jennifer-gymnast
561 253 4832 Ashley (Tony)
561 588 5444 Tammy (Facialist)

Mike Pezulo
El Brillo neighbor
561 655 6210(w)
800 854 9192(pgr)

Mogens, Larry
561 655 5510

Police PB
Jennifer Bruno (cop hire)/Pat
561 227 6358
561 838 5476
(Hm)Capt Gudger
561 227 6365
561 838 5470 Joe Recarey
561 308 1546 Tom Melinchok
561 838 5470 Srgt Trilych

Pompano Helicopter
1 800 957 4374
954 931 7186(Steve)

Stopek, Alan
Xyle'phloem
14372 Horseshoe Trace
Wellington, FL 33414
561 793 7303(w)
561 793 9674 (wf)

Maxwell, Ghislaine
358 El Brillo Way
Palm Beach, Florida 33480
001 561 655 4870
001 561 832 3816 com
001 407 346 7141 Mercedes
001 407 655 3704

Vet
Jack Liggett
561 659 2208

Michael & Sally — A.R. Lovelz
PB house managers
1 561 818 8361 (Pp)
1 561 818 8398 (Ep)
Email: pbmanager@earthlink.net

RANCH (RH)

Bodie John
Plane rental StFe
001 505 884 4530

212-695-7171
212-489-1818 home

Ellis Freedman
001 212 758 9593 (h)
001 212 351 3092/'91 (w)

Grumbridge, Malcolm
Solicitor
The Hogarth Group
1A Airedale Avenue
London, England W4 2NW
0208-995 1515 (w)
Email: mcg@thehogarth.co.uk
(Hm)31 Cleveland Avenue
London, W4 15N
0208-995 0975 (h)
0208-995 1373 (f)
0208-994 0929 (w) switch board
0385 365 616 Car
0385 248887 Portable
44 20 8995 1515 wf

Lemaine, Pierre
00 33 1 4329 4465 / 5184
00 33 1 4325 4080 (f)
00 33 1 4402 3414 / 000926
00 33 1 4345 5191 (h)

Marden Scott and Sarah Nurse
001 212 595 1619(h)
011 212 702 8680(w)

Marden Scott and Sarah Nurse
001 212 595 1619(h)
011 212 702 8680(w)

Marden, Scott & Sarah
001 212 702 8602(w)

212 595 1619(h)
212-595-1617 work
212-595-1619
212-272-6050

Miranda, Bob
001 914 739 6879 (h)
001 212 345 6408 (w)

Moss Brian /Carolin Coleman
01865 881165
01865 881153

Nesson, Mauri
001 212 724 9070
001 303 925 8817 Aspen

Oliver, Keith
Peters & Peters
2 Harewood Place (w)
Hanover Square
London, W1R 9HB
0207-629-7991(w)
0207-499-6792(wf)
Email: keoliver@petersandpeters.
(Hm)Flat 1 (h)
Statham Court
20 Tollington Way
Holloway, London N7 6FP
0207-409-9703 Direct
07785 232 122 (p)

Onakewe, Rodolph
47 Rue de Chaellot
Paris,
33 1 4723 0063

Ord, Robert
01491 652642(h)
0385 307809(p)

0836 208089

Paul Cox
7532206

Peters & Peters
Keith Ollver/Helen Mcdowell
2 Harewood place
Hanover Sq
London W1
0207-629 7991
0207-491 3035
0207—499 6792(f)
0385 232 122

Pisar, Samuel
011 331 4766 0212(w)
011 331 4622 8203(wf
011 331 4501 8718 (h)
954 457 9267 holiday #
212 744 0727 (h) NY
011 331 4401 4401 Caroline
Gravisse
011 331 4415 9415 Caroline
Gravisse (f)
212 744 0836 (f)
011 331 4501 2384 (hf)
011 3314486 4676 Mme.
Gravisse
212 829 8800 x15 Leah Pisar (w)
917 664 8243 Leah Pisar (p)
212 829 8800 x15 Leah Pisar
work

Posen, Felix
24 Kensington Gate
London, W8 5NA
0207-584-9330 home
0207-584-0915 off.
Email: nesop@dircon.co.uk
0207-584-0904 (f)
(0)1342-833133 Crowhurst
(0)1342-833568 (f)

Shaw Derek
0205 820944

Shelly Aboff
001 203 532 0453 (w)
001 203 622 5905 (h)

Tony Busby
0865 60684 X3593

Travis, Paul
0342 844686

Tutle, Jim
(732) 248 1847
0867 358822 X3577
0867 358822 X3577

White, Justin
0765 724 372
0765 724 372

RUGS

Pierre, Jerome
Gardener at PB house
561 369 4354
561 547 3575
561 541 7955 (p)

SECURITY (SC)

Scotland Yard
0207-230 1212

South Ken
0207-741 6212

The Home Office
0207-273 2124

SWITZERLAND (SW)

Bristol Hotel
10 rue du Mart-Blanc
Geneva, Switzerland 1201
4122-732-3800
4122-738-9039
331-42-669-145 Paris

The Corveglia Club
010 41 8234864

The Steffani
010 41 82 22101

TRAVEL (T)

Aero Leasing
(1) 814 3700 (Zurich)
(22) 984510 (Geneva)

Air France
1-800-237-2747
0820 820 820
1023994284 frequent flier (GM)
1023994343 frequent flier number
(JE)

Air Hansen
(Helicoptor)
0252-290-089
0252-860-287

American Airlines
Kay Leonard,
Special Services:
Val Cushing - Gatwick
293 567783
75261 9047
800 433 7300
1-800-882-8880 AA Frequent
Flyer Dept.
340 774 6464 St T Brenda Boone
(special sev
305 526 7710 Susan Michado Miami special se

American Express
American Express
1-800-297-6453
1-800-297-3276 Membership Re-
wards
877 877 0987x57323 Amad
Abdullah (Cent. Travel)
877 877 0987x6775 Ian Roche
(Cent. Cards)

AT&T
1-800-225-5288

British Airways
001 800 247 9297
0845 779 9977uk
91088094 Pin 9919 club number
(GM)
91859156 club member (JE)
0208-759 5511 Claire McArdle
0208-564 1680 Jilly Rutherford
718 425 5585 Roz Olivier/Special
Services
718 425 5654 Alan Jacob-
son/special services
212 452 5353 Roz home (emer-
gencies)

718 553 5585 Penelope Foy
(special services
718 425 5585 Bernette Berry -
Spec. Rep.

Citicar

3515 37th Avenue
Long Island City, NY 10021
718-707-9090
800-456-3548
718-361-9800 Ellen/Tackie
800-456-3548 Toll-Free Number
718-361-8834 when ph system is
down

Concord Tickets
David Gladwin

19 Main Street, Keyworth
Nottingham NG12 5AA, UK
0115 9372455 (t)
0115 9376930 (f)
612 931-0490 (Fisher) Susie Simon (h)
212 268-9088 (Wilpon) Michael
Holtz

Continental Airlines

001 800 525 0280
#SM147662 frequent flier number
(GM)

Delta Airlines

001 800 323 2323
2102103435 frequent flier number
(GM)
1-800-325-1999 Flight information
number
2001009253 frequent flier number
(JE))

Delta Dash

1-800-638-7333

DHL Courier

800-225-5345

Flight Options

26180 Curtiss-Wright Parkway
Cuyahoga County Airport
Cleveland, OH 44143
877 357 1263 (w)
216 797 3325(wf)

Flyaway

081-759 1567/2020

Frequent Flyer Clubs
Delta One Pass

001 713 952 1630
001 800 221 1212
#2102103435 frequent flier num-
ber

Garnero, Jr., Mario B.

011 55 11 9970 1020
Email:
mbgarnero@brasilinvest.co
646 251 2271 (p) Europe
011 331 4720 1884 Paris

Helicopters
Jean-Jacques Moinet
Nice Helicopteres

Aeroport Nice Cote d'Azur
Terminal1
06281
Nice, Cedex 3
04 93 21 34 32
04 93 21 35 64 (f)
Email:
nicehelicopteres@wanadoo.
06 14 356 353 (p)

Hickery, Eileen
Special Services, NY
101-69585 BA

Immunisation
071-439 9584

Kent, Geoffrey
Abercromble & Kent
9301 North A1A
Suite 1
Vero Beach, FL 32963
561 388 0145(w)
800 588 0145(w)
561 388 2756 fax
01144 207 559 8797 London
Number

London Airways
0207-403 2228

Lonsdale
Karen
0207-636 1313

Net Jets
Richard Santulli asst. Carol 732
326 3728
914 536 5254 Peggy Culver
Feign
212 879 7577 Peggy (h)
732 326 3833 Peggy (w) asst Erin
00 35 121 446 8484 Portugal

Nite & Day
570 Moonacha Road
WoodBridge, NJ 07075
201-933-7556

Northwest Airlines
001 800 225 2525

Omar
Travel Agent
Alto Travel
827 Ridgewood Ave.
N. Brunswick, NJ 08902
001 908 435 0555
001 908 435 0660(f)

Phone
1800 414 9898(ny)
212 338 8300 (9366)
(Hm)UK 0181-288 3310 (1211)
ring h answ picks 2512*21*2512
h.no. tel no.&#
*71 enter 1 no. se deact * 710
send wait tone end
01 610 317 7726 Voicestream
00 800 99 0011 ATT access for
France
72# enter number activate call
forward on site
73# enter number deactivate forward from site

Pisa Brothers
Rockefeller Center
630 Fifth Avenue
New York, New York 10111
212 265-8420
212 265-8753 (f)

Plane Charter
Chauffair
01252 377 880
01252 377 872 (f)

Platinum Travel
1800 525 3355
371385847234008 Pla(GM)
3713 8182 5931 004 Pla (JE)

371846368841034 AMX (GM)
3718 463688 41000 AMX (JE)
5263 2710 0944 295 Mast (GM)

Raytheon Travel Air
George Kocher
One Pomperaug Office Park
Suite 305
Southbury
CT. 06488
203 267 5200(w)
917 863 8755(p)
Email:
george_kocha@raytheon.com
203 287 5202 (f)
1 888 835 9782 Book flight
1 888 u fly rta
316 676 1793 Karen Jenkins
316 676 3820 Karen Jenkins Fax
877 357 1263 Flight Options

Red Carpet Limousine Company
310-552 0099

Saphire Travel
01170 522 2226

Shopper's Travel
303 Fifth Avenue, Suite 1007
New York, NY 10016
212-779-8800

Sprint
212-750-9895-3742
800 366 2663 conference call
scheduling

SR Reservations
081-439 4144

Steppes East
Marc Bullough
Mick Lany
285 810267

Travel Consolidator Europe
Kevins Travel Contac
0207 373 6465
0207 637 8485 cheap concorde
tickets
011 33 156213000 Succes Voyage—Pascaline

Travel Consolidators
See other numbers
800 243 2784 CHEAP
44 12 93 78 9000 Laker Airlines
212 779 8800 Ragoo
1 800 377 1000 Very Cheap
Tickets (coach)
1 800 755 4333 Very Cheap
Tickets
800 451 7200 Cheap Seats
212 570 1179 Cheap Seats
44-1332-331-132 Peter
Koukoularides (Lonsdale)
340 774 1040 Connie
011 3902 8645 5203 Paris
Concorde Mr. Capellini
01 705 22 22 26 Saphire/charters
Gatewick-St.T
800 538 2583 Jet Blue
310 973 7938 Traveling Traveler/Sabatian
888 973 7938 Sabatian
800 799 8888 Ticket Planet ext.
230 Sal
212 753 1100 Homeric Tours
800 468 7477 Go Trips-Stacy PB
877 409 5838 24 hr. hotline code
#E5516
732 690 4625 Raghu cell
0870 444 7224 cheapflights.co.uk
212 243 3500/Lucy
FranceTravel-airfrancediscount
0207 637 8485 cheap concorde
tickets
212 760 3737 FlyTime Travel -
Tashi

800 223 5866 Navigant
877 877 0987 Amex. Centurian Travel
1 800 443 7672 Amex Plat. Travel
800 443-7672 Platinum/Heather ext. 63793
800 715-4440(22339 Global Travel
310 276 2741 1st & Busi./Charlie
212 983 0779 UN Travels and Tours
323 933-8763 Domestic only mi. broker/John
800 239 8269 Virgin specialist

TWA

001 800 221 2000
#188925144 frequent flier numbers (GM)
34663436 frequent flier number (JE)

United Airlines

001 800 241 6522
#00385250614 frequent flier # G.M.
00316924999 frequent flyer # J.E.

US Air
Frequent Traveler Center
P.O. Box 5
Winston Salem, NC 27102-0005
001 800 872 4738
001 800 428 4322   (
001 800 428 4322
#138515311 frequent flier number (GM)

USA International

218 West 47th Street (B'Way)
New York, NY

Virgin Atlantic Airways

029-356-200
001 800 862 8621
#00 900 043 506 frequent flier number (GM)
00 779 044 628 frequent flier number (JE)

Epstein, Jeffrey
Fed ex Sat delivery only
c/o Dan and Nancy Sowle
Highway 41, Landon Store
Stanley, NM 87056
505 832 4339

Epstein, Jeffrey
Zorro Ranch
49 Zorro Ranch Road
Stanley, NM 87056
Email: zorroranch@aol.com
505 832 2675 Line 1 (office)
505 832 2696 Line 2 (office)
505 832 2676 (office f)
505 832 2697 Hotline Security
505 832 2698 Office modem
505 832 2240 BunkHouse LR
505 832 2505 Bunk 1
505 832 2262 Bunk 2
505 832 2245 Bunk 3
505 832 2504 Bunk 4
505 832 2247 Bunk 5
505 832 1708 Shop Wood Shop
& Greenhouse
505 832 2352 Log cabin
505 832 1348 Guest lodge cabin
505 832 1364 Guest lodge (f) &
modem
505 832 0690 JE - 1
505 832 0691 JE - 2
505 832 0595 JE - 3
505 832 1394 JE - 4
505 832 5411 JE (f)
505 832 1392 JE modem
505 832 1746 GM line
505 832 1389 GM (f)
505 832 9781 GM modem
505 832 1748 Guest line
505 832 1390 Staff - 1
505 832 1391 Staff - 2
505 832 6784 Brice & Karen (h)
505 832 1393 Kate & Mike (h)
505 832 0897 Deidre & Floyd (h)
505 832 2699 Larry (h)
505 832 1427 HVAC - MH
505 991 0026 Mike (Nextel)
505 991 0027 Deidre (Nextel)
505 991 0028 Floyd (Nextel)
505 991 0029 Manolito (Nextel)
505 991 0025 Kate (Nextel)
505 780 0004 Extra 1 (p)
505 780 0002 Extra 2 (p)
505 660 9585 Mercedes - front
seat
505 660 3976 Mercedes - back
seat
505 660 6240 Mercedes G500
(jeep)
505 690 5480 JE Suburban
505 690 1821 99 Suburban
505 699 8055 Tahoe
505 670 9754 Hummer
505 765 1200 Bradbury Stamm
(w)
505 842 5419 Bradbury Stamm (f)
505 466 2668 Tom Pascuzzi
(doctor) (p)
505 832 2238 Stables
505 699 7301 Karen (Cell)
505 832 2676 Office Fax

Healy, Shannon
Zorro Ranch
107 Camino Cabo
Santa Fe, NM 87508
505 466 2668(h)
505 660 1683(p)
570 454 8081 Mom (Cheryl)
516 331 6339 Dad

Kelly, John
Attorney General
3510 Wolters Place, N.E.
Albuquerque, New Mexico 87106
505 848 1867 (w)
505-768-1529
(Hm)500 Fourth Street NW
Suite 1000
Albuquerque, NM 87103-2168
505-268-4508 (h)
505 235 5084 (p)
505 848 1889 (wf)

Kerney, Gary
Landmark National
2817 Crain Highway
Upper Marlboro, Maryland 20774
301-574-3330(w)
240 463 3237(p)
Email:

okerney@landmarknational.
(Hm)292 Cape St. John
Annapolis, Maryland 21401
805 581 4173 (gson)
410 533 2485 Gary home
301-574-3301 (wf)
home 410-349-1778
240 463 3237 cellular
240 463 3236 Emergency

King, Bruce
Governor - New Mex

Suite 400
1120 Paseo De Peralta
Santa Fe, NM 87503
505-827-3020
505-827-3026
     505-827-7300 Home
505-832-4239

King, Rhonda
Rhonda King Realty
Hwy 472
2.5 mi west of Stanley
P.O. Box 606
Stanley, New Mexico 87056
505-832-4603 Work
505-982-4289 Fax
505-832-4229 Home
505-250-0730 Portable

Massage - New Mexico
505-269-1755 Diana (p)
505-271-9532 Diana
505-989-3902 Laura Christianson
505-982-1176 Daniella Urbassek
(German)
505 982 2283 Sabrina
505 660 6192 Sabrina
505 984 8356 Rachel
505 424 7416 Rachel
505 669 1269 Rachel
505 989 9846 Linda
Spankman-Yoga
505 471 1244 Melinda Walker -
Reflexologist
505 984 8142 Sabina (German)

505 983 6742 Maureen (GM re-
ally likes)
505 989 4264 Stina - GM still to
try
505 228 4505 Heidi (p)
505 438 3467 Nicki(Bill Siegel
recommended)

Richardson, Bill
505 476-2200 o
505 944 7410 f
505 699 8222 (p)
505 476 2245 office direct
505 469 6881 Sec agent w/Gov
(Tony)

Santa Fe Institute
1399 Hyde Park Road
Santa Fe, NM 87501
505-984-8800
505-982-0565

Singleton, Dr. & Mrs.
San Cristobal Ranch
Lamy, NM 87540
505-988-9720 (H)

RM

Aboff Shelley
001 407 333 2338
001561 333 9517

Cowley, Dick
0207-822 3691 (h)

Domb, Sam
230 Central Park South #18F
New York, NY

Hatsuhana (Japanese)
17 East 48th Street
0101 212 355 3345

Helmsley Palace
0101 212 888 7000

Il Cantinori
32 East 10 (at Broadway)

Il Tre Merli

Houston Street
West Broadway
691 7098

Isabelle's
359 Columbus Avenue
0101 212 724 2100

Jour et Nuit
212-925-5971

Karen Pets
1195 Lexington Ave.
b/w 81st & 82nd Sts.
212 472-9440

Klinger, Georgette
480 Madison Ave.
New York, NY 10021
212-838-3200
407-659-1522 Florida
Series #201482 Norma Jean

Le Club
88th (2-3)

Le Comptoir
227 East 67th Street
New York, NY 10021
212-794-4950

Lowell Hotel
Fuad Chartounian-contact
28 East 63rd St.
New York, NY
212-838-1400
212 319 4230

Madison Gourmet
212 288 8276(66)
212 737 3331 (84)

Madison Towers
22 E. 38th Street
(Corner of Madison & 38th)
3rd floor
New York, NY
001 212 685 7155

Madre, Le

168 West 18th
New York, NY
001 212 727 8022

Mark Hotel

New York, NY
212 744 4300

Massage - California

310 572 9693 Tracey
310-840-6989 Anastasia
310 396 0951 Danielle Schweitzer
310-450-1751 Rachel
714-841-1171 Lydia
310-392-2559 Scott Connelly
310-281-1270 Jackie Iverson
323-871-8829 Lisa Versaci
310 457 9894 Gypsy (h)
310 429 0254 Lori Bregman
310 463 6358 Jen (one of gypsy)
310-854-6366 Sports connection
310 463 5759 Sophie Biddle (p)
310 394 7048 Sophie Biddle
818-216-6974 Tiffany Gramza
323-270-7470 Tiffany Gramza (p)
310 394 1086 Scott Hobbs
323-254 8566 Marie Sabe
(Courtney Love's)
818-618 6907 Marie (p)
310 458 0883 Amber
323 314 4043 Crissy (Lisa
Sullivan:s friend
310 457 9388 Gypsy (w)
212 615 6948 NY # Gypsy (can
leave vm)
323 572 1632 Chauntae Davis
323 666 9942 Marianna (p)
702 743 0620 p Gypsy(p)

310 880 3495 Tanya (Petrella's
friend)
310 702 0169 Chauntae (p)
310 709 8877(p) Alex
Zosman(Gara's friend)
310 709 8877 Elizabeth Zosman
310 435 3930 Christy Tharpe
Los Angeles

Mayfair Regent

65th bet Park/Mad
001 212 288 0800

McMullan, Patrick

Photographer
12 Fifth Avenue, #1-R
New York, N.Y. 10011
212-674-2153

Mercer Kitchen

99 Prince
001 212 966 5454
001 212 966 0010(f)

Morgan Hotel

001 212 686 0300

Mr Chow

324 E. 57th
New York
10022
212 751 9030
0207 589 7347
(Hm)151 Knightsbridge

Visitors Message (P.B)

- Alison Chambers   (561) 758-1011
- Johanna   (561) 650-0185
- Jennifer   (561) 575-9814
- Cerdyn Adriano   (561) 478-0496
- Nicole   (561) 832-6777
- Kristen   (561) 707-3565
- Alice   (917) 774-4452
- Dawn   (561) 776-5679
- Ceche (Brazil)   00 5511 83834951
- Paula   (917) 518-2454
- Alicia   (305) 555-8013
- Manuela   (212) 300-6136
- Marie   (561) 644-1639
- Courtney Wild   (561) 202-0188
- Teale   (917) 603-2296
- Netlie   (917) 204-9696
- Svetlana   (917) 774-3061
- Cheri Lynch   (561) 373-1412
- Britney   (561) 644-7226
- Johanna   (561) 714-0546
- Brittany   (561) 547-2415
- Ceche   (201) 563-7171
- Jenny   (917) 330-1033
- Katya   (917) 678-2772
- Emmy   (323) 821-3699
- Nina   (917) 294-1627
- Allison   (631) 267-6215

2

- Andrea   (561) 798-6103
- Kelly   (561) 707-1789
- Melissa   (561) 641-7658
- Debra   (561) 625-0378
- Heidi   (954) 452-8582
- Katya   (954) 467-0412
- Alicia   (917) 345-3107
✗ - Carolina   (305) 321-4022

Important e-mail / addresses

* Jeffrey E. Epstein: jeffrey e@mindspring.com (P.B)
                    jeeproject@yahoo.com (N.Y)
                    zorrovanch@aol.com (N.M)
                    epstein@wanadoo.fr (Paris)

* * * Ghislaine Maxwell: gmex1@mindspring.com (NY)

                  — In House —
— Tim Newcombe (Citrix Systems Programmer)
               (614) 361 – 8625 Cell.
               (614) 481 – 7628 H.
(12)755-7050 — Charley Palmer (Chef- Aureole Restaurant) NYC
70)7.74-0323 — Joe Degeno (Chef- Aspen, CO,)
(Important) — Christophe (French Driver) P.B (561) 350 – 1700
  witness   ⤷ (Jet Aviation)   (561) 233 – 7242
                          (561) 233 – 7240

      → Secret Service Personnel escorting
        Mr. Berek, Ehud Former P.M of Israel on
        J. Epstein planes. —
* * * → Jean-Luc Brunel "Scout" for young females —
        Karin Models   (212) 226 – 4100
      — David Copperfield (Magician) (702) 235 – 5555
      — Eva Andersson (Former model & mother of nacked pic)
        (Dubin)   (212) 288 – 4844
      — David Cook Palm Beach (2004-2005) Witness,
        interacted and chat daily w/ underage girls. —

Epstein Black Book #2

This second Jeffrey Epstein address book pre-dates the first, and is being included second because it did not surface until nearly a decade after the first - this one being made public in 2021.

The book, which contains 349 names, offers a window into the late sex offender's social circle a full decade before the era covered by his previously known "little black book." More than 200 names listed in the book did not appear in Epstein's later address book.

Prominent entries not previously associated with Epstein include Morgan Fairchild, Suzanne Ircha, Carl Icahn, John A. Catsimatidis, Sandy Warner, and Martin Peretz.

A key difference between this book and the first is that the "finders" of this address book did not release full contact information for each recipient - only their name and location (plus additional notes when applicable).

The origins of this book are their own remarkable story: Denise Ondayko, a former musician, said she was walking down Fifth Avenue in the mid-'90s when she spotted an address book on the ground and picked it up out of curiosity.

More than two decades later, 2020, Ondayko was cleaning out an storage unit she had rented when the long-buried book emerged from a box. After a relative thumbed through it — and saw the entries for Epstein's numerous properties — the relative recognized who the owner was.

The book was subsequently sold on eBay, and its contents (names and cities only) were made public.

301 East 66th St.	Miscellaneous	New York, NY	US		
Dan Abraham	Person	New York, NY	US	Thompson Medical	
Frederick Adler	Person	West Palm Beach, FL	US	Venad Management, Inc.	
Cath Adler	Person	West Palm Beach, FL	US	Venad Management, Inc.	
Aero Leasing	Entity	Zurich, Geneva,	CH		
John Alessi	Person	Royal Palm Beach, FL	US		House maint. man
Ron Altbach	Person	New York, NY	US	HKM	
Tim Ambrose	Person	Interlochen, MI	US		
Marjan Amogli	Person	London, UK	UK		
Anderson & Shepard Ltd.	Entity	London, UK	UK		
Eva Andersson	Person	New York, NY	US		
Jean Appelt	Person			Citibank	
Ted Arison	Person	Miami, FL	US	Carnival Cruise Lines	
Placido Arango	Person	Madrid, Spain	ES	Grupo Sigla	
Bill Archer	Person	Westerville, OH	US		
Stanley Arkin	Person	New York, NY	US	Arkin, Schaffer & Kaplan	
Lorinda Ash	Person	New York, NY	US	Gagosian Gallery	
Linda Aslanian	Person	New York, NY	US		
Andre Balazs	Person	New York, NY	US	The Mercer	
Bandar Prince	Person	Aspen, CO	US		
Renee Preisler Barasch	Person	New York, NY	US	RPB Design	
Elena Leonidovna Barmakova	Person	Malibu, CA	US		
Richard Barnett	Person	Bayside, NY	US		

Jonathan Barrett	Person	New York, NY	US	
Anthony Barrett	Person	New York, NY	US	Ossa Properties
Gwendolyn Beck	Person	Palm Beach, FL	US	
Nicky Barrett	Person	Greenwich, CT	US	Ivey, Barnum & O'Mara
Doug Barton	Person	Gahanna, OH	US	New Albany Company
Gerald Barton	Person	New Albany, OH	US	New Albany Company
Jerry Beck	Person	Columbus, OH	US	The Limited
Harry I. Beller	Person	Monsey, NY	US	
Michaela Bercu	Person			
Stanley Bergman	Person	New York, NY	US	
Bob Berlin	Person	Scarsdale, NY	US	Paine Webber
Sophie Biddle	Person	New York, NY	US	
Abe Biederman	Person	Brooklyn, NY	US	Lipper & Co.
Nadia Bjorlin	Person	West Palm Beach, FL	US	
Conrad Black	Person	London, UK	UK	
Leon Black	Person	New York, NY	US	Apollo Management, L.P.
Jennifer Blair	Person	Alvaro, TX	US	
Dennis Block	Person	New York, NY	US	Wil, Gotshal & Manges
Dominique Bluhdorn	Person	New York, NY	US	Spade & Archer
Bill Boardman	Person			BankOne
David Bonderman	Person	Washington, DC	US	Texas Pacific Group
Beth Anne Bovino	Person	Cherry Hill, NJ	US	
Kelly Bovino	Person	Santa Monica, CA	US	
Randy Bowie	Person	New Albany, OH	US	The Limited
Bruce Brickman	Person	New York, NY	US	Brickman & Associates

Name	Type	Location	Country	Affiliation	
Bristol Hotel	Entity	Geneva, Paris,	CH, FR		
Horace "Woody" Brock	Person	Menlo Park, CA	US	Strategic Economic Decisions	
Fred Brooks	Person	Greenwich, CT	US	Connecticut Economics Corp	
Andrea Brown	Person	Newton, MA	US	Harvard Radcliffe Hillel	
Coco Brown	Person	New York, NY	US	Brown Companies	
BSI Geneva	Entity	Geneva,	CH		
Michael S Buchholtz, M.D.	Person	Huntington, NY	US		
Tiffany Burns	Person	Burlington, VT	US	WVNY TV	
David M. Byrne	Person	,		Oatman Associates	Driver
George Carmody	Person	New York, NY	US	Carmody Law Office	
Bill Carter	Person	Worthington, OH	US	Price Waterhouse	
Francois Catroux	Person				
John A. Catsimatidis	Person	New York, NY	US	Red Apple Group	
Jimmy Cayne	Person	New York, NY	US	Bear Stearns	
Didier Cazaudumec	Person	New York, NY	US		
Hale Champion	Person	Cambridge, MA	US		
Chicago Car	Entity				
Bill Ciralosky	Person	Toledo, OH	US		
Nancy Ciralosky	Person	Toledo, OH	US		
Claridges	Entity				
Jay Cochran	Person				
Jeffrey Cohen	Person	New York, NY	US	Wasserstein, Parella & Co. Inc	
Steve Cohen	Person	New York, NY	US	Gold & Wachtel	

Name	Type	Location	Country	Affiliation	Notes
Bob Crow	Person	New York, NY	US	Crow, Crow & Ver	
Diane Cummings	Person	New York, NY	US		
Paul Curran	Person	Spring Lake, NJ	US	Kaye, Scholer	
Mike Cutlip	Person	Chicago, IL	US	Hong Kong Bank ICA Division	
Ron Daniel	Person	New York, NY	US	Harvard University, McKinsey & Co Inc.	
Dayle Davison	Person	New York, NY	US	Citibank	
Michel de Yougoslavia	Person	Palm Beach, FL	US	Sotheby's Int. Realty	
George Delson	Person	New York, NY	US	George Delson & Associates	
Michael Dennis	Person	New York, NY	US	Azure Dev Inc.	
Alan Dershowitz	Person	Cambridge, MA	US		
Dawn Devito	Person	Watertown, MA	US		yoga instructor in P.B.
Alex Di Carcaci	Person	London, UK			
Donna	Person				
Drake Hotel	Entity	Chicago, IL	US		
Milt Dresner	Person	Southfield, MI	US		
Marie Helene du Chatel	Person	New York, NY	US		
Glen Dubin	Person	New York, NY	US	Dubin & Swieca	
Laurie Durning	Person				
Dr. David M. Eisenberg	Person	Boston, MA	US	Harvard Medical School	
Warren Eisenstein	Person				
John C. Elam	Person	Columbus, OH	US	Vorys, Sater, Seymour & Pease	

William S. Elkus	Person	Pacific Palisades, CA	US	Nathan Todd & Company
Mandy Ellison	Person	New York, NY	US	
Ralph Ellison	Person	Palm Beach, FL	US	
Donald Engel	Person	New York, NY	US	Bear Stearns
EPSTEIN - PORTABLES	Miscellaneous			
EPSTEIN - PORTABLES EUROPE	Miscellaneous			
Jeffrey Epstein	Person			
Arnold H. Epstein	Person	Kendall Park, NJ	US	
Mark Epstein	Person	New York, NY	US	Izmo Family of Companies, Inc.
Mark Epstein	Person	Stone Mountain, GA	US	
Karen Epstein	Person	Stone Mountain, GA	US	
Paula Epstein	Person	West Palm Beach, FL	US	
Exercise people	Miscellaneous			
Morgan Fairchild	Person	New York, NY	US	
Mitchel Feigenbaum	Person			
Frederic Fekkai	Person	New York, NY	US	Frederic Fekkai Beauty Center
Frederick (Ted) W. Field	Person	Los Angeles, CA	US	
Ted Fields	Person			
Mark Fisher	Person	New York, NY	US	
Bobby Foman	Person			
Jeanette Foman	Person			

Lyn Fontanilla	Person	New York, NY	US	
Jojo Fontanilla	Person	New York, NY	US	
Chris (Kip) Forbes	Person	New York, NY	US	Forbes Magazine
Katie Ford	Person	New York, NY	US	Ford Models
Lynn Forester	Person	New York, NY	US	Firstmark Holdings
James S. (Jim) Forsbach	Person	New Albany, OH	US	The Limited, Inc.
Marius Fortelni	Person	New York, NY	US	
Four Seasons	Entity	New York, NY	US	
Ellie Fox	Person	Woody Creek, CO	US	
Eric Fraad	Person			
Richard Freedman	Person			
Samuel Fried	Person	Bexley, OH	US	The Limited, Inc.
David M. Fromer	Person	New York, NY	US	Hacher Group
Cyril Fung	Person	Hong Kong,	CN	
Christina Galbraith	Person	New York, NY	US	
Eric Gany	Person	Wilton, CT	US	
Garage	Entity	New York, NY	US	
Cheryl Gaydas	Person	New York, NY	US	Fairchild Corporation
Darlene Gaydas	Person	New York, NY	US	
William Geffers	Person	Chicago, IL	US	The Industrial Bank of Japan
Les Gelb	Person			Council on Foreign Relations
Ann Getty	Person	San Francisco, CA	US	
Jim Gibson	Person	Washington, DC	US	
Kenneth Gilman	Person	Columbus, OH	US	The Limited, Inc.

Howard Gittis	Person	New York, NY	US	MacAndrews
Hubert de Givenchy	Person	Paris, France	FR	
Dan Glickman	Person	Washington, DC	US	
Bob Gold	Person	Westport, CT	US	McDermott, Wohl Emery
Stanley Gold	Person	Burbank, CA	US	Shamrock Holdings, Inc.
Dr. Nick Goldberg	Person			The Brain Institute
Bob Goldsandt	Person	Los Angeles, CA	US	Product Resources
Jerry Goldsmith	Person			
Isabel Goldsmith	Person	Beverly Hills, CA	US	
Bob Goodman	Person	Englishtown, NJ	US	
Francis Goodman	Person	Brooklyn, NY	US	
Rita Goodman	Person	Englishtown, NJ	US	
Alan Gordon	Person			
Edward S. Gordon	Person	New York, NY	US	Edward S. Gordon Company
Matt A. Gorman	Person	Bethesda, MD	US	U.S. Treasury Department
Stephen Jay Gould	Person	Cambridge, MA	US	Museum of Comparative Zoology, Harvard University
Alan (Ace) Greenberg	Person	New York, NY	US	Bear Stearns
Ted Greenberg	Person	New York, NY	US	ABD
Christina Greeven	Person	New York, NY	US	Manhattan File
David Grosof	Person	Clayton, MO	US	Central Institute for the Deaf
Pamela Gross	Person	New York, NY	US	
Charles Hack	Person			

Susan Guttfreund	Person			
John Guttfreund	Person			
Elena Hahn	Person			J.P. Morgan
MaryLynn Halland	Person	New York, NY	US	
Carl Hamman	Person	Mount Stirling, OH	US	Lower Gwynne
Steve Hanson	Person	New York, NY	US	
Jill Harth	Person			American Dream
Galila Hashemi	Person	London, UK		
Alex Hayes	Person	New York, NY	US	
Carrie Hayes	Person	New York, NY	US	Missbrenner
Gregory Hedberg	Person	New York, NY	US	Hirschel & Adler Art Gallery
Christy Hefner	Person	Chicago, IL	US	Playboy Enterprises Inc.
Paula Heil	Person	New York, NY	US	Millennial Arts
Dennis Hersch	Person	New York, NY	US	Davis, Polk & Wardwell
Emanuelle Hess	Person	Neuilly, France	FR	
Judith Hess	Person	New York, NY	US	
Ashley Hester	Person	Los Angeles, CA	US	
Danny Hillis	Person	Glendale, CA	US	Walt Disney Imagineering
Charlie Hinson	Person	Columbus, OH	US	Limited Store Planning, Inc.
Dr. Hirshfield	Person			
Heidi Holterbosch	Person			
Shaunt Hovnanian	Person	Red Bank, NJ	US	Hovanian Grove
Joe Hunter	Person	New York, NY	US	Ford Models

Ambassador Jon M. Huntsman	Person	Salt Lake City, UT	US	Huntsman Chemical	
Carl Icahn	Person	Mount Kisco, NY	US		
Darren K. Indyke	Person	New York, NY	US		
Suzanne Ircha	Person	New York, NY	US		
Allison Jacobs	Person	New York, NY	US		
Francis Jardine	Person	Cape Town,	ZA		
William Jeffers	Person	Chicago, IL	US	The Industrial Bank of Japan	
Pamela Johananoff	Person	Little Rock, AR	US		
Elizabeth Johnson	Person	New York, NY	US		
Anton Katz	Person	New York, NY	US		
John Kelly	Person	Albuquerque, NM	US		Attorney General
Lainie Kelson	Person	New York, NY	US		
Christine Kenneally	Person	New York, NY	US		
Bobby Kennedy	Person	Bedford, NY	US		
Mary Kennedy	Person	Bedford, NY	US		
Senator Edward Kennedy	Person	McLean, VA	US		
Gary Kerney	Person				
Jack Kessler	Person	New Albany, OH	US	New Albany Company	
Kristina Kincaid	Person	New York, NY	US	Victoria's Secret	
Bruce King	Person	Santa Fe, NM	US		Governor - New Mexico
Robert Kissen	Person	London, UK	UK		
Robin Klein	Person	Los Angeles, CA	US		
John Warner Kluge	Person	New York, NY	US		
Eva Koch	Person	New York, NY	US		
Mrs. Koppel	Person				

Name	Type	City	Country	Affiliation	Note
Jesse Kornbluth	Person	New York, NY	US		
Charles Kotick	Person	New York, NY	US	Aronsohn & Berman	
Michael Kramer	Person				
Kristina Kraverica	Person	Los Angeles, CA	US		
Henry Kravis	Person	New York, NY	US	Kohlberg, Kravis & Roberts	
Heidi Kucker	Person	New York, NY	US	Christie's	
Lauren Kwintner	Person	New York, NY	US		
Sean Lancaster	Person	Washington, DC	US	Bristol Associates, Inc.	BAC I-II Expert
Lanesborough Hotel	Entity	London, UK	UK		
Christina Lange	Person				
Alice Larkin	Person	New York, NY	US	Betsy's	
Nathan Rabbi Laufer	Person	Teaneck, NJ	US	Wexner Heritage Foundation	
Ann Lawesson	Person	Granna,	SE		
Christopher Lawford	Person	Katonah, NY	US		
Jean Lawford	Person	Katonah, NY	US		
Robin Leach	Person	New York, NY	US	Leach Entertainment Enterprise	
Larry Leeds	Person	New York, NY	US	Buckingham Research	
Elliot H. Levine	Person	New York, NY	US		
Robin E. Levy	Person	Los Angeles, CA	US	Elite Talent	
Kathy Lindman	Person	New York, NY	US		
Kenny Lipper	Person	New York, NY	US	Lipper & Company	
Lynn Forester	Person	New York, NY	US	Firstmark Holdings	
Carol Mack	Person	New York, NY	US		

Earl Mack	Person	New York, NY	US		
David Mahoney	Person	West Palm Beach, FL	US		
Bob Mallard	Person	New York, NY	US	Lehman Brothers	
Bruce Margolius	Person	Park City, UT	US		
Mark Hotel	Entity	New York, NY	US		
Donald Marron	Person	New York, NY	US	Paine Webber	
Masseuse/Masseur	Miscellaneous				
Mast Industries	Entity	Hong Kong, Milan	CN		Pres. John Welch
Ghislaine Maxwell	Person	London, UK	UK		
Mayfair Regent	Entity				
Thomas C. McMillen	Person	Washington, DC	US	United States House of Representatives	Congressman
Jerry McNamara	Person			Goldman Sachs	
Samantha McQuiston	Person	London, UK	UK		
John Meade	Person	Washington, US	US	O'Connor & Hannan	
Jerry Merritt	Person	New Albany, OH		The Limited, Inc.	
Mark Middleton	Person	Washington, DC	US	The White House	
Celina Midelfart	Person	Oslo, Norway	Norway		
Charles Miller	Person	Mamaroneck, NY	US	Miller & Raved	
Howard Millstein	Person	New York, NY	US		
Paul Millstein	Person	New York, NY	US	Millstein Properties Corp.	
Ross Milroy	Person	Boca Raton, FL	US		
Steve Minick	Person	New Albany, OH	US	The New Albany Company	

Name	Type	Location	Country	Organization	Role
David Mitchell	Person	New York, NY	US		
George Mitchell	Person	Portland, ME	US	Verner, Liipfert, Bernhard, Mc	Special Counsel
Larry Mogens	Person				
Rosa Monckton	Person	London, UK	UK	Tiffany & Co.	
Mike Moritz	Person	Columbus, OH	US	Baker & Hostetler	
Nathan Myhrvold	Person	Redmond, WA	US	Microsoft Corporation	Chief Technology Officer
Erin Nance	Person	Athens, GA	US		
Robert E. Nederlander	Person	New York, NY	US	Nederlander Organ, Inc.	
New Albany	Entity	New Albany, OH	US		
New Albany Bath & Tennis Club	Entity	New Albany, OH	US		
New Albany Country Club	Entity	New Albany, OH	US		
New Albany Property Investment	Entity	New Albany, OH	US		N.A. Property
New York Academy of Art	Entity	New York, NY	US		
Larry Newman	Person	Sand Point, NY	US		
Larry Esq. Newman	Person	New York, NY	US	Friedman & Kaplan	
Mr. & Mrs. W.A. Nitze	Person	New York, NY	US		
Robert Nunnery	Person	New York, NY	US		U.S. Customs
Jack O'Rourke	Person	Washington, DC	US		
Bob Oatman	Person	Gahanna, OH	US	R.L. Oatman & Associates, Inc.	Protective Operation
Wayne Owens	Person	Washington, DC	US		Congressman
Mark Packer	Person	New York, NY	US	Canastel's	
Joel Pashcow	Person	Great Neck, NY	US	RPS Realty Trust	

Name	Type	Location	Country	Organization	Title
Stacey Pashcow	Person	New York, NY	US		
Gabriel Perahia	Person	Geneva,	CH		
Marty Peretz	Person	Washington, DC	US	The New Republic	
Ronald Perelman	Person	New York, NY	US	Revlon	
John Peters	Person	Burbank, CA	US	Peters Entertainment	
Lauren Petrella	Person	Willowick, OH	US		
Caryl Philips	Person	Dayton, OH	US		
Pierre Hotel	Entity	New York, NY	US		
PILOT INFORMATION	Miscellaneous				
Sue-Ann Pisack	Person	New York, NY	US		
Stuart Pivar	Person	New York, NY	US		
Suzanne Ponsot	Person	New York, NY	US	American Friends of Israel	Executive Director
Gene Pressman	Person	Larchmont, NY	US	Barney's of New York	
Kim Price	Person	Alexandria, VA	US	Barrueta	
Paul Prosperi	Person	Palm Beach, FL	US	Algoa Deny	
George Pryor	Person	New Albany, OH	US	First Intercontinental Realty	
Nina Pustilnik	Person	New York, NY	US	First Boston	
Thomas H. Quinn	Person	Washington, DC	US	O'Connor & Hannan	
Lewis S. Ranieri	Person	Merrick, NY	US	Ranieri & Co., Inc.	
Steven Rattner	Person	New York, NY	US		
Marty Raynes	Person	New York, NY	US	M.J. Raynes	
Patty Raynes	Person				
Ed Razek	Person	Galena, OH	US		
Nick Ribis	Person	New York, NY	US	Trump Organization	

Joan Rivers	Person	New York, NY	US	
Jacque Robertson	Person	New York, NY	US	Cooper Robertson & Partners
David Rockefeller	Person	New York, NY	US	Rockefeller Financial Service
Dave Rodgers	Person	Lake Worth, FL	US	
Marshall Rose	Person	New York, NY	US	Georgetown Group
Henry Rosovsky	Person	Newton, MA	US	Harvard University Dean
David Ross	Person	New York, NY	US	Whitney Museum of American Art
Leonard Ross	Person	Beverly Hills, CA	US	Rossco Holdings Incorporated
David Roth	Person			National Line
Peter Thomas Roth	Person	New York, NY	US	Karbra Co.
Edmund Baron Rothschild	Person	Geneva,	CH	
Edouard de Rothschild	Person	Paris, France	FR	
Celine Rousselet (Cazals)	Person	Paris, France	FR	
Steve Ruchefsky	Person			
Bernard Sabrier	Person	Geneva,	CH	Unigestion, S.A.
Oliver Dr. Sacks	Person	New York, NY	US	
Elizabeth Schafer	Person	New York, NY	US	
Larry Schafran	Person	New York, NY	US	L.G. Schafran & Partners
Jeff Schantz	Person	North Woodmere, NY	US	
Douglas A Schoettle	Person	New York, NY	US	

Robert S. Schwartz	Person	Columbus, OH	US	Schwartz, Kelm, Warren & Rubenstein	
Claudia Scier	Person	New York, NY	US		
Kathryn Scott	Person	Arlington, VA	US	Kathryn Scott Associates	
Joan Severance	Person	Studio City, CA	US		
Donald B. Shackelford	Person	Gahanna, OH	US	State Savings Bank	
Rhonda Shearer	Person	New York, NY	US		wife of Jay Gould
Stanley Shopkorn	Person	New York, NY	US	Ethos Capital	Managing General Ptn
William (Bill) Siegel	Person	New York, NY	US	Chris-Craft Industries	
Bruce Slovin	Person	New York, NY	US	MAC Andrews & Forbes Group Inc.	President
Dennis Smith	Person	Southampton, NY	US		
Richard Snyder	Person	New York, NY	US		
Laura Yorke Snyder	Person	New York, NY	US		
Bruce Soll	Person	Columbus, OH	US	The Limited, Inc.	
Michael W. Sonnenfeldt	Person	Tenafly, NJ	US	Emmes & Co., Inc.	
Sophie Van Hauen	Person	London, UK	UK	Charlotte Morgan	
Ellen Spencer	Person	Amelia Island, FL	US		
Bob Starodoj	Person	Aspen, CO	US	Mason & Morse Real Estate	
John Stefanidis	Person	London, UK	UK		
Saul Steinberg	Person	New York, NY	US	Reliance Group Holding Inc.	Chairman
Pamela Stephens	Person	Columbus, OH	US		
Michael Stevens	Person	St. Tropez, France	FR		
Nina Stevens	Person	St. Tropez, France	FR		

Name	Type	Location	Country	Organization
Linda Stone	Person			Microsoft
Craig Tafoya	Person	Davie, FL	US	Limitless
Felicia Taylor	Person	New York, NY	US	CNBC
Elizabeth Tepper	Person	New York, NY	US	ABB Service Worldwide
Allan R. Tessler	Person	Teton Village, WY	US	International Financial Group
Susan Thomases	Person	New York, NY	US	Wilkie Farr & Gallagher
Lenny Toboroff	Person	New York, NY	US	Riddell
Cathy Tolbert	Person	New York, NY	US	
Trilaterial Commission	Entity	New York, NY	US	
Donald Trump	Person	New York, NY	US	The Trump Organization
Marty Trust	Person	Manchester, NH	US	Mast Industries, Inc.
Steve Tuckerman	Person	Columbus, OH	US	Tuckerman Optical Co.
Christy Turlington	Person	Los Angeles, CA	US	
Tony Valukas	Person	Chicago, IL	US	Jenner & Block
John Viggiano	Person	New York, NY	US	Dignitary Protection
Larry Visoski	Person	Boynton Beach, FL	US	
Linda Wachner	Person	New York, NY	US	Warnaco, Inc.
William B. Wachtel	Person	New York, NY	US	Gold & Wachtel
Francis Wahl	Person	Geneva,	CH	
Philipe Wahl	Person	Rome,	IT	DeDem Automatica
Ric Wanetik	Person	Columbus, OH	US	Ric Wanetik & Associates
CC Wang	Person	New York, NY	US	U.S. Summit Corp.
Vera Wang Becker	Person	New York, NY	US	Vera Wang Bridal House, Ltd.

Sandy Warner	Person	New York, NY	US	J.P. Morgan
Patsy Warner	Person	New York, NY	US	
Bob Wesselman	Person	Worthington, OH	US	NA Country Club
Bella Wexner	Person	Columbus, OH	US	
Les Wexner	Person	London, UK	UK	The Limited, Inc.
White House	Entity	Washington, DC	US	
Amber Williamson	Person	Santa Monica, CA	US	
Tobie Wood	Person	Beverly Hills, CA	US	
Fred Yaffe	Person	Bloomfield Hills, MI	US	Yaffe & Co.
Dimitri Yugoslavie	Person	New York, NY	US	Sotheby's
Barry Zelin	Person	New York, NY	US	Gruntal
Ira Zicherman	Person	Brooklyn, NY	US	Bear Stearns
Mort Zucherman	Person	New York, NY	US	Boston Properties

Epstein Palm Beach House Manual

This is the 56-page Epstein Palm Beach house manual was made public in the sex trafficking case against close Epstein associate Ghislaine Maxwell.

This manual is dated February 14, 2005.

Epstein's longtime housekeeper Juan Alessi said that he was told to "see nothing, hear nothing, say nothing" when guests came to the house, and an instruction in the manual reads, "NEVER disclose Mr. Epstein or Ms. Maxwell's activities or whereabouts to anyone."

This gives a behind the scenes look at Epstein's estate, and the secrecy that pervades it.

HOUSEHOLD MANUAL

358 EL BRILLO WAY
PALM BEACH, FL 33480

LIST OF CONTENTS

- Introduction

- Grooming & Guest Relations

- Proper Language

- Answering the telephone

- Pre-arrival information gathering

- Guest pick-up and drop-off

- Escorting guests to their room

- Pre-arrival preparations

    - Master Bedroom
    - Master Bathroom
    - Master Bathroom Toiletries
    - Ms Maxwell's Bathroom
    - Ms Maxwell's Bathroom Toiletries
    - Guestrooms
    - Guest Bathrooms
    - Guest Bathrooms Toiletries
    - All Bathrooms
    - Exterior
    - The Cabana
    - Vehicles and Bicycles
    - Interior
    - Prepare and Purchase Shopping List   (See pp. 30-32 for lists)

- Daily duties while Mr Epstein, Ms Maxwell, and guests are in residence

    - Morning preparation
    - Pool Area
    - Cabana
    - Kitchen
    - Downstairs Areas
    - Master Bedroom
    - Master Bathroom
    - Ms Maxwell's Bathroom
    - Guestrooms
    - Early evening
    - Before you leave at night

- Shopping Lists
    - Pre-Arrival
    - On-hand at all times

- Cleaning Schedule

    - Daily
    - Weekly
    - Monthly (Week 1, Week 2, Week 3)
    - Every six months (April, October)

- Maintenance Schedule

    - Check every month
    - Check every three months (March, June, September, December)
    - Check every six months (April, October)

- Bedroom cleaning

- Bathroom cleaning

- Laundry and dry cleaning

- Office Supplies

- Mail and Deliveries

- Resetting the Telephone

- Serving Breakfast

- Standby duties

- Emergency procedures

- Supplement: Contact Telephone Numbers

INTRODUCTION

This manual is designed to give you the proper guidance and assistance to perform your duties to the best of your ability, while ensuring a consistently high level of service.

Gathering as much information as possible will help you with the day to day running of the home.

By using your communications skills - listening and observing, you will be able to anticipate the needs of Mr Epstein, Ms Maxwell and their guests.

Checklists will assist you in making sure that all tasks have been completed and that not even the smallest details have been overlooked.

GROOMING & GUEST RELATIONS

Appearance is extremely important if high standards are to be maintained. A favorable first impression goes a long way. Personal cleanliness, good presentation, and a genuine and polite "aim to please" approach are very important.

- Try and anticipate the needs of Mr Epstein, Ms Maxwell and their guests.

- Make guests feel pampered and welcome.

- Always address guest by their name, (eg: Mr Smith or Ms Smith)

- Do not discuss personal problems with guests.

- Be cautious of voice levels and noise while working in rooms, kitchen and hallways.

- Unobtrusive is the key.

- Remember that you see nothing, hear nothing, say nothing, except to answer a question directed at you. Respect their privacy.

- Use your judgment when conveying information to Mr Epstein. If the matter is not urgent, leave a note for him, clearly stating what it is you need to know.

- Wear the appropriate clothing while Mr Epstein, Ms Maxwell and their guests are in residence. Dark blue trousers with white golf shirts to be worn daily, long sleeve white shirts for dinner service.

- Items in pockets must not create a bulge or be visible.

- Do not address Mr Epstein, Ms Maxwell and their guests with your hands in your pockets.

- Do not eat or drink in front of Mr Epstein, Ms Maxwell and their guests. Do not chew gum.

- When you are attending to Mr Epstein, Ms Maxwell and their guests, cellular phones must be placed on "vibrate." At no time should these phones "ring."

- Avoid using strong perfume or aftershave lotion. This could cause an allergic reaction.

- Channel all questions and concerns through the Estate Manager.

- SMILE!

PROPER LANGUAGE

What you say is as important as what you do. Your language must include good diction and exclude swear words and slang. Pay attention to how you speak to Mr Epstein, Ms Maxwell and their guests.

You do not say:

"Yeah"
"Sure"
"No problem"
"You bet"
"Gotcha"
"Right"
"I dunno"

You do say:

"Yes, Mr _____ "
"Of course, Ms _____ "
"My pleasure"
"It is no trouble at all"
"With pleasure"
"I would be very pleased to"
"You are quite right"
"I have no idea, but I will find out immediately"

To a compliment you say:

"You are very kind"
"Thank, you, Ms _____. I enjoy doing it."

To a justified criticism or mistake you say:

"I am very sorry; it will not happen again."
"It was completely my fault; I will make the changes immediately."

To a guest you say:

"If I can be of any additional assistance, please let me know."
"Is there anything else that you might need."
"I am very pleased that you enjoyed your stay, Mr _____ "
"It was lovely to see you again, Mrs _____ "

What to say when entering a room:

"May I come in"

What to say after entering the room:

Greet Mr Epstein, Ms Maxwell, and /or their guests, "Good Morning, Mr _____"

You do not expound on the weather or any other subject, unless asked. You have no idea how they are feeling.

You provide your service, then ask, "Is there anything else I might do for you," and if not, leave the room.

ANSWERING THE TELEPHONE

How you answer the telephone will leave a long-lasting impression on all those who call. It immediately tells the caller the service standard. When you answer the phone, the quality of your voice is of utmost importance. The person on the other end of the line cannot see your expression or gestures, so any impression that person receives depends entirely on your voice. Speak clearly and distinctly. Do not slam down the receiver at any time!

- All calls should be answered in three rings or less.

- If the incoming line is one of Mr Epstein's or Ms Maxwell's, answer as follows:

  "Good morning / afternoon / evening, Epstein / Maxwell residence.

- If Mr Epstein or Ms Maxwell have advised th at they do not wish to receive any calls, you are to reply as follows:

  "Mr Epstein / Ms Maxwell is not available. Ma y I take a message?"

  Complete a phone message slip with the following information: Name (spelt correctly), date and time of call, telephone number including the area code.

  Place the message on the pantry countertop if it is for Mr Epstein, and for Ms Maxwell, on her desk.

- If Mr Epstein and Ms Maxwell choose to receive a call, you are to reply as follows:

  "May I ask who is calling? Just a moment please."

  Ring the extension where they are located and advise them who is calling.

- There is a "Do Not Disturb" setting on the telephone system. This option is to be set as directed in the pre-arrival check off list.

- Telephone directories are to be updated every six months, or as the new tel ephone directories are available.

- A copy of Mr Epstein and Ms Maxwell's telephone directories must be placed to the right of each telephone (except for the Guestrooms).

- Always check that there are notepads and pens. These must be placed to the right of each telephone.

- A pair of reading glasses must be placed in front of each telephone (except for the Guestrooms).

- An extension card must be placed under the front of each telephone.

- Unless otherwise instructed, **NEVER** disclose Mr Epstein or Ms Maxwell's activities or whereabouts to anyone. If the caller is insistent, you simply ask to take a message, a time and a number, where the caller can be reached. Do not be bullied and do not show any reaction or impatience, simply be firm.

- Advise Ms Maxwell of any strange telephone calls or enquiries.

- Advise Ms Maxwell of any unusual behavior, such as strangers lurking around the vicinity of the property.

- Entrance gates to the property must remain closed when Mr Epstein is not in residence.

- **The security of the house and of Mr Epstein, Ms Maxwell and their guests, is your first consideration and should be uppermost in your consciousness.**

PRE-ARRIVAL INFORMATION GATHERING

This is all the information necessary to meet the needs of Mr Epstein, Ms Maxwell and their guests. If possible, this should be done 24 hours prior to arrival.

- Obtain a list of all guests who will be joining Mr Epstein and Ms Maxwell.
- Confirm travel itinerary.
- Ask about any special requests or dietary requirements.
- Ask about any gifts that Mr Epstein may want placed in the guestrooms.

GUEST PICK-UP AND DROP-OFF

All guests should have a staff member waiting for them at the appropriate terminal gate.

- Double check arrival information.
- Always have a written copy of the guest's travel itinerary (flight arrival times, etc) on hand.
- Check the number of people in the party to insure that the vehicle can accommodate all arriving guests.
- If you are unfamiliar with the guest, prepare a sign clearly stating the guest's name.
- Welcome guest by name.
- Advise guest of your name.
- Offer to carry any luggage that guest may have with them.
- Escort guest to luggage pickup area if necessary, gather luggage and escort guest to vehicle.
- Advise guest on travel time. Provide demographics on the area.
- Keep conversation to a minimum.
- When you are driving Mr Epstein or Ms Maxwell, keep your hands on the wheel. Your cellular phones should be placed on "vibrate." At no time should you answer private calls.

ESCORTING GUESTS TO THEIR ROOM

- Upon arrival, gather guest's belongings and escort to pre-assigned room.
- Inquire from guest where they would like their luggage and place it appropriately.
- Offer to unpack luggage.
- Show guest how to use the telephone.
- Show guest how to use the remote control for the television.
- Ask guest to complete "Emergency contact information" form and return to you.
- Ask guest if they have any food allergies.
- Ask guest what they would like to be served for breakfast and at what time.
- Tell guest to enjoy their stay and let them know how you can be reached.

PRE-ARRIVAL PREPARATIONS

CHECK OFF LIST

MASTER BEDROOM

- ❏ A/C is set at 60 degrees.

- ❏ All light fixtures are working.

- ❏ Shutters must be closed.

- ❏ Remote controls for the television are working.

- ❏ Telephones are on "Do not disturb."

- ❏ *JE* and *GM* telephone directories placed to right of telephone.

- ❏ Telephone extension card placed under front of telephone.

- ❏ Alarm clock must be set to the correct time and date.

- ❏ Two lighted pens on both bedside tables.

- ❏ Regular pens on both bedside tables.

- ❏ *Jeffrey Epstein* large and small notepads on both bedside tables.

- ❏ Reading glasses on both bedside tables.

- ❏ Eye masks on both bedside tables.

- ❏ Box of tissues on each bedside table (Replace if less than 1/3).

- ❏ Flashlight with new batteries.

- ❏ Bottled water and drinking glasses on both bedside tables.

- ❏ Gun placed in beside table drawer.

DATE: _____   **SIGNATURE:** _____

MASTER BATHROOM

☐ Check that water is hot and runs clear.

☐ Fresh bar of soap placed to the right of the washbasin.

☐ Two fresh facecloths on the washbasin and two in the shower.

☐ Electric toothbrush (Replace head every 4 weeks).

☐ New toothbrush placed in a clean drinking glass to the left of the washbasin.

☐ Toothpaste is more than ½ full.

☐ Mouthwash.

☐ Razor and shaving cream (more than ½ full).

☐ Electric razor plugged in and charged.

☐ Tissues (replace if less than ⅓).

☐ Q-Tips.

☐ Round cotton pads.

☐ Clean all fixtures, shower and steam room.

☐ New pair of exfoliating gloves in the shower.

☐ Tidy and replace any toiletries which are running low.

☐ Three large blue towels and one hand towel to be ready for massage in towel room.

☐ Shutters must be open.

DATE: _____   **SIGNATURE:** _____

MASTER BATHROOM TOILETRIES
CHECK OFF LIST

- ❏ *Gillette MACH 3* Razor with extra blades (change blade after every use)
- ❏ Shaving Cream (*Kiehl's Close Shavers Squadron*)
- ❏ *Secret Original Solid* Deodorant
- ❏ *Lever 2000* soap
- ❏ *Noxzema Plus* Face Wash
- ❏ Facial moisturizers (*Kiehl's Ultra Facial Moisturizer, Babor*)
- ❏ *Aquaphor* Hand Cream
- ❏ *California Mango* Lotion
- ❏ Bubble bath and shower gels (variety)
- ❏ Shampoo / Conditioner (*White Rain Coconut Essence, Biolage, Nexxus Simply Silver*)
- ❏ Hair finishing cream (*Paul Mitchell Stickworks*)
- ❏ *Peter Thomas Roth* Sunscreen (face and body)
- ❏ *Kiehl's* Lip Balm with SPF
- ❏ Q-Tips
- ❏ Round cotton pads
- ❏ Toothpaste (*Arm & Hammer Dental Care* and *Mentadent*)
- ❏ Toothbrush (Oral B / Hard)
- ❏ Electric Toothbrush (*Braun Ultra Plaque Remover*)
- ❏ *Scope* mouthwash
- ❏ Dental Floss (*Johnson & Johnson Reach / Mint waxed*)
- ❏ Baby Powder (*Johnson & Johnson*)
- ❏ *Mason Pearson* Hairbrush
- ❏ Hair Comb
- ❏ Tweezers
- ❏ Fingernail clippers and file

DATE: _____   **SIGNATURE:** _____

MS MAXWELL'S BATHROOM

☐ Two big white towels placed next to the bath.

☐ Soap, shampoo and bubble bath by the side of the tub.

☐ Check that water is hot and running clear.

☐ Water must be directed to the faucet and not the sprayer on the tub.

☐   Two fresh washcloths on the washbasin and two next to the bathtub.

☐ Fresh bar of soap placed to the right of the washbasin.

☐ Electric toothbrush (Replace head every 4 weeks).

☐ New toothbrush placed in a clean drinking glass to the left of the washbasin.

☐ Toothpaste is more than ½ full.

☐ Mouthwash.

☐ Q-Tips.

☐ Round cotton pads.

☐ Tidy and replace any toiletries which are running low.

☐ Tissues (replace if less than ⅓).

☐ Unlock the closets.

☐ Photographs to be placed.

DATE: _____   **SIGNATURE:** _____

MS MAXWELL'S BATHROOM TOILETRIES

CHECK OFF LIST

- ❏ Facial Moisturizer (*La Mer*)
- ❏ *Babor* Foam Mask
- ❏ *Kiehl's* Cucumber Toner
- ❏ *Kiehl's* Washable Cleansing Milk
- ❏ *La Mer* Eye Balm
- ❏ *Evian* Face Mist
- ❏ *Clarins Crème Masvelt* Body Shaping Crème
- ❏ *Babor* Natural Body Peeling
- ❏ *Lancôme Exfoliance* Gel
- ❏ Body Lotion (*Frédéric Fekkai, Clinique Deep Comfort Body Moisture*)
- ❏ *Aquaphor* Hand Cream
- ❏ *Secret Original Solid* Deodorant
- ❏ Round cotton pads
- ❏ Q-Tips
- ❏ Toothbrush (Oral B / Hard)
- ❏ Electric Toothbrush (*Braun Ultra Plaque Remover*)
- ❏ Toothpaste (*Arm & Hammer Dental Care* and *Mentadent*)
- ❏ Dental Floss (*Johnson & Johnson Reach / Mint waxed*)
- ❏ *Scope* mouthwash
- ❏ Sunscreen (*Lancôme Sôleil SPF 30 Face Creme*)
- ❏ *Kiehl's* Lip Balm with SPF

- *Lever 2000* soap

- Bubble Bath, Bath Gel, Bath Salts (variety)

- Razor and shaving gel

- Shampoo / Conditioner (*Frédéric Fekkai Technical & Apple Cider*)

- Aquis Hair Towel

- *Mason Pearson* Hair Brush

- *Babor* Hand & Nail Repair

- Nail polish remover (*Cutex*)

- Fingernail clippers and file

- Tweezers

- *OB* tampons (light & heavy)

DATE: _____ **SIGNATURE:** _____

GUESTROOMS

Hint: All guestrooms must appear as though the arriving guest is the first to ever stay in the room.

❏ Bed linen must be fresh.

❏ All light fixtures are working.

❏ Remote controls for the television are working.

❏ Instructions on "How to work the television" placed next to the television.

❏ Alarm clock must be set to the correct time and date.

❏ Telephones are on "Do not disturb."

❏ Telephone extension card placed under front of telephone.

❏ Pens and *Jeffrey Epstein* large and small notepads on bedside table.

❏ Eye masks on both bedside tables.

❏ Small bouquet of fresh flowers.

❏ Gifts if indicated by Mr Epstein.

❏ Bottled water and drinking glasses on bedside table.

❏ Selection of fresh fruit.

❏ Side plate, fruit knife, napkin.

❏ Flashlight with new batteries.

❏ Closets must be cleared. Check that there are sufficient wooden hangers that are hung evenly.

DATE: _____   **SIGNATURE:** _____

2/14/2005   16

GUEST BATHROOMS

- ☐ Towels and bathrobes are fresh.

- ☐ Fresh bar of soap and shampoo in bathtub and shower stall.

- ☐ Two fresh washcloths on the washbasin and two next to the bathtub.

- ☐ Fresh bar of soap placed to the right of the washbasin.

- ☐ New toothbrush and toothpaste on the counter to the left of the washbasin.

- ☐ Clean drinking glass.

- ☐ Tissues (replace if less than ⅓).

- ☐ Check guest supplies and replace what is needed.

- ☐ Hairdryer is working.

- ☐ Replace toilet paper with new roll. Fold end into a "V."

DATE: _____   **SIGNATURE:** _____

GUEST BATHROOMS TOILETRIES

CHECK OFF LIST

- ☐ Toothbrush (Oral B / Hard)

- ☐ Toothpaste (*Arm & Hammer Dental Care, Mentadent*)

- ☐ Dental Floss (*Johnson & Johnson Reach / Mint waxed*)

- ☐ *Scope* mouthwash

- ☐ Shaving Cream (*Kiehl's, Gillette*)

- ☐ *Schick Triblade* Disposable Razors (Men & Ladies)

- ☐ *Aquaphor* Hand Cream

- ☐ Facial cleansers and moisturizers (variety)

- ☐ Round cotton pads

- ☐ Body Lotion (*The Body Shop Body Butter, California Mango*)

- ☐ *Secret Original Solid* Deodorant

- ☐ Sunscreen (*Clinique Body & Face SPF 15 & 30*)

- ☐ Lip Balm (*Kiehl's with SPF*)

- ☐ *Hawaiian Tropic* After Sun

- ☐ Tweezers

- ☐ Fingernail kit

- ☐ Hairbrush

- ☐ Comb

- ☐ Shampoo / Conditioner (*Biolage, The Body Shop Coconut, Frédéric Fekkai*)

- ☐ *Lever 2000* soap

- ☐ Q Tips

- ☐ Bath / Shower Gel

- ☐ *Tampax* and *OB* tampons (regular), *Always* pads (with wings)

DATE: _____   **SIGNATURE:** _____

2/14/2005   18

ALL BATHROOMS

CHECK LIST

All bathrooms must contain the following extra items

- ☐   Toilet paper (white two-ply)
- ☐   Bath towel
- ☐   Hand towel
- ☐   Washcloth
- ☐   Hand soap
- ☐   Bath soap (*Lever 2000*)
- ☐   Kleenex tissue
- ☐   Tylenol
- ☐   Tums
- ☐   Sudafed
- ☐   Halls cough sweets
- ☐   Box of matches
- ☐   Toilet brush
- ☐   Toilet plunger

DATE: _____   **SIGNATURE:** _____

EXTERIOR

- ❏ Pressure wash pool deck, sidewalks, terrace and patios.

- ❏ Pressure wash outdoor furniture.

- ❏ Place cushions on pool and terrace furniture.

- ❏ Have the pool cleaned.

- ❏ Check that pool water temperature is between 82 – 88°F

- ❏ Float in the pool is properly inflated.

- ❏ Pool "toys" are clean and in working order.

- ❏ Pool lights working.

- ❏ Towels are in the wooden basket.

- ❏ Telephone is connected and in working order.

- ❏ Landscape lights working.

- ❏ Wash windows.

- ❏ Check fence for holes where Max can get out.

- ❏ Awnings are clean and working.

DATE: _____   **SIGNATURE:** _____

THE CABANA

- ☐ Check that computer will access the Internet and Bloomberg.
- ☐ Place paper in the copier.
- ☐ Plenty of pens and paper.
- ☐ Two pairs of reading glasses on the desk.
- ☐ Telephone directory placed to the right of the telephone.
- ☐ Tissues (replace if less than ⅓).
- ☐ Tidy the desk, but do not throw any papers away.
- ☐ Stereo in working condition.
- ☐ Two bathrobes and towels in the bathroom.
- ☐ Fresh bar of soap placed to the right of the washbasin.
- ☐ New toothbrush and toothpaste placed to the left of the washbasin.
- ☐ Clean drinking glass.
- ☐ Replace toilet paper with new roll. Fold end into a "V."
- ☐ Suntan oil and insect repellent.

DATE: _____   **SIGNATURE:** _____

VEHICLES AND BICYCLES

- ❏ Drive all vehicles to make sure that they are in good running condition. No flat batteries.

- ❏ Check that cars are full of petrol (never below ¼).

- ❏ Place $100 in the glove compartment or center console of each car.

- ❏ Two bottles of water.

- ❏ *JE* and *GM* telephone directories.

- ❏ Reading glasses.

- ❏ *Jeffrey Epstein* large and small notepads with pens.

- ❏ Box of tissues.

- ❏ Two pairs of sunglasses.

- ❏ Check that bicycles are clean and tire pressure is correct.

DATE: _____   **SIGNATURE:** _____

INTERIOR

Living Room

- Plump the cushions.

- Check that stereo system and headphones are working.

- Clean and tidy all table top surfaces.

- Tidy up the magazines. Throw out fashion magazines over two months old.

- Place books that are lying around back on bookshelves.

Ms Maxwell's Desk

- Check that the DSL computer line is working.

- Place paper in the copier.

- Plenty of pens and notepads.

- *JE & GM* telephone directories placed to the right of the telephone.

- Tissues (replace if less than ⅓).

Kitchen

- Polish marble counter tops in kitchen.

- Empty dishwasher.

- Check all expiration dates on food in refrigerator and pantry.

- Dish pantry must be organized.

- Napkins cleaned and pressed for trays.

General

- Buy *The NY Times*, *The Wall Street Journal*, *Palm Beach Post* and place in the pantry. Buy the *Daily Mail* and place on Ms Maxwell's desk.

- Current TV Guide next to television.

- "How to work the TV" instructions next to television.

- Check that all light bulbs are working. Dust and straighten lampshades.

- Check that the water is hot and running clear.

- Check that all air conditioners are in working order.

- Check that all telephones are working.

- Flashlights on each desk and in the kitchen. Check batteries.

- Reading glasses, pens and notepads at every telephone.

- All clocks are set at the correct time and date. (See p. 55 for instructions.)

- All electrical appliances and stereo systems are working.

- Place box of matches next to all candles.

- Dust and straighten paintings.

- Straighten the fringe on all rugs. Check for stains.

- Check that all smoke detectors are working. Check fire extinguishers.

- Clean all air vents.

- Make sure that all drapes are hanging neatly with hooks in place.

Stationary

- Three sizes of *Jeffrey Epstein* notepads.

- Two sizes of *Ghislaine Maxwell* and *Lady Ghislaine* notepads.

- Letterhead stationary and envelopes. One pack from each of Mr Epstein's residences and business. Mr Epstein's personal stationary (writing paper, notepads, envelopes, compliment slips).

- *Jeffrey Epstein* and *Ghislaine Maxwell* cards and envelopes.

DATE: _____   **SIGNATURE:** _____

DAILY DUTIES (IN RESIDENCE)

CHECK OFF LIST

Morning preparation

- ❏ Buy newspapers.
- ❏ Check that the petrol in all vehicles is more than ¼ full.
- ❏ $100 in glove compartment or center console of each vehicle.
- ❏ Replace empty water bottles.
- ❏ Check that there are pens, notepads, telephone directories and tissues.
- ❏ Any CD's lying around should be placed back in the correct covers.

Pool Area

- ❏ Check that pool temperature is between 82 - 88°F
- ❏ Wipe down all outside tables and chairs.
- ❏ Place reading glasses, pens, notepads and a telephone on the pool table outside.
- ❏ *JE* and *GM* telephone directories placed to the right of the telephone.
- ❏ Replenish and place towel basket next to pool.
- ❏ Check that pool "toys" are clean.

Cabana

- ❏ All exercise equipment is put away.
- ❏ Stereo is switched off.
- ❏ Empty dustbin.
- ❏ Pens, notepads and reading glasses on desk.
- ❏ Check that there is enough paper in the printer.
- ❏ Tidy desk and place books neatly to one side. Do not throw away any papers.
- ❏ Replace soiled hand towels and bathrobes.
- ❏ Check soap, toothbrush, toothpaste and clean drinking glass.
- ❏ Clean the toilet and check toilet paper.
- ❏ Replace tissues if less than ⅓.

Kitchen

- ☐ Make the coffee.
- ☐ Wipe down the counter tops and cupboard doors.
- ☐ Take out the trash.
- ☐ Check that Max has food and water.

Downstairs Areas

- ☐ Plump the cushions.
- ☐ Remove any trash and dirty glasses.
- ☐ Tidy magazines and replace any books on bookshelves.
- ☐ Any CD's lying around should be placed back in the correct covers.
- ☐ Check that there are pens, notepads and reading glasses next to each telephone.
- ☐ Check that the telephone extension card is placed under the front of the telephone.
- ☐ Replace hand towel in powder room. Clean sink and toilet. Replenish toilet paper.
- ☐ Check that the printers have enough paper.

Once Mr Epstein, Ms Maxwell and guests come downstairs

- ☐ Make breakfast.

Master Bedroom

- ☐ Make up the bed with fresh bed linen.
- ☐ Check the phones are on "Do not disturb."
- ☐ Tidy bedside tables and remove any trash and dirty glasses.

Master Bathroom

- Replace used towels.
- Two clean hand towels by the sink.
- Two facecloths by the sink and in the shower.
- Three large blue towels and one hand towel on the chair for massage.
- Clean all fixtures including shower and steam room.
- Replace tissues if less than ⅓.
- Check that there is enough toothpaste.
- Clean the drinking glass.
- Tidy all toiletries and replace any that are running low.
- Remove clothes from the hamper and launder.
- All other clothes and shoes should be put back in the closet.

Ms Maxwell's Bathroom

- Replace used towels.
- Clean bathtub and all fixtures.
- Replace tissues if less than ⅓.
- Check that there is enough toothpaste.
- Clean the drinking glass.
- Tidy all toiletries and replace any that are running low.
- Remove clothes from the hamper and launder.
- All other clothes and shoes should be put back in the closet.

Guestrooms

❑ Make the beds (change linen every other day).

❑ Remove any trash and dirty glasses.

❑ Straighten any out of place clothing, private belongings, newspapers and magazines.

❑ Remove dirty clothing and launder.

❑ Replace used towels.

❑ Clean bathtub and all fixtures.

❑ Replace tissues if less than $\frac{1}{3}$.

❑ Clean the drinking glass.

❑ Tidy vanity and toiletries.

Early evening

❑ Check if there are any incoming faxes. Replenish fax paper.

❑ Walk through the house and tidy.

❑ Turn on all lights inside and out.

❑ Turn down bed in Master Bedroom.

❑ Check the phones are on "Do not disturb."

❑ Tidy Master Bedroom and replace any soiled towels and bathrobes.

❑ Turn down beds in Guestrooms.

❑ Tidy Guestrooms and replace any soiled towels and bathrobes.

❑ Place bottles of water and drinking glasses by each bedside.

Before you leave at night

❑ Make sure that Max is inside.

❑ Check that all doors to the outside are shut and locked.

❑ Check that the garage doors are closed.

DATE: _____   **SIGNATURE:** _____

PRE-ARRIVAL SHOPPING LIST

Dairy Products

- ½ gallon regular milk
- 1 quart skim milk
- 1 quart half and half
- 4 Lurpak European butter
- 1 large container Dannon regular plain yogurt
- 1 Philadelphia cream cheese
- 1 tub plain cottage cheese
- ½ pint heavy cream
- 1 dozen eggs
- **½ pound Boar's Head Swiss cheese**
- Häagen Dazs ice cream - coffee, chocolate, vanilla, strawberry

Fresh produce

- 2 green vegetables of choice (such as French green beans, broccoli)
- Cleaned baby spinach and medium greens
- **8 ripe tomatoes**
- Grape tomatoes
- 3 avocadoes
- European cucumber
- 1 Iceberg lettuce (not in a packet)
- 1 regular lettuce (not in a packet)
- 6 endive
- Fresh baby carrots
- Fresh Rosemary
- Fresh Thyme
- Dill
- Fresh Mint
- Italian parsley
- **Olives**
- Scallions
- Garlic
- 2 Sweet onions
- 2 Red onions
- 2 Sweet potatoes
- 6 Baking potatoes
- Ginger
- 1 bag juice oranges
- 6 eating oranges
- Small bunch red and green grapes
- 2 Mango
- 6 ripe bananas
- **Berries (strawberries, raspberries, blueberries – whatever is in season)**
- 4 Fugi apples
- ½ Watermelon
- 4 Lemons
- **Figs**

Fresh meat, poultry & fish

- ½ pound Boar's Head black forest ham
- ½ pound cracked pepper turkey breast
- Ms Maxwell or David will advise any additional meat, poultry or fish to purchase.

Beverages

- **Apple Juice**
- Cranberry juice
- 4 Diet Coke (place in refrigerator)
- 4 Coke (place in refrigerator)
- **Gatorade**
- Large bottle Perrier water (place in refrigerator)
- Vitamin water (place in refrigerator)
- **Tonic Water**

Breads, Cereals and baked goods

- **Cheerios**
- **Kix**
- 6 assorted bagels
- 1 pack Tortilla wraps
- 1 pack Pita bread

Treats
- **Chocolate**
- **Cheetos**

Other
- **"Skippy" Chunky Peanut Butter**

Carmine Giardini's Market

- **Homemade mozzarella**
- 1 inch wedge parmesan cheese
- Smoked salmon
- 6 Laughing Cow mini cheese
- 6 Baby Bell Cheeses
- Bric cheese
- ½ pound Cheddar cheese
- 1 fresh salmon

DATE: _____   SIGNATURE: _____

3/3/2005

30

SHOPPING LIST

The following items should be in stock at all times

** Regardless of quantity used, all open packets must be replaced after each visit **

Beverages

- ❏ Fiji water (large and small)
- ❏ Maxwell House coffee
- ❏ Starbucks ground Colombian coffee
- ❏ Diet Coke
- ❏ Coke
- ❏ Sprite
- ❏ Diet Sprite
- ❏ Pepsi
- ❏ Diet Pepsi
- ❏ Tonic Water
- ❏ Club Soda
- ❏ Perrier Water
- ❏ Vitamin Water
- ❏ Cranberry juice
- ❏ English breakfast tea (packets and tea leaves)
- ❏ Earl Grey tea (packets and tea leaves)
- ❏ Mint tea
- ❏ Chamomile tea
- ❏ White wine - Chablis Premier Cru (6 bottles)
- ❏ Red wine – Brouilly (6 bottles)
- ❏ Veuve-Clicquot champagne (4 bottles)
- ❏ Absolut Vodka
- ❏ Tanqueray Gin
- ❏ Whiskey
- ❏ Heineken Beer (6 pack)
- ❏ Corona Beer (6 pack)

Spices and condiments

- ❏ Hellmann's mayonnaise
- ❏ Dijon mustard
- ❏ 6 Low sodium chicken stock
- ❏ Colivita extra virgin olive oil
- ❏ Sea salt
- ❏ Sugar (White, Brown)
- ❏ Sweet & Low
- ❏ Equal

Canned goods

- ❏ Pomi tomatoes chopped and strained
- ❏ Tomato paste

Miscellaneous

- ❏ Assortment of Barilla Pasta
- ❏ Rice
- ❏ Assorted LU cookies
- ❏ Oreos
- ❏ Eukanuba dog food

Household products

- ❏ Paper towels
- ❏ Toilet paper (white two-ply)
- ❏ Kleenex tissues
- ❏ Tide with Bleach
- ❏ Downy fabric softener
- ❏ Bounce dryer sheets
- ❏ Palmolive Dish soap
- ❏ Murphy's oil soap
- ❏ Soft scrub
- ❏ Windex
- ❏ Clorox Bleach
- ❏ Fantastik All purpose cleaner
- ❏ Cascade Dishwasher detergent
- ❏ Glad zipper storage bags (Large)
- ❏ Glad zipper storage bags (Small)
- ❏ Garbage bags
- ❏ Sponges
- ❏ Latex Gloves
- ❏ Off! Insect repellent
- ❏ Air freshener
- ❏ Formula 409 bathroom cleaner
- ❏ Lysol toilet bowl cleaner
- ❏ Brasso
- ❏ Liquid drain opener
- ❏ Oven /Grill cleaner
- ❏ Silverware cleaning product
- ❏ Light bulbs
- ❏ Batteries
- ❏ Lenscrafters Pre-Moistened Disposable Towelettes

Pharmaceuticals

- 2 bottles Bayer aspirin
- Tylenol
- 2 Aleve
- 2 Robitussin cough medicine
- Nyquil
- Robitussin cough sweets
- Halls cough sweets
- Bandages
- Antiseptic for cuts

- Neosporin
- Echinacea
- Zinc lozengers
- Vitamin C
- Vitamin B
- Vitamin E
- Folic Acid
- Multi vitamin twin tab 1 a day
- Calcium twin tab

DATE: _____

2/14/2005

SIGNATURE: _____

CLEANING SCHEDULE

The most important aspect of household cleaning and maintenance is routine. Certain tasks have to be completed every day to keep things at a high standard. A home that is properly cleaned stays "in place" much longer than those that have been only surface cleaned. Always remember to clean from the top down and from the inside out. Always vacuum last. When leaving a room, turn to check it after you complete it.

DAILY

- ☐ **Dishes, dishwasher** – wash dishes, use dishwasher if needed. Remember: crystal, fine china, silver, cutlery knives, hand-painted bowls or serving platters and pots and pans do not normally go in the dishwasher.

- ☐ **Kitchen** – Clean counter tops, clean sinks, move items on the counter top and clean under them. Clean smudges and finger prints from cabinets, doors and light switches, clean microwave oven, clean and shine inside and out. Clean refrigerators.

- ☐ **Kitchen appliances** – Shine toaster, coffee maker. Note: appliances not left out should be cleaned before putting away.

- ☐ **Sink** – Remove any deposits, clean and shine.

- ☐ **Garbage** – Empty trash, replace bag, wipe off.

- ☐ **Floors** – Remove chairs and small items, sweep well. Mop with warm water.

- ☐ **Glass** – Clean glass doors and tables as needed.

- ☐ **Furniture** – Clean, dust, shine tables, chairs, plump cushions.

- ☐ **Bedrooms** – Make beds as needed, neaten personal belongings, clean all the mirrors, look for streaks.

- ☐ **Bathrooms** – Shine faucets, toilet paper holder, make-up mirrors, towel rack, toothbrush holder. Clean and refill vanity items, check for tissue and toilet paper, wipe bath, sink, mirror, shower walls, place fresh towels.

- ☐ **Clocks** – Check time and date.

- ☐ **Phones** – Clean with disinfectant.

- ☐ **Vacuum** – Heavy traffic areas as needed. Comb tassels on carpets.

DATE: _____   **SIGNATURE:** _____

- **Baseboards** – Dust with a soft cloth.

- **Wood furniture** – Dust and polish tables, chairs, shelves, frames, cabinets.

- **Sofas and chairs** – Vacuum all cushions, fluff pillows, spot-clean as needed.

- **Lamps** – Dust lampshades. Check light bulbs. Straighten shades.

- **Computers and desks** – Clean and wipe screen, dust, replace objects exactly where you found them.

- **Dust and polish** – All glass tables, mirrors, pictures, porcelain and art objects.

- **Walls** – Remove fingerprints from walls, switches, doors.

- **Cabinets and drawers** – Clean thoroughly inside and out. Straighten or repack.

- **Shelving** – Clean thoroughly. Rotate areas requiring fresh shelf paper.

- **Massage Tables** – Wipe and sanitize.

- **Carpets** – Vacuum. Be sure you get the stairs, get behind doors, under furniture, spot-clean as needed.

- **Bathrooms** - Shine faucets, mirrors, towel racks. Wipe and clean bath and shower tiles, doors and walls. Remove mold with mildew remover. Remove soap build up.

- **Toilet** – Clean bowl, seat, lid, base, tank top. Check toilet paper.

- **Marble** – Polish marble in bathrooms.

- **Refrigerator** – Clean thoroughly. Throw out spoiled food. To eliminate odors, place a bowl of cotton balls soaked in plain vanilla extract in the fresh food section.

- **Windows** – Clean all windows inside and out, clean window ledges.

- **Blinds** - Dust quickly over each blind. If necessary, clean with ammonia and water.

- ❏ **Front Entrance** – Sweep and mop, clean door mats.

- ❏ **Outdoor furniture** – Pressure wash.

- ❏ **Pool** – Clean. Check that water temperature is between 82 - 88°F.

- ❏ **Exercise equipment** – Wipe all equipment, sides and fronts, vacuum behind, check.

- ❏ **Garage** – Vacuum / sweep out as needed.

- ❏ **Cars** – Wash and wax exterior, clean and vacuum inside.

DATE: _____   **SIGNATURE:** _____

MONTHLY

Divide your list of monthly duties into weekly cleaning schedules. This will make it easier for you to deep-clean each area properly. This does not mean that you do not need to perform your daily and weekly duties.

WEEK 1

- ❏ Clean windows -- wash the insides, clean sills.
- ❏ Clean blinds.
- ❏ Clean light fixtures.
- ❏ Clean ceilings, walls, doors, baseboards and air vents.
- ❏ Clean ceiling fans.
- ❏ Clean /vacuum air conditioners and humidifiers.
- ❏ Air all rooms. Open the windows and doors to allow fresh air into the room.

WEEK 2

- ❏ Clean and organize closets in bathrooms and bedrooms.
- ❏ Clean drawers and shelves in bathrooms and bedrooms.
- ❏ Turn mattresses.
- ❏ Re-fold linen closets and order as needed.
- ❏ Re-stock utility closets.
- ❏ Wipe books.
- ❏ Discard old magazines.
- ❏ Polish wood furniture.
- ❏ Clean bed frames, vacuum under beds and bedroom furniture.
- ❏ Wash bath mats.
- ❏ Clean steam room walls and floor thoroughly to prevent scum and mildew from forming and avoid bad odors.

WEEK 3

- ❏ Clean and organize crockery and glassware in butler's pantry.
- ❏ Clean kitchen floors thoroughly.
- ❏ Clean refrigerator and freezer.
- ❏ Clean pots and pans.
- ❏ Clean kitchen cabinets inside and out.
- ❏ Clean and organize kitchen drawers.
- ❏ Clean and check pantry supplies.
- ❏ Clean silverware.

** Chipped and broken items must be removed and reported to the Estate Manager.

DATE: _____   **SIGNATURE:** _____

EVERY SIX MONTHS

APRIL

(Check list to be completed and si gned by 28th April)

- ☐ Rotate seasonal clothing. Dry clean items if necessary.
- ☐ Wash mattress covers and launder any blankets.
- ☐ Take all books down from shelves and clean.
- ☐ Clean upholstery and throw cushions.
- ☐ Dry clean drapes.
- ☐ Check for pests throughout property.
- ☐ Inventory all crockery, glassware, linens, etc.
- ☐ Steam clean all carpets.
- ☐ Car maintenance if necessary.
- ☐ Drain and clean pool.

DATE: _____   **SIGNATURE:** _____

OCTOBER

(Check list to be completed and signed by 28th October)

- ❏ Rotate seasonal clothing. Dry clean sweaters and other items if necessary.
- ❏ Wash mattress covers and launder any blankets.
- ❏ Take all books down from shelves and clean.
- ❏ Clean upholstery and throw cushions.
- ❏ Dry clean drapes.
- ❏ Check for pests throughout property.
- ❏ Inventory all crockery, glassware, linens, etc.
- ❏ Steam clean all carpets.
- ❏ Car maintenance if necessary.
- ❏ Drain and clean pool.

DATE: _____   **SIGNATURE:** _____

MAINTENANCE SCHEDULE

Preventive maintenance is the best way to keep your home and grounds in good condition. Maintenance that is carried out on a regular basis, will ward off major repairs.

CHECK EVERY MONTH

(Check list to be completed and signed by the 28th of each month)

- ❏ **Fire Extinguisher** – Check to make sure that it is fully charged.

- ❏ **Security alarm** – Test system.

- ❏ **Sink stoppers** – Clean out debris, soak stoppers in vinegar and water to clean.

- ❏ **Garbage disposal** – Flush with hot water and baking soda, put ice cubes through to sharpen.

- ❏ **Hot water heating system** – Test relief valve and replace if necessary; check pressure gauge and drain expansion tank if necessary.

- ❏ **Steam heating system** – Check safety valve and steam-pressure gauge and have replaced if necessary; check water-level gauge and add water if needed; drain water until clear to eliminate sediment.

- ❏ **Air conditioners / heaters** – Clean or replace filter; clean condenser, evaporator coils and condensation drain.

DATE: _____   **SIGNATURE:** _____

2/14/2005   42

CHECK EVERY THREE MONTHS

MARCH

(Check list to be completed and signed by 28th March)

- ☐ **Faucets -** Check for leaking faucets. Replace washers if necessary.

- ☐ **Bathtub drain assembly –** Clean out debris; inspect rubber seal; replace if necessary.

- ☐ **Shower drain assembly –** Clean out debris and scrub strainer.

- ☐ **Range hood fan –** Clean grease filter.

- ☐ **Dishwasher -** Run the unit with a quart of white vinegar added to the tank. This removes any deposits left behind in the tub and helps keep the drain clear.

- ☐ **Hinges and locks –** Lubricate as needed.

- ☐ **Awnings –** Lower and clean. Check motor.

DATE: _____   **SIGNATURE:** _____

JUNE

(Check list to be completed and signed by 28ᵗʰ June)

- ❏ **Faucets -** Check for leaking faucets. Replace washers if necessary.

- ❏ **Bathtub drain assembly** – Clean out debris; inspect rubber seal; replace if necessary.

- ❏ **Shower drain assembly** – Clean out debris and scrub strainer.

- ❏ **Range hood fan** – Clean grease filter.

- ❏ **Dishwasher -** Run the unit with a quart of white vinegar added to the tank. This removes any deposits left behind in the tub and helps keep the drain clear.

- ❏ **Hinges and locks** – Lubricate as needed.

- ❏ **Awnings** – Lower and clean. Check motor.

DATE: _____   **SIGNATURE:** _____

SEPTEMBER

(Check list to be completed and signed by 28th September)

- ❏ **Faucets -** Check for leaking faucets. Replace washers if necessary.

- ❏ **Bathtub drain assembly** – Clean out debris; inspect rubber seal; replace if necessary.

- ❏ **Shower drain assembly** – Clean out debris and scrub strainer.

- ❏ **Range hood fan** – Clean grease filter.

- ❏ **Dishwasher -** Run the unit with a quart of white vinegar added to the tank. This removes any deposits left behind in the tub and helps keep the drain clear.

- ❏ **Hinges and locks** – Lubricate as needed.

- ❏ **Awnings** – Lower and clean. Check motor.

DATE: _____   **SIGNATURE:** _____

DECEMBER

(Check list to be completed and signed by 28th December)

- ❏ **Faucets** - Check for leaking faucets. Replace washers if necessary.

- ❏ **Bathtub drain assembly** – Clean out debris; inspect rubber seal; replace if necessary.

- ❏ **Shower drain assembly** – Clean out debris and scrub strainer.

- ❏ **Range hood fan** – Clean grease filter.

- ❏ **Dishwasher** - Run the unit with a quart of white vinegar added to the tank. This removes any deposits left behind in the tub and helps keep the drain clear.

- ❏ **Hinges and locks** – Lubricate as needed.

- ❏ **Awnings** – Lower and clean. Check motor.

DATE: _____

SIGNATURE: _____

CHECK EVERY SIX MONTHS

APRIL

(Check list to be completed and signed by 28th April)

- ☐ **Toilets** – Check for leaks in flushing mechanism; repair if necessary.

- ☐ **Interior caulking** – Inspect caulking around bathtubs, showers and sinks; replace if deteriorating.

- ☐ **Washing machines** – Clean water inlet filters; check hoses for leaks and replace if necessary.

- ☐ **Clothes dryers** – Vacuum lint from ducts and surrounding areas.

- ☐ **Refrigerator** – Wash and check door gasket; clean condenser coils with a gentle brush.

- ☐ **Range hood fan** – Wash fan blades and housing.

- ☐ **Hot water heating system** – Lubricate circulating pump and motor.

- ☐ **Wiring** – Check for frayed cords and wires; repair if necessary.

- ☐ **Foundation** – Check for cracks and moisture, repair if necessary.

- ☐ **Roof** – Inspect roof surface; repair if necessary.

- ☐ **Gutters and downspout** – Clean out, inspect and repair weaknesses; check for proper drainage and adjust if necessary.

- ☐ **Exterior caulking** – Inspect caulking and replace if deteriorating.

- ☐ **Window sills, door sills and thresholds** - Fill cracks, caulk edges and repaint; replace if necessary

- ☐ **Drain-waste and vent system** – Flush out system.

- ☐ **Irrigation system** – Check, drain and repair if necessary.

- ☐ **Fences** – Inspect and repair if necessary.

- ☐ **Garage doors** – Clean and lubricate hinges, rollers and tracks; tighten screws.

DATE: _____   **SIGNATURE:** _____

OCTOBER

(Check list to be completed and signed by 28th October)

☐ **Toilets** – Check for leaks in flushing mechanism; repair if necessary.

☐ **Interior caulking** – Inspect caulking around bathtubs, showers and sinks; replace if deteriorating.

☐ **Washing machines** – Clean water inlet filters; check hoses for leaks and replace if necessary.

☐ **Clothes dryers** – Vacuum lint from ducts and surrounding areas.

☐ **Refrigerator** – Wash and check door gasket; clean condenser coils with a gentle brush.

☐ **Range hood fan** – Wash fan blades and housing.

☐ **Hot water heating system** – Lubricate circulating pump and motor.

☐ **Wiring** – Check for frayed cords and wires; repair if necessary.

☐ **Foundation** – Check for cracks and moisture, repair if necessary.

☐ **Roof** – Inspect roof surface; repair if necessary.

☐ **Gutters and downspout** – Clean out, inspect and repair weaknesses; check for proper drainage and adjust if necessary.

☐ **Exterior caulking** – Inspect caulking and replace if deteriorating.

☐ **Window sills, door sills and thresholds** - Fill cracks, caulk edges and repaint; replace if necessary

☐ **Drain-waste and vent system** – Flush out system.

☐ **Irrigation system** – Check, drain and repair if necessary.

☐ **Fences** – Inspect and repair if necessary.

☐ **Garage doors** – Clean and lubricate hinges, rollers and tracks; tighten screws.

DATE: _____   **SIGNATURE: _____**

BEDROOM CLEANING

- If weather permits, open windows to air the room.

- Strip the bed.

- Place pillows, duvet, bedspreads and blankets on a chair. Never on the floor.

- Empty trash containers and pick up any other trash. Check under the bed.

- Make the bed with fresh linen.

- Make sure that the closets are empty. Check that the hangers are not broken and are hung evenly.

- Dust all furniture and picture frames.

- Dust and straighten lamp shades. Seams must face the wall. Replace the light bulb if necessary.

- Spot clean all mirrors and glass.

- Wipe all walls, doors, and light switches.

- Telephone must be free of dust. No sticky spots. Cord must hang properly.

- Make sure that the television, remote control and radio are in working order and free of dust.

- Alarm clock must be set to the correct time and date.

- Close the windows.

- Make sure that the drapes hang evenly and all hooks are in place.

- Vacuum the carpet.

BATHROOM CLEANING

- Empty trash containers and pick up any other trash.

- Replace soiled towels. All towels to be even in width and hung evenly lengthwise. No seams exposed.

- Replace soiled bathrobes. Robes must be washed after each visit.

- Check guest supplies and replace what is needed.

- Replace toilet paper with new roll. Fold end into a "V"

- Replace soap with new bar.

- Clean mirrors using glass cleaner. Start at the top and work down to the bottom.

- Clean vanity and sink using all-purpose cleaner.

- Clean toilet using toilet bowl cleaner. Squirt under rim of bowl and let stand a few minutes. Clean the rim, seat, hinges, base, all porcelain and hardware. Flush.

- Clean the shower stall and walls. Place the dirty bathmat in the tub or shower stall and stand on the mat while cleaning. Use all-purpose cleaner and wipe down the walls and glass door. Clean marble with damp cloth. Clean the shower head and soap dishes. Rinse shower stall with hot water after removing the bathmat. Dry shower walls, floor and door. Wipe down shower curtain. Place bottom of curtain outside of tub. Arrange curtain in pleats.

- Clean the bathtub. Kneel on dirty bathmat. Using tissue, remove all hair and foreign material from tub and drain. Using all-purpose cleaner, scrub thoroughly, paying attention to sides of the tub. Rinse with hot water. Dry the entire surface. Polish fixtures with a dry, clean cloth.

NOTE:

All surfaces must be clean of hair, smudges, debris, fingerprints, soap build-up and scum.
No dripping faucets.
No clogged drains.
If guests are in residence, clean under toiletries left on the vanity and put back in a neat, orderly manner.

LAUNDRY AND DRY CLEANING

- The first rule in laundry is read the label. Determine if you can wash an item, or if you must take it to be dry-cleaned.

- Sort clothes – white in one pile, colored in another, delicate in yet another.

- Check pockets!

- Wash towels separately.

- Wash all new towels and linen before use.

- Rotate your towels and sheets so as not to wear them out.

- Worn towels should be transferred to staff quarters for staff use.

- Bed linens are taken to Snow White Laundry.

- Clothes that require dry cleaning are taken to Spartan Cleaners. If the garment is stained, be sure to show the cleaner where it is soiled, mentioning what you think the stain is. When you collect the clothes, check that the garment is properly cleaned and the stains have been removed.

- Detergents – Tide with Bleach; Downy fabric softener; Bounce dryer sheets.

- Organize the linen closet. All sheets, pillow cases and towels identically folded. The folded end should face outward. Separate stacks according to which bedroom they belong in.

OFFICE SUPPLIES

The following supplies should be in inventory at all times:

- Copy / printer paper.
- Toner and ink cartridges for printers and fax machine – a minimum of 2 per unit.
- Pens and pencils.
- Red and green markers.
- Black markers.
- Rulers.
- Pair of scissors.
- Scotch tape.
- Shipping tape.
- Photographic print paper.
- Personalized notepads, cards, envelopes (Call Cecilia Steen to order).
- FedEx and parcel slips.
- Disposable cameras.
- Film for cameras.

MAIL AND DELIVERIES

When Mr Epstein and Ms Maxwell are in residence:

- Personal cards, notes and invitations are to be placed on the pantry countertop.

- Correspondence for Ms Maxwell is to be placed on her desk.

When Mr Epstein and Ms Maxwell are not in residence:

- Mr Epstein or Ms Maxwell's assistant must be notified if any packages are delivered.

- General mail, including invoices and bank statements, are to be sent via FedEx to Eric Gany in New York, twice a week.

- Include all personal mail in a separate envelope addressed to either Mr Epstein or Ms Maxwell.

RESETTING THE TELEPHONE

Assure that the telephones are always set to the proper date and time. The household phones may be reset by performing the following:

- Without picking up the receiver, dial 692 on the kitchen phone.

- Follow by dialing 2 digits for the year, 2 digits for the day, 2 digits for the month and finally, dial 4 digits for the military time.

- The phone should display the new date and time as well as make a noise to indicate that it has been reset.

- Pick up the receiver and then hang-up. This will return the phone to its normal mode.

SERVING BREAKFAST

Mr Epstein's breakfast preferences:

- Glass of water

- Coffee

- 1 Sweet and Low or Equal

- Creamer filled with Half & Half, warmed in the microwave for 25 seconds.

- Mr Epstein will indicate what food he would like to eat.

Ms Maxwell's breakfast preferences:

- Maxwell House coffee served with milk

- Freshly squeezed orange juice

- Glass of water

- 1 Weetabix with sliced banana. Milk and sugar on the side.

When service breakfast to guests:

- Pre-set table or breakfast trays for the number of guests present.

- As guests arrive, inquire whether they would like coffee, tea, or fruit juice.

- Always make sure that coffee is fresh.

- Reconfirm that guests have no allergic reaction to any specific foods.

- Take the breakfast order. Inquire whether they would like to wait for any remaining guests (if applicable), before you begin preparation.

- Always serve from the left, and clear from the right if possible.

- Clean breakfast area as soon as guests have departed.

STANDBY DUTIES

When necessary, you will be required to be on "standby" duty. During this time, you are to make yourself available for any duties that need to be carried out, or respond to an emergency that may arise.

In order for you to be able to respond promptly, you should not travel more than one hour from your home base. This means that if you are called, the maximum time it will take you to return, is one hour.

To properly perform this duty, you should know the following:

- You could be called upon at any time, day or night.

- Have the necessary contact details for Mr Epstein, Ms Maxwell, the Estate Manager and other relevant staff members.

- Call the Estate Manager and other relevant staff members and advise them of an emergency. This should be done immediately.

- When speaking to the Estate Manager or other relevant staff members, provide accurate and detailed information.

- The security of the house, Mr Epstein, Ms Maxwell and their guests are your first consideration. Always handle a crisis in a calm and professional manner.

EMERGENCY PROCEDURES

In the event of an emergency, you may be required to decide on a course of action to protect Mr Epstein, Ms Maxwell, their guests, other staff members and yourself.

REMEMBER TO STAY CALM AND DO NOT PANIC

FIRE

Call the Fire Department or 911 as soon as possible. Tell them the exact location and nature of the fire.

Ask all guests to leave their rooms.

Never use the elevator. It could stop between floors.

When you exit the building during a fire, close all doors as you exit to confine the fire.

Make sure that everyone leaves with you.

Heat, smoke and gases emitted by burning materials can quickly choke you. If you are caught in heavy smoke, get down on the floor and crawl. Take short breaths, breathing through your nose.

If your clothes catch fire, don't run. Stop where you are, drop to the ground, cover your face with your hands to protect your face and lungs and roll over to smother the flames.

Do not overestimate your ability to put out a fire. Most fires cannot be easily or safely extinguished. Do not attempt to put the fire out once it begins to quickly spread.

HURRICANE SEASON

The season generally runs from June through November with the peak period being in August and September.

During this time, it is necessary to monitor all weather systems on a daily basis, either via the television, internet or radio. Guests must be advised of the situation.

All outdoor furniture and loose items must be stored inside. Potted plants are moved into areas with the least wind or placed indoors.

All shutters are closed.

MEDICAL EMERGENCY

Call 911 as soon as possible. Give them as much information as you can. Tell them what happened and the current condition of the patient.

If you are unable to get help, drive the patient to the Good Samaritan Hospital, 1309 North Flagler Drive, West Palm Beach. Call the hospital on route and tell them that you are on your way.

EMERGENCY CONTACT INFORMATION

GUEST NAME: _____

ALLERGIES: _____

CONTACT NAME: _____

CONTACT TELEPHONE:

HOME _____

WORK _____

PORTABLE _____

THANK YOU!

---

www.ingramcontent.com/pod-product-compliance
Lightning Source LLC
LaVergne TN
LVHW041331080426
835512LV00006B/404